Complex Dilemmas in Group Therapy

Complex Dilemmas in Group Therapy

PATHWAYS TO RESOLUTION

Edited by
Lise Motherwell, Psy.D., C.G.P.
Joseph J. Shay, Ph.D., C.G.P.

Brunner-Routledge
Taylor & Francis Group
NEW YORK AND HOVE

Published in 2005 by
Brunner-Routledge
270 Madison Avenue
New York, NY 10016
www.brunner-routledge.com

Published in Great Britain by
Brunner-Routledge
27 Church Road
Hove
East Sussex BN3 2FA
www.brunner-routledge.co.uk

10 9 8 7 6 5 4 3 2 1

Library of Congress Cataloging-in-Publication Data
    Complex dilemmas in group therapy : pathways to resolution / Lise
Motherwell, Joseph J. Shay, editors.
        p. ; cm.
    Includes bibliographical references and indexes.
    ISBN 0-415-94819-3 (hardback : alk. paper)
    1. Group psychotherapy—Methodology. 2. Group psychotherapy—Case
studies.
    [DNLM: 1. Psychotherapy, Group—methods. WM 430 C7367 2005] I.
Motherwell, Lise, 1955- II. Shay, Joseph J. III. Title.

RC488.C584 2005
616.89'152—dc22   2004009404

To my group members whose courage inspires me and to my
teachers who taught me to learn from my groups

LM

To all the members of my groups for their wisdom, courage, and
perseverance, which have made an immeasurable difference in my life

JS

Table of Contents

Preface

Imagine you have been running a therapy group for several years when suddenly the same group which has functioned well to now suddenly goes off the rails. One patient monopolizes the sessions with her anger and incessant talking, another assaults your competence, several others drop out precipitously, and your group, formerly passionate and vibrant, is now close to death. Anxious and confused, you dread meeting with your group again, even though group therapy has been the highlight of your practice for many years. How do you understand what has happened, and what do you do?

The idea for this book began 10 years ago when, as a neophyte group therapist, I found myself facing many such dilemmas. Each month, I looked forward to receiving the *Group Circle*, the American Group Psychotherapy Association's newsletter, because it had a column called "Consultation, Please" in which senior clinicians responded to a complex dilemma. What a great training tool! When Joe Shay, my co-editor on the *Northeastern Society for Group Psychotherapy Newsletter,* suggested we add a similar column to the newsletter, I agreed and asked if he would like to edit a book of clinical dilemmas with me so that we could offer similar consultation to students, neophyte group therapists, and senior clinicians who would inevitably find themselves faced with complicated situations in their own work.

Toward that end, we asked seven clinicians each to write a theoretical chapter addressing an important concept or current issue in group therapy. We then asked two senior group therapists to respond to each of three complex dilemmas we created for each chapter. The groups and patients in these dilemmas are fictitious although some of the scenarios are based on situations we have encountered in our practices or supervisions over the years. Overall, *Complex Dilemmas in Group Therapy* includes chapters and responses from fifty clinicians.

Seasoned clinicians know that group therapy is a complex endeavor. Even the most well-trained and competent among us have had experiences where we feel deskilled, helpless, confused, or baffled by events in our groups. The multiple transferences, enactments, projections, boundary crossings, and countertransference reactions in group therapy can create a kaleidoscope of unpredictable events and interactions. This book is a guide to help clinicians make theoretical and clinical sense of such unpredictable group therapy events.

Complex Dilemmas in Group Therapy is intended to be consultative rather than supervisory in nature. Whereas consultation is time-limited, supervision is usually ongoing and can follow the group process over a period of time. We chose to make this book consultative because we wanted readers to see how two different clinicians might respond to the same dilemma at one moment in time. In reading the responses, you will find that two authors may respond with completely different advice or focus on similar aspects of a dilemma but from a different vantage point. Although one might argue that there is a wrong way to do group therapy, you will see in the varied responses that there is no one right way.

Since this is a book on group therapy, it seemed only fitting to work with a *group* of experienced therapists. One of the great pleasures of this project for us has been the opportunity to interact with so many outstanding clinicians, researchers, and theoreticians—truly a *who's who* of professionals. We cast a wide net for our authors; our chapter writers and respondents come from all over the United States, Canada, and Great Britain. They write from a range of theoretical positions: from self psychology to object relations theory to Redecision Theory to System-Centered Theory and more. Some are researchers, many are theoreticians, and virtually all are clinicians who spend a large portion of their time conducting and thinking about group therapy.

It is with great pleasure that we offer their wisdom to you.

Finally, Joe and I have come to know and value each other at a much deeper level, both professionally and personally. Just as in any well-functioning group, we strove to capitalize on our complementary abilities, respect each other's weaknesses, and to make sure to experience joy in the process.

Lise Motherwell, PsyD, CGP

Joseph J. Shay, PhD, CGP

Editors
Lise Motherwell, PsyD, CGP, is faculty in the Center for Psychoanalytic Studies at Massachusetts General Hospital, an Associate in Psychology at Massachusetts General Hospital, and an Instructor at Harvard Medical School. She is President of the Board of the Northeastern Society for Group Psychotherapy and a past treasurer of the Massachusetts Psychological Association. She has written articles and presented extensively on group therapy.

Joseph J. Shay, PhD, CGP, is the Director of Psychological Services and Psychology Training at Two Brattle Center in Cambridge, Massachusetts, and an Instructor in Psychology in the Department of Psychiatry at the Harvard Medical School. He is also on the staff of the joint McLean Hospital/Massachusetts General Hospital training program. Dr. Shay has co-edited, with Dr. Joan Wheelis, *Odysseys in Psychotherapy* (2000), and has written and presented widely on the nature of psychotherapy, the heart of the change process, and complex concepts in group therapy.

Contributors
Yvonne M. Agazarian, EdD, CGP, FAGPA, is Founder of the Systems-Centered Training and Research Institute in Philadelphia, Pennsylvania. She has published chapters in books, journal articles, and six books including *The Invisible & Invisible Group* (with Richard Peters, 1981), *Systems-Centered Therapy for Groups* (1997), *Autobiography of a Theory* (with Susan Gantt, 2000), and *A Systems-Centered Approach to Inpatient Psychotherapy* (2001).

Anne Alonso, PhD, CGP, DFAGPA, is a Clinical Professor of Psychology and Psychiatry at Harvard Medical School, serves as Director of *The Center for Psychoanalytic Studies* at the Massachusetts General Hospital, and is the Founder and Director of the Endowment for the Advancement of Psychotherapy, Massachusetts General Hospital/Harvard Medical School. Dr. Alonso has published prolifically and serves on several editorial boards, including the *International Journal of Group Psychotherapy*, *Group*, and *The Journal of Psychotherapy Practice and Research*.

David A. Altfeld, PhD, CGP, FAGPA, has been Codirector and Faculty of the Supervisory Training Program for the past 20 years at the National Institute for the Psychotherapies (NIP), and is Senior Supervisor at NIP. He has supervised residents and interns in group therapy in the Department of Psychiatry at Cornell University Medical Center and the New York University Medical Center. He developed and published an experiential group model of supervision in the *International Journal of Group Psychotherapy*.

Sally H. Barlow, PhD, CGP, ABPP, ABGP, is Professor of Psychology at Brigham Young University (BYU) in Provo, Utah. She is also a Past President of Division 49 (Groups) of the American Psychological Association, and has taught group courses to clinical psychology students at BYU and psychiatric residents at the University of Utah Medical School for many years. She publishes journal articles, books, and book chapters on group and individual psychotherapy, and presents papers nationally and internationally.

Harold Bernard, PhD, CGP, FAGPA, ABPP, is Clinical Associate Professor of Psychiatry at New York University School of Medicine. Currently President of the American Group Psychotherapy Association, Dr. Bernard has written numerous papers and chapters, and has co-edited three books: *Handbook of Contemporary Group Psychotherapy, Basics of Group Psychotherapy,* and *Psychosocial Treatment for Medical Conditions: Principles and Techniques.*

Richard M. Billow, PhD, is Director, Adelphi University Postdoctoral Program in Group Psychotherapy, Long Island, New York. He is the author of *Relational Group Psychotherapy: From Basic Assumptions to Passion* (2003) and has written many journal articles.

Bonnie J. Buchele, PhD, CGP, DFAGPA, ABPP, is a Training and Supervising Analyst with the Greater Kansas City Psychoanalytic Institute and is in private practice in Kansas City. She is a Past President of the American Group Psychotherapy Association and has authored a number of publications. Recently she has been consulting with leaders of groups for persons traumatized by the events of 9/11.

Arnold Cohen, PhD, is an Instructor in Psychology in the Department of Psychiatry at Harvard Medical School. He has taught courses in group psychotherapy at Boston College School of Social Work, Simmons School of Social Work, and the Northeastern Society for Group Psychotherapy. He is on the Board of the American Group Psychotherapy Association, is a Past President of Northeastern Society for Group Psychotherapy, and has written chapters on group psychotherapy.

Suzanne L. Cohen, EdD, CGP, FAGPA, is a Clinical Instructor in Psychology in the Department of Psychiatry at Harvard Medical School, a Clinical Supervisor at Massachusetts Mental Health Center, and on the faculty of the Northeastern Society for Group Psychotherapy Training Program. She has published in the *International Journal of Group Psychotherapy* and *Group,* and is a reviewer for the *International Journal of Group Psychotherapy*.

Barbara R. Cohn, PhD, CGP, FAGPA, is Associate Clinical Professor of Medical Psychology at Columbia University and Director of Psychology Education at St. Luke's Roosevelt Hospital Center in New York City. She is the Book and Media Editor of the journal *Group* and has published journal articles on group therapy. She directs a psychology internship and a psychology fellowship in group psychotherapy, and teaches group therapy to psychology interns, psychiatric residents, and in American Group Psychotherapy Association institutes and workshops.

Elaine Jean Cooper, LCSW, PhD, CGP, FAGPA, is Clinical Professor at University of California School of Medicine at San Francisco, Department of Psychiatry. She is author of *Group Intervention* and is on the Editorial Board of the *International Journal of Group Psychotherapy*. She is a Past President of the Northern California Group Psychotherapy Society. She has written numerous journal articles and book chapters.

Eleanor F. Counselman, EdD, CGP, FAGPA, ABPP, is an Assistant Clinical Professor in Psychiatry (Psychology) at Harvard Medical School and is on the faculty of the Center for Psychoanalytic Studies and the Center for Group Psychotherapy at Massachusetts General Hospital. She is also on the faculty of the Northeastern Society for Group Psychotherapy and the Boston Institute for Psychotherapy. She is Editor of *The Group Circle* (newsletter of the American Group Psychotherapy Association) and on the Editorial Board of the *International Journal of Group Psychotherapy*. She has published many articles in the field of group and individual psychotherapy and supervision.

Hylene S. Dublin, MSW, LCSW, CGP, FAGPA, is in private practice and on the faculty of the Institute for Clinical Social Work of Chicago. She has been on the faculties of the Northwestern University, University of Illinois, and University of Chicago Departments of Psychiatry where she conducted group psychotherapy training programs for psychiatric residents, psychologists, social workers, and nurses. She has been Director of the Illinois Group Psychotherapy Society Training Program for years and been a Past President of the Illinois Group Psychotherapy Society. She has published many articles, book reviews, and book chapters.

Allan B. Elfant, PhD, CGP, FAGPA, ABPP, is in private practice in State College, Pennsylvania. Dr. Elfant has held faculty positions at Pennsylvania State University, Texas A&M University College of Medicine and Brooklyn College, City University of New York. He is a frequent presenter at national and regional conferences and has written several journal articles.

Sara J. Emerson, LICSW, CGP, FAGPA, is in private practice in Cambridge, Massachusetts and is on the faculty of the Boston Institute for Psychotherapy. She is a Clinical Supervisor at Two Brattle Center, Cambridge and on the Board of the Northeastern Society for Group Psychotherapy.

Pamela L. Enders, PhD, CGP, is a Training Supervisor in the Department of Psychiatry at the Massachusetts General Hospital and an Instructor at Harvard Medical School where she supervises psychiatric residents and fellows in group psychotherapy. She is a past member of the Board of Directors of the Northeastern Society for Group Psychotherapy.

Nina Fieldsteel, PhD, FAGPA, is on the faculty of the Center for Psychoanalytic Studies at Massachusetts General Hospital and an Instructor at Harvard Medical School. She was on the faculty and a senior supervisor at the Postgraduate Center for Mental Health, and a Training Analyst at Blanton Peale Institute and the Institute for Psychotherapy and Psychoanalysis of New Jersey. She has published numerous articles on ethics and termination in psychotherapy and was the Founding Editor of *Group: Journal of the Eastern Group Psychotherapy Society* from 1976 to 1981, and on the Editorial Board of the *International Journal of Group Psychotherapy* for 15 years.

Bernard Frankel, PhD, BCD, CGP, FAGPA, is Clinical Professor at Adelphi University and is on the faculty of the Derner Institute and the Post-Doctoral Program in Psychoanalysis and Psychotherapy. He is Senior Consultant in the Adelphi Group Psychotherapy training program. He was voted Outstanding Practitioner at the National Academy of Practice in Washington, DC. He has been a private practitioner of group, marital, and family therapy for 45 years.

Joel C. Frost, EdD, CGP, FAGPA, ABPP, is an Assistant Clinical Professor of Psychiatry at Harvard Medical School. He supervises groups in the Departments of Psychiatry and Social Work at the Beth Israel Medical Center in Boston. He has written numerous articles on group therapy and has a special interest in therapist self-disclosure.

Jerome S. Gans, MD, CGP, FAGPA, DFAPA, is Associate Clinical Professor of Psychiatry at Harvard Medical School and a Clinical Associate in Psychiatry at the Massachusetts General Hospital. Dr. Gans is Book Review

Editor for the *International Journal of Group Psychotherapy*. He runs the Training-Group (T-Group) for psychiatric residents at the Massachusetts General Hospital/McLean combined residency program and is a Supervisor at the Center for Psychoanalytic Studies at the MGH, where he co-teaches the second year course on supervision. Dr. Gans has published widely on group and individual psychotherapy.

Ramon Ganzarain, MD, FAGPA, is Emeritus Associate Professor of Psychiatry and training analyst at the psychoanalytic institute, Emory University, Atlanta. He taught group therapy in Chile, at the Menninger Clinic in Kansas City, and in Atlanta. He has published two books, *Fugitives of Incest* and *Object Relations Group Psychotherapy,* and many articles and chapters. Dr. Ganzarain has served on the Board of Directors of the American Group Psychotherapy Association and the International Group Psychotherapy Association.

Allan H. Gelber, PhD, CGP, is in private practice in Phoenix, Arizona. He is Director of the Arizona Center for Mental Health, P.C. and the Training and Education Chair of the Arizona Group Psychotherapy Society. Dr. Gelber teaches and supervises individual and group psychotherapy.

Macario Giraldo, PhD, is in private practice in McLean, Virginia, Director of the National Group Psychotherapy Institute and on the faculty of the Washington School of Psychiatry. He has published two textbooks, written several articles, and presented ongoing seminars applying Lacanian theory to the psychoanalytic group.

Steven Haut, MSW, BCD, CGP, FAGPA, is in private practice in Boston and Concord, Massachusetts. He has been on the faculty in group psychotherapy at Boston University, Boston College, Simmons College, Tufts University, and the Northeastern Society for Group Psychotherapy Training Program. He is a consultant to hospitals and mental health centers on group psychotherapy. He is a Past President of Northeastern Society for Group Psychotherapy, Past President and Co-founder of the Children's Group Therapy Association, and has been an invited speaker at national and international conferences on group psychotherapy.

David M. Hawkins, MD, CGP, DFAGPA, is in private practice in Chapel Hill, North Carolina. He is Associate Consulting Professor of Psychiatry at Duke University Medical Center and at the University of North Carolina at Chapel Hill. He provides consultation and training in psychodynamic group psychotherapy through monthly groups in Chapel Hill and in Atlanta, Georgia. He is a Past President of the American Group Psychotherapy Association and of the American Academy of Psychotherapists.

Barry Helfmann, PsyD, CGP, ABPP, is Managing Partner of Short Hills Associates in Clinical Psychology. He is a Past President of the New Jersey Group Psychotherapy Association and the New Jersey Psychological Association, and has served as Chair of the National Registry of Certified Group Psychotherapists. He has published articles related to group practice and was voted the New Jersey Psychologist of the Year in 1994.

Earl Hopper, PhD, is a psychoanalyst, group analyst, and organizational consultant in private practice in London. He is the author of many books and articles, including *The Social Unconscious: Selected Papers* and *Traumatic Experience in the Unconscious Life of Groups*, and an internationally renowned lecturer and teacher. Dr. Hopper is a Past President of the International Association of Group Psychotherapy and a Past Chairman of the Group of Independent Psychoanalysts of the British Psychoanalytical Society. Currently he is a member of the Executive Committee of the Group Analytic Society in London.

Arthur Horne, PhD, is Distinguished Research Professor of Counseling Psychology at the University of Georgia and the current President of the Division of Group Psychology and Group Psychotherapy of the American Psychological Association, as well as Past President of the Association for Specialists in Group Work. He has co-authored five books and co-edited five, has served on editorial boards of seven journals, and is the editor of the *International Journal for the Advancement of Counseling.*

Anthony S. Joyce, PhD, is Professor and Coordinator of the Psychotherapy Research and Evaluation Unit in the Department of Psychiatry, University of Alberta. He presents and publishes widely on both group and individual therapy research. He is a Past President of the Canadian Group Psychotherapy Association. Dr. Joyce serves on the Board of Editors for the *International Journal of Group Psychotherapy.*

Robert H. Klein, PhD, CGP, FAGPA is Clinical Professor of Psychiatry at the Yale School of Medicine, New Haven, Connecticut. He is Co-editor of *Group Psychotherapy for Psychological Trauma* and *Handbook of Contemporary Group Psychotherapy.* Currently President of the American Group Psychotherapy Association, he maintains a private practice in Milford and Westport, Connecticut.

Marti B. Kranzberg, PhD, CGP, FAGPA, is in private practice in Dallas, Texas. She is immediate Past President of the Dallas Group Psychotherapy Society and has served on the Board of the Southwest Group Psychotherapy Society. She has published several articles and a chapter on Redecision Therapy and group. She has also written more than a dozen articles about the shifting ground of mental health practice in *The Group Circle,* newsletter of the American Group Psychotherapy Association.

Steven Krugman, PhD, is on the faculty of the Department of Psychiatry at the Massachusetts General Hospital and teaches for the Center for Psychoanalytic Studies at MGH. He is a psychologist in private practice in Boston and Newton, Massachusetts. Dr. Krugman is a Co-founder of Group Solutions Network, a group referral network. He has published papers on individual and group psychotherapy, men's development, and shame.

Morris Nitsun, PhD, is a consultant clinical psychologist in Camden and Islington Mental Health National Health Service Trust, a psychotherapist in private practice at the Group Analytic Practice (London), a Visiting Lecturer at University College (London), and on the teaching staff of the Institute of Group Analysis. He has lectured and run workshops internationally, is widely published, and is well known for his book, *The AntiGroup*.

Jeanne Pasternak, LCSW, CGP, FAGPA, is in private practice in Houston, Texas and is the Chairwoman of the National Registry of Certified Group Psychotherapists. She is a Past President of the Houston Group Psychotherapy Society and has served on the Board of Directors of the American Group Psychotherapy Association. She has presented workshops on adolescent group psychotherapy locally and at the American Group Psychotherapy Association annual meetings and has served on the training faculty for the Boston Threshold Group Psychotherapy Conference in Belfast, Ireland.

William E. Piper, PhD, CGP, is Professor, Head of the Division of Behavioural Science, and Director of the Psychotherapy Program in the Department of Psychiatry at the University of British Columbia. Among his 150 publications are four books. He has served as President of the Canadian Group Psychotherapy Association, President of the Society for Psychotherapy Research, and Editor of the *International Journal of Group Psychotherapy*.

Theodore A. Powers, PhD, is an Assistant Professor in the Psychology Department of the University of Massachusetts at Dartmouth. He is the co-author of a *Concise Guide to Brief Dynamic and Interpersonal Therapy* and has authored or co-authored a number of other papers and chapters. He has lectured extensively on individual and group dynamics and time-effective strategies for change.

Helen Riess, MD, is Assistant Clinical Professor at Harvard Medical School and Director of Education for Psychotherapy Supervision at Massachusetts General Hospital. She has published in a number of journals, including the *International Journal of Group Psychotherapy*, on time-limited group therapy and is co-author of the book *Integrative Group Treatment for Bulimia Nervosa* (2002).

J. Scott Rutan, PhD, CGP, DFAGPA, is currently Senior Faculty at the Boston Institute for Psychotherapy. He is a Past President and Distinguished Fellow of the American Group Psychotherapy Association. He is on the Editorial Board of the *International Journal of Group Psychotherapy, Revista Italiana di Gruppoanalist, Group Dynamics: Theory, Research, and Practice,* and *Group.* He has written extensively on group psychotherapy including a seminal book entitled *Psychodynamic Group Psychotherapy* (with Walter Stone, MD).

Victor L. Schermer, MA, LPC, CAC, CGP, is a psychologist in private practice and clinic settings in Philadelphia, Pennsylvania. He is Executive Director of the Study Group for Contemporary Psychoanalytic Process and Director of the Institute for the Study of Human Conflict. He is co-editor with Robert H. Klein of *Group Psychotherapy for Psychological Trauma* and author or editor of four additional books on group psychology, psychotherapy, and related subjects.

Elizabeth L. Shapiro, PhD, is the Associate Director of The Center for Psychoanalytic Studies at Massachusetts General Hospital, an Assistant Clinical Professor in the Department of Psychiatry at Harvard Medical School, and is in private practice in Lexington, Massachusetts. Dr. Shapiro has led workshops and published articles on psychodynamic psychotherapy.

Meg Sharpe, BA (Hons), MInst GA, CGP, received her training in sociology. She is a member of the Institute of Group Analysis (London), the Society of Analytical Psychologists, the International Association of Group Psychotherapy, and the International Society of Analytical Psychologists. She is a member of the International Advisory Panel, *Journal of Therapeutic Communities and of Group Analytic Practice,* London. She has presented internationally on large groups.

Brenda L. Smith, MSW, LICSW, CGP, is in private practice in Boston and Concord, Massachusetts. She is Senior Consultant to John Hancock Financial Services and a cofounder of the Children's Group Therapy Association. She has presented workshops at local, national- and international conferences on group psychotherapy.

Mark Sorensen, PhD, CGP, FAGPA, is on the faculty of the Training Program for Northeastern Society for Group Psychotherapy. He has lectured extensively about group therapy at the local and national level and supervised group therapists in a number of agencies and institutions. He has published in the *International Journal of Group Psychotherapy,* is a past Director of Group Therapy at Westwood Lodge Psychiatric Hospital, and is currently serving on the Board of Directors of the National Registry of Certified Group Psychotherapists.

Gil Spielberg, PhD, CGP, FAGPA, is a Training and Supervising Analyst at the Institute for Contemporary Psychoanalysis in Los Angeles. He received his psychoanalytic training at the Institute for the Psychoanalytic Study of Subjectivity (New York) and the Center for Advanced Group Studies (New York). Dr. Spielberg has taught at the California School of Professional Psychology–San Diego, and the University of California, San Diego and Los Angeles. Dr. Spielberg practices in both Los Angeles and La Jolla, California.

Walter N. Stone, MD, CGP, FAGPA, is Professor Emeritus, University of Cincinnati College of Medicine, Department of Psychiatry. He is a Past President of the American Group Psychotherapy Association and currently on the Board of the International Association of Group Psychotherapy. He is author of *Group Psychotherapy for People with Chronic Mental Illness* and co-author of *Psychodynamic Group Psychotherapy* in addition to numerous articles on self-psychological perspectives in groups.

Hillel I. Swiller, MD, CGP, FAGPA, DLFAPA, is Clinical Professor and Director of the Division of Psychotherapy, Department of Psychiatry, Mount Sinai School of Medicine. He is co-editor (with Anne Alonso) of *Group Therapy in Clinical Practice.* He is a Past Chairman, Section on Psychiatry, New York Academy of Medicine.

Shawn M. Taylor, PhD, is in private practice in Chicago, Illinois and an Adjunct Assistant Professor at Northwestern University. She is the current Chair of the Research Special Interest Panel at the annual meetings of the American Group Psychotherapy Association, as well as a member of Division 49 (Groups) in the American Psychological Association.

Kathleen Hubbs Ulman, PhD, is Assistant Professor in Psychology at Harvard Medical School, the Director of the Center for Group Psychotherapy at Massachusetts General Hospital, and a Past President of the Northeastern Society for Group Psychotherapy. She has conducted Training Groups for Northeastern Society for Group Psychotherapy and the Boston Institute for Psychotherapy and presented workshops on group therapy nationally and internationally.

Marsha Vannicelli, PhD, is Clinical Associate Professor at Harvard Medical School and on the faculty at the Massachusetts School of Professional Psychology. Dr. Vannicelli is the author of two books on group psychotherapy, *Removing the Roadblocks: Group Psychotherapy with Substance Abusers and Family Members* (1992) and *Group Therapy with Adult Children of Alcoholics* (1989), and more than 50 articles. She is a former member of the Editorial Board of the *Journal of Studies on Alcohol* and *International Journal of Group Psychotherapy.*

Robert Weber, PhD, CGP, FAGPA, is Training Supervisor at Massachusetts General Hospital's Center for Psychoanalytic Studies and the Center for Group Therapy. For 10 years, Dr. Weber was the Director of Group Therapy at Cambridge Hospital, a teaching affiliate of the Harvard Medical School, where he is a Clinical Instructor. He has published many journal articles in the field of group therapy. Recently, he revised the Basic Group Training Curriculum for the Certification Program of the National Registry of Certified Group Psychotherapists.

Section I
Boundary Issues

Overview

In *Analyze This*, Robert De Niro plays a gangland boss who has panic attacks. He begins treatment with a psychiatrist, Billy Crystal, who is about to get married. Crystal finds that the boundaries of this relationship are different from those with his other patients. After all, the Mafia boss gets anything he wants when he wants it, including therapy sessions during Crystal's wedding ceremony! Although we can laugh at Crystal's dilemma, as therapists we know that boundaries and the group agreements that define them help to create a safe environment for doing therapeutic work.

Barbara Cohn, in her chapter *Creating the Group Envelope*, defines *boundaries*, discusses the use of the term in group therapy, and delineates specific guidelines proposed by various clinicians.

Then follows the first dilemma of this book, *Sizing Up the Group*, in which several members precipitously leave a group following a series of dramatic losses. The therapist feels the pressure to appease the growing discontent among the surviving group members and wonders if the time is right to add new members. Whereas respondents Steven Haut and Jeanne Pasternak both view this dilemma in terms of group boundaries, they address the issue differently. Haut believes the group will feel safer if the leader addresses such existential concerns as life and death, sickness and health, and omnipotence and powerlessness. Pasternak, speaking from a practical viewpoint, encourages the leader to address directly the current violations of the group agreements.

In *Show Me the Money*, a frustrated and confused group therapist is caught in a dance with group members who unilaterally change how they pay for group. Elaine Jean Cooper, writing from a psychodynamic and systems perspective, focuses on the replay of early family dynamics as well as the deteriorating health of the group system, and she encourages the group leader to focus on boundary maintenance. In contrast, Steve Krugman, writing from a relational perspective, asserts that therapists and patients co-construct therapeutic dilemmas so the leader must analyze not only the patients' roles, but also his or her own.

In the third dilemma, *All for One and One for Some?*, the group therapist suddenly finds himself dealing with issues of jealousy, possessiveness, sibling rivalry, and confidentiality when he adds his individual therapy patients to his group without informing the group. Both our respondents, David Hawkins and Victor Schermer, emphasize the leader's need to attend to important transference and countertransference issues. Hawkins notes that the patients' and therapist's anxieties dovetail with each other and need to be separated, while Schermer acknowledges that the boundary has been disturbed but worries little because "every crisis is an opportunity."

Creating the Group Envelope

BARBARA R. COHN, PHD, CGP

In his well-known poem, "Mending Wall," Robert Frost tells us, "Good fences make good neighbors" (Lathem, 2002, p. 33). We know intuitively what he means by this: We human beings need reliable structures, with delineated boundaries, to live our civilized lives and to deal with one another constructively. If no boundaries exist (in this case, no clear perimeters between the land of one and the land of another), chaos rules, and all our efforts go to defend our territories and to maintain our survival rather than to recognize the position of the other and to have time and energy to attend to our own growth. Frost describes physical space in the poem: His perimeter is a wall of irregular rocks that needs to be repaired annually because it becomes eroded by the weather and "hunters" who have no regard for its value.

Most of us remember the poem as a beautiful reminder of the value of "fences," but Frost questions the necessity of a wall, stating, "He [the neighbor] is all pine and I am apple orchard. My apple trees will never get across and eat the cones under his pines" (Lathem, 2002, p. 33). Thus, Frost suggests that clear differences in the internal structure of the two properties make the wall less important. He develops a concept of boundary that refers not simply to the perimeter or external boundary, but also to delineations within the territories—that is, a concept of internal boundaries. As a metaphor, we know that "good fences" refers not simply to physical space, but also to psychic space and, for our present purposes, to the group space as well.

The term "boundary" is used freely in common discourse to indicate the point or line of separation between one person or activity and the next.

Psychological boundaries can be understood as the separation of the internal from the external experience for each individual as well as the maintenance of the distinction between self and other (Johnston, 2001). Additionally, boundaries can be drawn within the individual, between various aspects of the internal world, such as the boundaries separating ego from id, or self from object representations (Gabbard & Lester, 2003). Although the term "boundary" often refers to a delineating area or line, it is also used to refer to a set of behaviors, which can be thought of as the "rules of the game" (Johnston & Farber, 1996).

The role of therapeutic boundaries is important because of the emotional and regressive nature of the psychotherapeutic endeavor. Depending on the particular theory and technique employed by the therapist, a patient may be asked to engage in often painful remembrance of childhood events; to experience intense transference toward the therapist and fellow group members; or, in the case of a more interpersonal or intersubjective treatment, to participate in affectively laden, here-and-now exchanges in which self boundaries are often permeable and sometimes indeterminate.

The group contract

We can think of group psychotherapy as a living social system in which a particular activity, psychotherapy, is the task. To establish the boundary between the inside of this system and the outside, therapists construct a group contract. Singer, Astrachan, Gould, and Klein (1975) write, "It is through the contract that the leader derives his authority to work: to propose activities, to confront a member, to make interpretations. And it is by virtue of the contract that certain activities can be declared 'out of bounds' .... A clear contract provides valuable guidelines by which both leader and member can legitimately act or make demands in or on the group" (p. 147).

Thus, the group contract delineates the group space from its surround, keeps the group focused on the task, and provides order and authority to the leader and the group members. Analogous to the Frost poem, the contract both locates the "wall" for the group and establishes that apple trees rather than pine trees will be planted within.

Some theorists use the term "therapeutic frame" to describe phenomena similar to those denoted by the contract. Langs (1974) emphasizes the importance of the establishment of the frame and the value of holding such factors as scheduling and the professional role of the therapist constant. Bleger (1966) suggests that, within therapy, the frame constitutes and organizes the most primitive and undifferentiated aspects of the patient's ego. He states that the development of the ego depends on the reliability of the frame. Although Langs is thought of as a theorist who uses a concept of "frame" that refers to a rigid, unyielding structure, Gabbard and Lester (2003, pp. 39–40) point out that Langs's concept actually includes two distinct aspects: the relative constants of the analytic relationship (structure), and the more human elements that define the interaction (process).

In group psychotherapy, the frame delineates the boundaries of the group and creates a group environment that is sufficiently predictable and "safe" to allow patients to take the risks necessary for growth. Day (1967) very likely had this group's inner sanctum in mind when he fashioned the phrase "the group envelope." As will be discussed subsequently, many group therapists agree with Kernberg (1973) and Singer and colleagues (1975) that the group leader's primary function is the maintenance of the group boundaries. Rice and Rutan (1981) write, "The leader is constantly faced with the task of deciding which of the boundaries present in a group are uppermost at a particular time and require his intervention" (p. 298).

Once the contract is established in dyadic therapy, it may serve as background in the treatment and can be relied on as an essential structure, but may slip out of awareness for both therapist and patient. In therapy groups, the contract or frame paradoxically sets up relative constants for group life, while at the same time provides dynamic factors that will lead to acting out and violation of the frame. The complexity of group processes, coupled with a range of member personalities, often results in frequent and unexpected departures from the frame. Thus, boundary crossings are, in fact, frequent occurrences in group life. Gans (1992) writes about this complexity with regard to the setting of fees in group therapy: "Unlike the comparable event in individual therapy, in group therapy the leader functions in a more intense and complicated emotional field" (p. 140). Even a single boundary crossing automatically becomes a group event that involves multiple patient reactions. Although such events invariably arouse anxiety and uncertainty in group members, including the leader, if they are regarded as welcome though complex signals, they can provide opportunities for individual and group learning. Some theorists (Agazarian, 2001) focus on the modification of internal group boundaries as a deliberate treatment technique: they require patients to choose "at the boundary" between thought and feeling as well as between a here-and-now experience versus a there-and-then experience.

Specifics of the group contract
The group contract addresses both external and internal boundary issues. External group boundaries include group membership, locale, and session length. Internal group boundaries refer to aspects of ongoing group life such as norms, roles, and orientation to task. Confidentiality, payment of fees, and a no-socializing policy are examples of internal group boundaries.

From the first moment of contact, usually on the telephone, therapist and prospective group patient interact with one another in ways that establish the role boundaries of their psychotherapeutic relationship. Implicit in their interaction is that the therapist will maintain a professional role that requires a nonjudgmental supportive stance. At the same time, the therapist withholds most personal information, although, in this initial contact, he or she may share certain facts about the group and the nature of the therapy. The patient, on the other hand, assumes a different stance. He or she discusses the reasons for seeking treatment, or alternatively, gets preliminary information about the group and sets up an appointment for a group screening. Regardless of how much personal information the patient chooses to reveal over the phone (and this may be affected by the nature of the therapist's questions), the initial contact starts to set up boundaries and promote a patient role that will encourage the revelation of personal information and dependency on the therapist—and ultimately on the group—for help.

If a therapist recruits an individual patient from his or her own practice for membership in a group, the role boundaries between therapist and patient in the group erroneously may be viewed as simple extensions of the existing dyadic relationship. In such a situation, differences between the dyadic and group roles need to be acknowledged and carefully spelled out to establish a workable patient-therapist relationship in the group.

Rutan and Stone (2001) discuss at length the boundary issues that surface when therapists see patients simultaneously in individual and group treatment. Although they suggest that several different guidelines can work effectively, they recommend an agreement in which information brought up in the individual format may be discussed in the group: "The patient's contract should include explicit agreement that the therapies are not separated by a boundary of confidentiality" (p. 208).

Rutan and Stone (2001) also discuss the importance of patient preparation and the group agreements in establishing the contract with prospective group patients. During these sessions, the therapist can inform the patient about how group therapy works and help the patient develop expectations of ways the particular group in question can help with his or her difficulties. Many group leaders try to translate the patient's presenting problem into an interpersonal issue that can serve as an initial goal of treatment. Others, although not so explicit, will help the prospective patient envision more general ways in which group membership can help. The therapist and patient together begin to establish the boundaries for their working relationship as they discuss the patient's goals for group, the group contract, and how the group might help the patient.

Rutan and Stone (2001) present the following group agreements or guidelines: Group members agree (a) to be present each week, to be on time, and to remain throughout the entire meeting; (b) to work actively on the problems that brought them to the group; (c) to put feelings into words, not actions; (d) to use the relationships made in the group therapeutically, not socially; (e) to remain in the group until the problems that brought them to the group have been resolved; (f) to be responsible for their bill; and (g) to protect the names and identities of their fellow group members (pp. 144–152).

They further point out that group therapists differ with regard to their policies concerning these factors. Although Rutan and Stone (2001) have opinions on what procedures work best, they state repeatedly that what is most important is clarity and consistency of the guidelines that are set up at the beginning of the treatment relationship. It is my belief that group members can tolerate and work successfully with many differences among themselves. In fact, such heterogeneity can engender a rich and stimulating group process, but the patients need to believe that the therapist has anticipated these differences, approves of them, and has incorporated them into the group contract.

Thus the "group envelope" can enfold or contain many individual differences among the patients, as long as the group members understand that these differences are grist for the mill rather than "errors" or "inconsistencies" made by the therapist. It is important to remember that boundaries invariably will be crossed by both patients and therapists: missed sessions, lateness, vacations, unpaid bills, and the like are unavoidable. However, the therapist must process these boundary crossings as an essential part of the treatment process. Just as Frost's "hunters" delight in knocking down the stone fences, group patients will sometimes violate the group boundaries and in so doing will bring to light invaluable aspects of their more basic selves.

Most group therapists set up a boundary that allows learning to be taken out of the group system by individual patients while at the same time protecting the identities of individual members. A guideline that keeps names and identifying material confidential while allowing, indeed encouraging, group members to incorporate experiences they have had in the group into their outside lives represents a workable confidentiality boundary. Such an agreement points to the importance of the "permeability" or "opening and closing" of the external group boundary, an aspect that systems theorists deem necessary for the maintenance of any living system (Durkin, 1981).

Another important aspect of the group contract that needs to be established at the time of entry into the group is a policy of fee payment. Gans

(1992) has written a valuable article on the complexities of money in group psychotherapy. In his article, Gans emphasizes the importance of setting up a clear group contract with patients that includes announcements about unpaid bills at the beginning of group and a clear payment policy that requires group members to pay for a "seat" or place in the group (p. 135). Gans believes that inevitable violations of the group contract in relation to fee payment bring rich and sometimes unique themes into the group process.

When some patients violate the established contract for fees and payment, other patients often begin to act out their feelings with regard to their group therapy fees. Group contagion and the leader's inability to handle individual and whole group issues underlying the acting out may lead to a situation not unlike the sorcerer's apprentice where multiple solutions may only compound the problem. With issues of money and the slippery slope of the group process, the tendency for one boundary violation to echo and reverberate throughout the entire group is great. Group leaders need to expect such boundary problems and to address them with curiosity and empathy, a particularly difficult task when the acting out involves payment issues (p. 149).

Group development, context, and task

Developmental factors help determine what we consider to be the important group boundaries at any given point of time in the life of the group. MacKenzie and Livesley (1983) suggest that an interaction exists between the group developmental stage and a determination of relevant boundaries:

> This process can be conceptualized in terms of the resolution of a series of boundary issues involving the group as a whole and its individual members. The term "boundary" is not used in a physical sense. Psychological boundaries exist when there is awareness that two entities are different; this information about differences constitutes the boundary. For example, the experience of intensive engagement in a group, together with an awareness of how this differs from past interpersonal experiences, begins to establish the external boundary of the group. Subsequently, realization of the members that they are different from each other focuses attention on the intermember boundaries. (p. 102)

The context in which the group occurs also affects the nature of the group boundaries. Many authors (see Klein & Kugel, 1981; Rice & Rutan, 1981) have written about the permeability of the external boundaries of psychotherapy groups on inpatient wards and in day treatment programs. Often external boundary maintenance becomes the most salient aspect of ongoing group life, and system events going on outside the group become highly relevant to an understanding of the group process. Yalom (1983) differs from the above authors in that he believes adherence to the group task rather than attention to hospital ward events reinforces the external boundary of inpatient groups. In writing about process groups in institutional settings, I have suggested that the "primary boundary maintenance function for a process group leader is actually performance of the group task: to focus the group on systems issues and their impact on the individual professional role" (Cohn, 1994, p. 341).

Thus, depending on the context, the goals of the group, and the stage of group development, boundary factors, or those elements that demarcate the group from the nongroup, can include a focus on various aspects of group life other than the initial group agreements. As will be discussed in the following section, therapeutic technique, as well as the therapist's values and theoretical orientation, all help determine the boundaries relevant to the particular group at hand.

Boundaries and group psychotherapy theory

For purposes of this discussion, I would like to make a distinction between psychodynamic and systems theories in their application to the subject of boundaries, despite the fact that many authors consider systems theory to be an aspect of psychodynamic theory (see Rutan & Stone, 2001). For others, the theory of living systems is considered to be a meta-theory that encompasses psychodynamic thinking as well as other theoretical models (Durkin, 1981; von Bertalanffy, 1966).

A review of psychoanalytic and psychodynamic group theory and practice since the time of McDougall (1920), Freud (1922/1951), Wolf and Schwartz (1962), Bion (1960), and Foulkes (1964) indicates that many seminal group thinkers did not use the concept of boundary as an important parameter in their writings on group theory and practice. This is not to say that their theories did not address the contract, norms, task, and roles—all factors that distinguish group events from nongroup events. However, the word and concept of "boundary" was not emphasized by these authors.

In contrast, systems theorists developed theory and technique that used a concept of "boundary" as a primary building block. Bringing together the writings of Lewin (1936) and von Bertalanffy (1966), writers such as Durkin (1981) created a rich body of thought, sometimes quite technical, which draws attention to the operation of both external and internal boundaries in groups. In his now classic work, *Living Groups*, Durkin (1981) presents a compendium of articles that greatly advances our knowledge of group boundaries, both in their structural and functional properties. In the section of his book titled *Glossary of Living Structure Terms*, Durkin presents a definition of boundary not as a noun, but as the verb, "boundarying." He defines boundarying as "the complementary processes whereby a living structure opens/closes its own boundaries" (p. 340). He describes how such opening and closing is essential to the maintenance of the group as a viable, "living" social system.

Many contemporary group psychotherapists use a combination of psychodynamic and systems thinking to understand the operation of boundaries in their groups. Brabender (2000), writing on the value of periods of chaos in the group process, states that group leaders need to reinforce boundaries particularly during phases of chaos—for example, when the dissolution of the prior organization of the group structure is occurring (p. 30). Contemporary relational concepts such as projective identification, empathic attunement, and containment (often thought to be process variables) can also be understood as boundary operations in that they help define the nature and limits of the group psychotherapeutic endeavor (Billow, 2000).

Working with group boundaries
As was discussed previously, attention to group boundaries is a primary focus for group psychotherapists. Yet therapists differ in the degree to which they think of group boundaries as a relatively stable aspect of the group (which, when crossed, provide the group with information about hidden themes) and as parameters that require active attention and even manipulation (Agazarian, 2001). Johnston and Farber (1996), in their study *The Maintenance of Boundaries in Psychotherapeutic Practice*, discuss this issue:

> The theoretical issue implied in the struggle between those advocating strict boundaries universally applied, and those advocating more flexible boundaries applied according to their impact upon the patient, reflects a larger issue in the field between those whose work is grounded in a positivistic model, and those who operate under post-positivistic assumptions . . . . The first school, exemplified by Langs, believes that precisely maintained boundaries yield "pure" intrapsychic phenomena (similar to the idea that total "neutrality" produces a "pure" transference). The second school, represented by Mitchell (1993), believes that the maintenance of boundaries is an interpersonal act organized by the patient's subjectivity—a part of the relationship, rather than a source of distortion. (p. 399)

Regardless of a therapist's approach to the group boundaries, metaphor and visualization are often used to apprehend and access the nature of these boundaries at any given point of time in the life of the group. For example, a supervisee who discusses a group with attendance problems describes the (external) boundary as "ragged and jagged." In another example, a woman's group discusses week after week the world of men as alien and discriminatory. The therapist visualizes the group boundary as a tightly fitted brick wall that grows progressively taller to keep out what is perceived as an ever-increasing, outside threat. In a third group, a therapist envisions the internal group structure as a delicate and complicated lattice work similar to the pieces of coral sitting on her desk; she does so after she listens to the members of a mature group reminisce about their first impressions of one another and contrast these one-dimensional views with their current complex and nuanced pictures.

Whether we refer to boundaries as a "group envelope," a "matrix," or a "thick, impermeable line," therapists tend to use visualization and metaphor to describe this complex phenomenon. I believe that such artful descriptions may be necessary tools for group therapists to fully understand and communicate the nature of the group boundaries both to ourselves and to our patients, as part of ongoing boundary maintenance. Just as Robert Frost in repairing his wall says, "good fences make good neighbors," we therapists in tending our group boundaries can well consider that "good boundaries make good treatments."

References

Agazarian, Y. M. (2001). *Systems-centered approach to inpatient group psychotherapy*. London & Philadelphia: Jessica Kingsley.

Bertalanffy, L. von (1966). *General system theory and psychiatry*. New York: Basic Books.

Billow, R. M. (2000). Relational levels of the "container-contained" in group therapy. *Group. 24*, 243–259.

Bion, W. R. (1960). *Experiences in groups*. New York: Basic Books.

Bleger, J. (1966). Psychoanalysis of the psychoanalytic frame. *International Journal of Psychoanalysis, 48*, 511–519.

Brabender, V. (2000). Chaos, group psychotherapy, and the future of uncertainty and uniqueness. *Group, 24*, 23–32.

Cohn, B. R. (1994). The process group in institutional settings: Special techniques for an endangered species. *International Journal of Group Psychotherapy, 44*, 333–347.

Day, M. (1967). The natural history of training groups. *International Journal of Group Psychotherapy, 17*, 436–456.

Durkin, J. E. (Ed). (1981). *Living groups: Group psychotherapy and general system theory*. New York: Brunner/Mazel.

Foulkes, S. H. (1964). *Therapeutic group analysis*. London: Routledge.

Freud, S. (1951). *Group psychology and the analysis of the ego*. New York: Liveright.

Gabbard G. O., & Lester, E. P. (2003). *Boundaries and boundary violations in psychoanalysis*. Washington, DC: American Psychiatric Press.

Gans, J. S. (1992). Money and psychodynamic group psychotherapy. *International Journal of Group Psychotherapy, 42*, 133–152.

Johnston, S. H. (2001). *Therapists' modifications of psychotherapeutic boundaries*. Unpublished dissertation.

Johnston, S. H., & Farber, B. A. (1996). The maintenance of boundaries in psychotherapeutic practice. *Psychotherapy, 33*, 391–402.

Kernberg, O. F. (1973). Psychoanalytic object relations theory, group processes and administration. *Annals of Psychoanalysis, 1*, 363–386.

Klein, R. H., & Kugel, B. (1981). Inpatient group psychotherapy from a systems perspective: Reflections through a glass darkly. *International Journal of Group Psychotherapy. 31,* 311–328.

Langs, R. J. (1974). The therapeutic relationship and deviations in technique. *International Journal of Psychoanalytic Psychotherapy, 4,* 106–141.

Lathem, E. C. (2002). *The poetry of Robert Frost.* Gordonsville, VA: Henry Holt.

Lewin, K. (1936). *Principles of topological psychology.* New York: McGraw-Hill.

MacKenzie, K. R., & Livesley, M. B. (1983). A developmental model for brief group therapy. In R. R. Dies & K. R. MacKenzie (Eds.), *Advances in Group Psychotherapy: Integrating research and practice,* Monograph I, American Group Psychotherapy Association Monograph Series. New York: International Universities Press.

McDougall, W. (1920). *The group mind.* New York: Putnam.

Mitchell, S. A. (1993). *Hope and dread in psychoanalysis.* New York: Basic Books.

Rice, C., & Rutan, J. S. (1981). Boundary maintenance in inpatient therapy groups. *International Journal of Group Psychotherapy, 31,* 297–310.

Rutan, J. S., & Stone, W. N. (2001). *Psychodynamic group psychotherapy* (3rd ed.). New York: Guilford Press.

Singer, D., Astrachan, B., Gould, L., & Klein, E. (1975). Boundary management in psychological work with groups. *Journal of Applied Behavioral Science, 11,* 137–176.

Wolf, A., & Schwartz, E. K. (1962). *Psychoanalysis in groups.* New York: Grune & Stratton.

Yalom, I. (1983). *Inpatient group psychotherapy.* New York: Basic Books.

Sizing Up the Group

Dear Consultant:

The attendance and membership of my ongoing group has been unstable lately. One patient, Jack, was hospitalized for depression and substance abuse two weeks ago (I expect him back in two weeks), and a month ago another left permanently with Lou Gehrig's disease. A third patient, Marguerite, comes to group erratically, and no matter what intervention I make, seems to have a hard time committing to weekly attendance. This is new behavior over the past few months (prior to that she attended group almost religiously). She says that she has been unable to come regularly because of work commitments, but I have a sense that something else might be going on. Along with the two people who have just left, another patient, Suzanne, has complained for some time now that the group is not helping her (even though she gets more time each week because of the limited membership). She berates me each week for my failing her, and then she tries to get other patients to side with her and further criticize me. They say that I don't talk enough in group, and that they are not making progress on their issues. When they are feeling particularly critical, they use Jack as an example of how unhelpful I am. They say if I was really a good therapist, he wouldn't have needed hospitalization, which I am beginning to feel myself.

Because the group is now down to four members (including Jack), I want to add several new members. Adding new members will increase the amount of input the members get from each other and I hope will help the group and me feel that the group will survive. I have interviewed one person whom I think will make a great group member, and I just got a referral for another. The person I interviewed is somewhat higher functioning than the rest of the group in that he is more insightful and less depressed. During the intake process, he asked me questions about the group and the kind of

13

people who are in it. Although I gave general answers about the age range and mixed gender, I did not reveal specific information about individual patients or that the group is going through a difficult time. I didn't really know how much to tell him, and I'm worried that the other potential new member might ask similar questions.

How do I respond to these kinds of questions ethically but also maintain confidentiality? When or under what circumstances should I bring in new patients? Will that destabilize the group further or strengthen it? Should they come in together or one at a time? What do I tell them, if anything, about what is going on in the group? How long should I wait between adding members? Should I wait until Jack has returned? How should I prepare new and current members for these changes in the group? I'd appreciate any guidance you can give me.

Dear Therapist:

Before I share my response to your questions, let me state my theoretical framework. My orientation is a composite of psychodynamic, social group work, systems theory, and existential philosophy. My stage of life development (age 58) and my 30-plus years of group experience, including a significant amount of child and adolescent group therapy, have a substantial impact on my point of view.

The tone of your description of the group reflects your significant concern about the group's survival and your effectiveness as a group therapist. Anxiety and self doubt frequently inhabit all good group leaders when their groups are in the process of negotiating very stressful events. The recent events of a member leaving with Lou Gehrig's disease, Jack's hospitalization, Marguerite's erratic attendance, and Suzanne's critical attitude about your effectiveness constitute major issues for the group. Therapy groups, by their very nature, do not negotiate these events gracefully. Thus, the group can simultaneously run successfully while the group leader feels badly about the way it is going. These problems also create an opportunity for growth in the members, the group, and the leader if they are negotiated successfully. Such successful negotiation is, in large part, dependent on maintaining the group's boundaries. The most productive answer to your questions lies in the understanding of the concept of boundaries. I would divide boundary issues into two categories. (The first I call the existential issues and the second involve the group contract.)

I feel that all groups initially surround themselves with a false cocoon-like boundary constructed by the wishes and yearnings for a leader who can omnipotently protect them from all harm. This cocoon insulates the group from the existential issues of the finiteness of life and the paper-thin line between sickness and health, life and death, and the limits about how much help one can get and give. The cocoon of your group has been shattered by Lou Gehrig's disease and Jack's hospitalization. Suzanne's wish for more from you expresses both anger and hurt and can be seen as speaking for the group wish for you to repair the cocoon. The wish is not only for you to have prevented Jack's hospitalization, but also to have prevented Lou Gehrig's disease. If you cannot accomplish this, what are the limits of the protection that you can provide to the members? Exploring the group's feelings about this will help them to grieve and accept the loss of the false cocoon. The more successfully the group can resolve the struggle between the wish for the power of the leader and group to be infinite, versus finite and real, the more the false cocoon can be replaced by realistic expectations.

Working within this new container, the group can be significantly more productive. In this context the more that problems of life, death, hospitalization, divorce, and the like can be experienced and tolerated in the group, the stronger and safer the group will feel. The members then start to realize that the group can contain and accept the parts of them of which they are most ashamed and frightened. In addition, the group's history and experience is enriched, and more expertise will be brought to future dilemmas.

I sometimes think of the group as a ship sailing into stormy weather where the members, and sometimes the leader, fear the ship is in danger of sinking. At these times members think about jumping ship. When a ship heads into stormy weather the first focus is to "batten down the hatches." In a group that is weathering a storm it is important to attend to all the boundaries. This is a time when basic boundary issues such as starting and ending the group on time can be critical. It is important for the members to know that no matter how difficult the issues, they are not swamping the group boundaries.

In the context of boundaries, it is important to explore Marguerite's sporadic attendance. Is Marguerite jeopardizing her group membership by breaking the contract on attendance? You may find it difficult to confront the violation in the contract when the group is shrinking and you feel its survival is questionable. The degree of difficulty in this situation is directly proportional to its importance.

Over the years, my experience has indicated that establishing a clear contract before starting the group and holding to it, even in the most difficult times, is vital. Your specific questions—what to tell prospective new group members, when to bring in new group members, how many new group members should arrive at a time, and the level of functioning criteria for the new group members—are best answered in your initial contract.

Deciding these issues in the midst of a group crisis is a time when leaders are most likely to be in the grip of countertransference and projective identification, and it is not the optimal time to make or change group policies.

The general answers you offered to the prospective new member were very sound, appropriate, ethical, and maintained confidentiality. My answer to the question of when to add new members is as soon as possible, consistent with your contract. I am assuming that the total number of members in the group has been set and that all the members know that number by the empty chairs in the room. These empty chairs are important as they outline a physical boundary that is yet to be filled. When the group is filled and that boundary closes, groups take off in a way not possible before. Some experienced leaders add a member as soon as an opening is available without prior announcement to the group. Others, myself included, give the group a specific number of weeks (e.g., one to four) to process the change.

My experience has been that it is not productive to try to time the addition of new members in relation to what is going on in the group for several reasons. What if Jack's return is delayed, or suppose he doesn't return? Suppose another crisis erupts in your group? I have seen group leaders change the starting date of a new member because of a group crisis and then the new member decides not to join the group. How long do you want to keep a new member waiting? Most importantly, groups are at best ambivalent about new members. If you have a silently held policy about when not to add new members, the group will divine this and then are likely to act out to prevent you from adding these members.

Adding more than one member at a time has its pros and cons. If you have a few new members to add at once, it would be a difficult but potentially exciting change for the group. On the other hand, spreading it out would mean that each new member, and the group, would have more time to process the entry. However, your group would then be in the turmoil of change for a more protracted time. It is a personal decision with no clear right or wrong answer. I would opt for adding new members as soon as these members are ready, even if at the same time.

Your question about the "somewhat" higher functioning potential member is influenced by the stress of the current group situation. To check this out, ask yourself these questions: When I established the group, would this member have fit in? A few months ago, when the group was functioning better, would I have seen him as fitting in? If he had been in the group these past few months, would he have regressed like the other members in this crisis? If future new members came along who were at a similar functioning level, would I accept them?

I agree with you that adding new members is a vote of confidence in the group and this will give new hope for the survival of the group. To summarize, the more the boundaries can be maintained and held in crisis and transition, the stronger the container for the group to work within. Your struggle with the group appears to be a very normative one for a group leader.

Steven Haut, MSW, CGP, FAGPA

Dear Therapist:
Your dilemma is common to all group therapists. How do we bear the anxiety when group members question the benefits of group, act out, or leave? We can't help but take it personally when a member leaves precipitously or others criticize us for not doing a good enough job. The challenge is to remind ourselves this is not personal, but instead a message from the member about how he feels. You are experiencing the frustrations of a parent who is trying to "do the right thing" and the kids are giving you grief. What a perfect time to reach out for a consultation!

Your group members are going through some important life events that are probably making the group members feel anxious. Given that two of the four members have experienced a major loss recently, I understand why the remaining two express anger and helplessness. Lou Gehrig's disease is painful to watch and I'm hopeful that the patient gave adequate notice and time to process the good-byes. If not, you will need to process the good-bye with the remaining members. Remember, although gone from the group, he is still very present for those who remain. What losses did his illness and precipitous leaving bring up for them?

Jack's absence from the group for the past few weeks will give you another opportunity to talk with the group about loss. Although you should encourage group members to talk about how they feel about Jack's absence, I would frame Jack's hospitalization positively. His participation in an intensive treatment program is a sign of independence and he should be supported for making such a commitment. Did everyone know about Jack's substance abuse? What are the boundaries surrounding substance abuse for your group? Jack seems to be addressing his difficulties, and I would give the group credit for helping him to seek treatment: "Perhaps it was our success with Jack that he finally decided to get intense treatment for his depression and substance abuse. Hospitalization takes courage and commitment to the healing process. I look forward to Jack's return in a couple of weeks." I would also make Jack's recovery an active subject in group by asking him, following his return, "How are you doing today with your sobriety?" This gives members permission to address the issue with Jack, and allows him to be forthcoming about a major problem in his life. It focuses on what the group is assembled to address—problems and successes. Most abuse is shameful and kept secret. Jack's hospitalization makes his struggle group information.

The two women remaining in this group may be telling you that they fear the ship is sinking, and likely worry it is their fault. Their criticism may be an expression of their concern about whether you can keep them safe. After all, one man gets a disease, and another is hospitalized. What will happen next?

Marguerite's erratic attendance is a boundary violation and I would wonder aloud about her message. Is she acting out her ambivalence about these important relationships? On an individual level, what is her history with people coming and going in her life? Perhaps your fear of losing another group member makes it difficult to confront her acting out. You need to confront Marguerite about the impact of her behavior on her relationships. It is hoped that others will join in, letting her know that they feel unimportant to her or angry when she puts her job before her commitment to them. It may feel easier to be angry with the leader than directly with another group member.

Erratic attendance interferes with the development of intimacy—a common problem for many group members. Marguerite may not feel safe in this group and doesn't know how to increase her level of intimacy when other members keep leaving. I would say to her that she may feel ambivalent about how she wants to use the group to resolve her life struggles. When she joined the group, she committed to weekly attendance and to work honestly with others in relationship. She has changed those boundaries and needs to reflect on how her behavior is her way of not valuing the people around her. She may not want to move to the next level of commitment in her therapy, or she may feel ready to terminate and not know how to do so honestly and directly.

It is always better for the group to feel that you, as their leader, value the boundaries to which they all committed. It is disheartening for members to see the leader allow acting out. Issues of "group survival" are important indicators of how we feel about our competence as group therapists. Your hope that a new member will help the group survive is a good example of Yalom's (1985) discussion of how the power of the group can make one feel inadequate. The group may have picked up on your anxiety. It is you who needs to keep the boat steady. A group can survive with four members. You can let them know that you plan to increase the size to six or eight, but that it is more important to add someone who is right for the group. The better the match, the more the group will cohere. Group cohesion is a significant curative factor and is achieved as members assume ownership of the group process.

To announce a new member is a clear statement that you intend for the group to survive. Optimally, it would be best to wait until Jack returned and made a commitment to continuing. I usually give the group two to three weeks' notice before a new member joins. I would not tell a new member that the group is going through a difficult time. Groups that are "working" should go through difficult times. Conflicts, illness, sobriety, commitment, and responsibility are all predictable group issues that cause instability but are available for examination in the group. As the group leader, you need to provide continued support for this expectably difficult work and the commitment group members have made to developing healthier relationships.

It is not a boundary violation to give information about the composition of your group to a potential new member. Confidentiality must be protected, but information about the work the group is doing is important (e.g., a member has just terminated because of a serious illness). Your confidence in being able to provide a safe environment for these members to do their work is conveyed through your ability to define the boundaries that will keep this a positive growth experience. An important curative factor in the group experience is accepting the reality that people come and go in our lives, yet we can benefit from the experience we have with each. If two people are ready to start the group and it is practical, I would start them together. I am open with members, new and old, that one may start this month and another may start next month because of scheduling. Those two new members may develop a bond and continue to relate to "when we started group."

Your final questions speak to the need for strong and clear boundaries. I remind my group that one benefit of group therapy is that there will always be next week, a designated time and place where everyone will again sit down and address the issues. They need not fear that conflicts will not get resolved, if everyone agrees to return and continue the discussion. I monitor my anxieties during the week between group meetings, understand what got stirred up for me, and get consultation if needed. I can then let the members have their own anxieties and learn to understand them. Everyone is anxious about a new person joining us—will he or she enhance or destroy the group? Will he or she like me? The new person is anxious, too. Each member's defenses are in play and it is your ability to keep the boundaries strong that allows each to learn which defenses serve the interest of developing relationships. How many times have I concluded a group session harboring the fear that not a single member would return next week? But then I comfort myself with the memory that I have been here before and that interesting work lies ahead!

Jeanne Pasternak, LCSW, CGP, FAGPA

Reference

Yalom, I. (1985). *The theory and practice of group psychotherapy.* New York: Basic Books.

Show Me the Money

Dear Consultant:

I need help with money management in my group. My group agreements require patients to pay me at the beginning of the group as they come into the room. I hand patients a receipt at the end of each month. They are allowed to miss two sessions per calendar year for free, regardless of when they join the group. This agreement rolls over again each January 1. An explicit part of the agreement is that billing and payment issues are group business and are discussed in the group.

For the past three months I have noticed that my patients in one group have been acting out around payment for group therapy. I started this group of five 2 years ago. Four of the original members are still in the group and a new member, Paula, joined the group last month, bringing the group back to five. Initially I had patients pay me at the beginning of the group each week. Until recently, most patients were pretty good at paying, but a number of events have led me to wonder whether the group is acting out some feelings toward me.

Two patients have begun to consistently forget their checkbooks, so I often do not get paid until the following week. One of them, Julia, recently decided to pay a month in advance so she wouldn't get behind. The other, Susan, who pays each week, announced she will be gone for three months because of a temporary work transfer. She's agreed to pay for her seat, but I wonder what her absence will do to the group dynamic.

I find I am having trouble keeping track of who's paid how much when. It's driving me crazy! A third patient, Anne, tends to use up a lot of the time in the group. A month ago she bounced her check to me, and then did it again several weeks later. I told her I wanted to be paid in cash after that. At first she paid me in a white envelope, which I did not open until the group was over. I found that she had shorted me $5. The following week I told her that her payment was short and she said she'd make up for it the next week. I said okay. When I opened the envelope that week she had shorted me another $10! Now I open the envelope each week and count it in front of the group. Although I know it's her issue, I find it embarrassing to have to count the money in the group and confront her if she hasn't paid the right amount. When I address the issue with her, she says she is really stretched financially even though she makes more than I do!

To make things worse, I want to raise my fee in this group because I haven't since the group started. I feel greedy, but I also work hard and want to be paid for my work. I'm afraid to raise the issue because I think some of the patients might leave and the group is already small, especially when Susan takes her leave. When I've addressed the financial issues in the group, the conversation falls flat, and, at times, I detect resentment as well. What can I do to better address the underlying dynamics? What are patients trying to tell me about my leadership and their dynamics? Should I have a different financial policy? Do you have any general recommendations about how to handle financial issues in group therapy?

Dear Therapist:

Over the years I have learned to respect a number of theories. Rather than pick one that will serve all purposes, I keep a collection in my armamentarium and pull them out as I need them. In reading your dilemma, four theories come to mind that would be useful in understanding your dilemma: psychodynamic (Rutan & Stone, 2001), psychoanalytic (Scheidlinger, 1980), systems (Durkin, 1975), and self psychology (Harwood & Pines, 1998; Lonergan, 1982). In the interest of space, I will reflect on two of these four theories to offer a flavor of how I think.

The hallmark of psychodynamic theory is that members' behavior in the group is connected to early family experiences. Is it possible that Julia, who pays a month ahead, does not want to take a risk that she will mess up and have you become angry or disappointed in her? Is she trying to avoid your rage as she did her parents? Anne pays with a bad check. Is she expressing hostility toward you that she cannot consciously own? Does she feel entitled to therapy without payment? Is she enraged about the abuse she endured as a child? Is Susan, who pays up front but leaves for three months, avoiding your rage at her absence? If so, is she repeating a childhood coping mechanism that allowed her to do what she wanted but appeased her parents?

You need to make the unconscious conscious by interpreting what the unconscious motivation might be for each individual and the group. It is notable that you seem surprised or feel something is wrong when people act out their money issues. Acting out is often a vehicle for patients to show and get help with their problem: Treatment means analyzing the meaning of their behavior. Thus, when you count Anne's payment in front of the group, you courageously confront her problem. Everyone in the group needs to understand this. An analysis of the members' behaviors may reveal fears they have about: (a) how strong you are; (b) whether you can take their anger; and (c) whether you can understand how their behavior is related to their central psychological problem. Their defensive reactions are only problematic if they are not understood (analyzed), so this is an opportunity to surface unconscious material. If you confront the "flat conversation" and the underlying resentment, there will be a wealth of new material underneath.

A good psychodynamic group will connect history with current functioning, group participation, and presenting complaint. From this perspective, other questions would be: Is Julia generally avoidant of conflict? Is this one reason that she is coming for help for intimate relationships that don't seem to last? Is Anne coming to the group because she has no friends and alienates people quickly? Does she relate similarly to group members? Is Susan coming to the group because she has difficulty making sacrifices for a relationship and, therefore, has friends drop her? Do people in the group feel close to her?

Systems theory is the study of living systems and what makes them sick or healthy. All systems (e.g., individual, group, and therapist) are part of a suprasystem; they also have subsystems. You are the organizing subsystem of the group (similar to the ego for an individual). For a system to be healthy, it has to have an optimum balance of information going in and out. This makes boundary maintenance very important. If the boundary is too tight, the system will stagnate. If it is too open, there will not be enough cohesiveness (glue) to hold it together. In your group the boundary appears to be too open. Patients are paying erratically; Susan is leaving for three months; you do not feel in control of the group; you don't feel comfortable raising fees; members are not cooperating with your rules. It appears that the "organizing subsystem" is not functioning well. Given this picture, the system has to be treated. You need to take control of the group and set strict guidelines, taking the risk that people might quit the group. It is better to have one or two people leave and have the group be therapeutic for those remaining. New people joining will pick up the healthier norms quickly.

You sound in a muddle about the fees you charge. Nothing is wrong with wanting to raise your fees, but you need to look at whether this serves your best interest. We all have to be practical and consider the "supply and demand" of our services. Sometimes, higher fees result in unexpected terminations. On the other hand, when we feel guilty about a fee increase, we often underestimate what group members can handle. Regardless, you need to process your fee arrangements with the group members.

Your current agreements about payment may be contributing to your group's less than optimal functioning. When you collect payment for group each week, you have to deal with these issues every week. I have people pay by the month, so the group and I can deal with other issues on other weeks. You admit that you are afraid of raising people's fees. Are you comfortable collecting fees at all? Are members playing on your discomfort, to everyone's disadvantage? It is generous of you to give members two weeks of vacation, no matter when they join the group. However, your policy may convey that you are uncomfortable making your own financial needs *a priority,* or that you do not want people to be angry with you.

I suggest three alternate possibilities for collecting fees in a group. First, members pay at the beginning of the month for the whole month and pay for the group as long as the group meets. No exceptions. The result is a group of serious group members who don't want to miss sessions that they have already paid for. They pay for their place in the group the way they pay rent for an apartment. You get paid a predictable fee. It also gives the group something to get angry about. Because you do not change your rule in response to dissatisfaction, members can re-experience the unfairness of childhood. Some things are just unfair. You have needs too.

Second, members pay for their last month of treatment before they begin group, and then they pay weekly or monthly. This plan assures that members will give their four weeks notice when they are ready to leave. They are less likely to quit in a rage.

Finally, the leader makes announcements at the beginning of each session, which include problems with payment. Bills are put on a table in the middle of the group, so everyone can see them. If members have an insurance plan with a co-payment, they pay the entire amount if they miss a session, because the insurance company will not pay for missed sessions (Gans, 1992).

You need confidence and sophistication to carry out these plans. Now compare these plans with what you chose to do. In your conscious effort to be fair (and nice), you have given members too much leeway, the way a permissive parent does with a child. The child becomes insecure because he gets the message that he is too weak to endure the strong limits that other children can. When you break the frame, you convey to the members that they are so fragile that they may fall apart if you are not nice. In fact, what you need to do is confront the group members on their resistance and interpret their transferential relationships to you as parent–leader. Until you do, you (and they) will continue to feel disempowered. Pay attention to your countertransference because it may reflect the impotence that all the members feel. As they project their impotence on you, you feel more and more helpless. When you can help them to reflect on their behavior and understand the meaning, you will feel more in control of the group and they will feel safe enough to do the work.

In conclusion, it is important not to oversimplify what goes on in a therapy group. Viewing the group through the lens of several theories can foster an in-depth view of the group process. Group process is multilayered and complex. This is the reason so many of us love to lead therapy groups: the surprises and new learning are never-ending.

Elaine Jean Cooper, LCSW, PhD, CGP, FAGPA

References

Durkin, H. (1975). The development of systems theory and its implications for the theory and practice of group therapy. In L. Wolberg and M. Aronson (Eds.), *Group Therapy* (pp. 8–20). New York: Stratton Intercontinental.

Gans, J. S. (1992). Money and psychodynamic group psychotherapy. *International Journal of Group Psychotherapy*, 42, 133–152.

Harwood, I., & M. Pines (Eds.). (1998). *Self experiences in group*. London: Jessica Kingsley.

Lonergan, E. (1982). *Group intervention*. New York: Jason Aronson.

Rutan, J. S., & Stone, W. N. (2001). *Psychodynamic group psychotherapy* (3rd ed.). New York: Guilford Press.

Scheidlinger, S. (Ed.). (1980). *Psychoanalytic group dynamics*. New York: International Universities Press.

Dear Therapist:

Your account reminded me of the long list of group money tangles I have experienced over the years. I thought of how much I had learned about money as the "infinite emotional calculus" that it is, and that only recently, I again found myself tripped up over an over-determined financial matter with a patient.

My remarks reflect my interest in relational psychoanalysis and inter-subjectivity as a theoretical framework for group: "The basic premise of the relational approach is that psychoanalytic data are mutually generated by therapist and patients, codetermined by their conscious and unconscious" (Billow, 2003, p. 44). The issue of money in group treatment touches patient and therapist alike and constitutes a web of connection among members and leader. It is one of the fundamental "exchanges" that structure the treatment relationship. Inevitably, it reflects feelings of self worth, of having and not having, of being given to and taking from, and of being owed.

Feelings of greed, shame and guilt, competition, and jealousy are embedded in the issues and conflicts surrounding money.

To add to the complexity, many mental health professionals are uncomfortable with their own needs for money, and may have entered the helping profession out of an aversion to competition and materialism. People who want to help others sometimes have difficulty asserting their own needs, and can feel very conflicted about charging fees, wanting to get paid, and being prosperous. At the same time, issues of greed may also color therapist-patient transactions. Many would like to avoid the exchange of money for emotional attention. The combination of a therapist who is uncomfortable in relation to money, and patients with their own feelings of deprivation, specialness, loss, jealousy, and the like can generate a big mess.

We do not know many things about this group and its history. How and when did the fifth original member leave the group? How did the group process the loss? Is the new member, Paula, the one who acts out? Although you, as therapist, share a great deal of your own feelings about the financial behavior of the group, we do not know how the group is functioning in any other areas, or how they feel about you.

The vignette suggests two complementary lines of thought. Along one line, money and "money management" is the issue and the group, in a sense, is supervising the therapist. Along the other, the conflict and confusion surrounding payment is likely to reflect other conflicts and feelings that are being displaced and disguised as issues about money.

It is possible to imagine that a subgroup is reacting to feelings about your rigidity and anxiety about money management. You have taken the useful position that feelings and attitudes about money belong in the group and should be openly discussed. However, your policy of allowing two free absences may signal your anxiety over conflict and issues of fairness. Finally, I found myself bridling at the idea of paying for group each and every time, and remembered utilizing such a policy in the past. Although it seems straightforward, it inadvertently focuses group conflict and hostility on the question of "why did you not pay today?" Fees become a lightning rod for hostility and passive-aggressive behavior. One can take too rigid a stance, focusing on who has or hasn't paid and why. Larger and deeper themes may get obscured by a focus on passive-aggressive resistance and the ensuing conflict. The question of what the deeper issues are, and why they can't be named, remains unexamined. At the same time, one can have a very lively process with this focus. In this case, however, the group is unreflective and unresponsive to the question.

Heading in the other direction, I wondered whether the displaced conflict concerned the loss of the fifth member and the premature introduction of a new person. Maybe there was more anger and resentment than you and the group knew how to manage directly (Your policy of two free absences strikes me as a conflict-avoidant stance.) Perhaps in your anxiety about money management and your concern about shrinking revenue, you rushed in the new member before the group was ready. Perhaps the older members of the group, sensing your discomfort and confusion, have been exploiting this area as an indirect expression of other feelings that are not yet safe enough to name.

Given your confusion, I might well seek a consultation to clarify what my role was in the group's behavior, and how to understand the larger situation. After sorting this out, I would ask the group's help in making sense of the complex communication. I might say, for example:

> I wonder if the group could help me sort something out. Over the past few months (maybe since original group member five left) I'm sure that some of you have noticed that the issue of bill paying has gotten more and more complicated. You've really gotten my attention, but the only trouble is I'm not sure what you want me to know or to notice. It's as if part of the group is trying to tell us something about how they feel but they're doing it disguised as a money issue. It feels like some of you are annoyed with me but are uncomfortable saying so more directly. I've also noticed that when I've brought this up before, the group goes flat. What are you trying to tell me?

Depending on how this went, I might then take a more direct stance vis-à-vis the contract. Gans (1992) argues that the "failure of the leader to attend to these violations [of the group contract] and promote group discussion around them is invariably destructive to the group" (p. 138). Dealing with issues regarding payment would be in the forefront of my thoughts about the group. I might say something like, "Your feelings about being taken advantage of in your marriage remind me that I sometimes feel that you're taking advantage of me and the group," or, "Perhaps there's a connection between your wish to be treated as a special person, which gets you in trouble at work, and your wish to be treated differently from everyone else in the group with respect to paying your bill?"

My objectives are threefold: to understand together what is being expressed in the acting out, finding words to express the feelings; to discover how I have contributed to the development of these behaviors; and to get the issue of fee payment back where it belongs—in the frame.

In the past, I would have felt more threatened and reacted with confrontation and limit setting. Over the years, I've come to believe that these behaviors around money are important communications—often unconscious, sometimes symbolic. The group, the individuals, and I will be better served if I take a firm but relaxed attitude toward these challenges. Firm means keeping the issue alive and not letting it go underground. Relaxed means keeping the interpersonal space open for exploration and play.

Steven Krugman, PhD

References

Billow, R. (2003). *Relational group psychotherapy: From basic assumptions to passion.* London & New York: Jessica Kingsley.

Gans, J. S. (1992). Money and psychodynamic group psychotherapy. *International Journal of Group Psychotherapy, 42,* 133–152.

All for One and One for Some?

Dear Consultant:

I have finally been able to collect enough members for a group, having been working at it for more than 6 months. I've had a few dropouts along the way, even before the first group meeting, because some people either didn't want to wait or lost confidence in me because I hadn't been able to get the group mobilized. I was beginning to lose confidence myself, so I actually did something that may have been a mistake. To ensure that I had enough group members to start, I persuaded some of my own individual patients to join. I now have a seven person group with four members who are in individual therapy with me and three who have other individual therapists. In the early sessions of the group, this differential became clear when group members discussed their treatment histories. Unfortunately, I had failed to inform everyone prior to the group's start that some of them were in treatment with me, and I had also not focused sufficiently with my own patients on how I would treat material that came from their individual sessions. They have been unclear about whether I would ever allude to information from individual sessions, or under what circumstances.

In addition, one of the people not in individual therapy with me has expressed a concern that her needs might be short shrifted because I would never really know what was going on for her unless she brought it up, and her shyness made that difficult to do. A second member, also not in therapy with me, asked whether I ever spoke about him in my individual sessions with the others, and didn't seem to believe me when I said I worked hard to protect everyone's confidentiality. My statement rang hollow even to me, although it is my goal.

To complicate matters even more, it's evident that two of my individual therapy patients are disappointed that I seem to have warm personal

29

relationships with both of them. Each of them has presumed in individual therapy that the specialness they have felt from me is very personal, and watching me be empathic to obvious competitors has brought out aggressive comments toward me in the individual therapies of each.

The group has spaces for nine people, and I'm wondering if I dare bring in any more of my own patients. I'm even wondering whether I should have mixed my individual patients with the others in the first place. What is a good boundary here? Should one have only one's own patients in a group or none of one's own? Also, because I'm not going to disband this group, how can I think about and then articulate my position on confidentiality and separation of material from one therapy to another? I'm hoping it's not too late.

Dear Therapist:

My theoretical approach is psychodynamic. I am mindful of transference and countertransference as central to the therapeutic process, and I address the group-as-a-whole as a system that is developing over time. This developmental trajectory provokes and contains the work of the individual members. Any group event can be understood from four perspectives, individual (intrapsychic), interpersonal, structural (roles being played in the service of developmental tasks), and group-as-a-whole (overarching themes in the group's life, often in relation to the therapist). The therapist's job is first and foremost to attend to the intactness of the group, as the cohesion necessary for therapeutic work will inevitably be buffeted by developmental forces. Usually this means attending to structural and group-as-a-whole issues before addressing individual and interpersonal perspectives.

In the beginning, the group-as-a-whole exists only in the therapist's imagination. The individual members have no real relationship with each other. They are anxious, as any of us would be undertaking a step as important as joining a therapy group. Waiting for the group to start, individuals may drop out for many reasons: their relationship to the therapist has been threatened by the referral; the negative side of their ambivalence was not sufficiently addressed; or, fears of the imagined group increase with no real experience of the group to mitigate them. If patients felt coerced by the therapist to join, they may have had time to realize that joining is not the right thing for them at this time.

This is a stressful time for the therapist who must address the patients' anxiety and also manage his or her own. To avoid making problematic decisions because of transferential or countertransferential pressures, clarity about the parameters of the group and the working agreement is very important. Some therapists see patients only in the group, others combine group and individual treatment; some combine patients they see individually with patients seen individually by other therapists and some don't. In fact, a number of approaches work well. The determining factor is that the therapist has established parameters that fit comfortably with his or her training and theoretical approach. He or she can then present patients and referring therapists with a clear description of the group's structure, the working agreement, and his or her role.

I make clear to patients that their therapy is confidential and that information from any source will be used in the service of that therapy. Data from individual or group sessions are about them and cannot be artificially separated. When members in group refer to their "private" session, I am quick to say, *"individual* session." In individual sessions, I ask, "How will you bring this back to the group?"

If the rule in real estate is "location, location, location," then in group therapy it is "consultation, consultation, consultation." To think through the parameters of your group with a consultant is the best preparation for doing your primary job: managing the boundaries and cohesion of the group. The best safeguard against creating group casualties is to seek consultation when countertransference pressures mount.

You have been open about your uncomfortable feelings. Some likely result from interpersonal problems that you bring to the table, have been problematic for you in other situations, and could be addressed in consultation or supervision. It is also informative to consider how your feelings reflect those of the group members, and what they tell us about how the members are relating to you (i.e., feelings they are evoking in you). You mention concern about losing confidence, making mistakes, disappointing patients, and being the target of aggressive comments. These are all feelings that group therapists (with support when needed) must work to recognize, tolerate, avoid acting out, and then investigate and use. In your dilemma, I believe this will be central to helping your members develop cohesion and become a working group.

Members enter a new group with similar concerns: Will I fit in? What are the rules? Will I be safe? Will my needs be attended to? Will I be able to connect with someone else? They are in "fight-flight," anxious about being in the room together. If they tolerate their anxiety long enough to begin participating, they will move into a "dependency" phase. They look to the leader to take care of them, want to be special to the leader, and are jealous of and competitive with the other members. They are, of course, angry at and afraid of the leader.

From my psychodynamic perspective, you now have three tasks in addition to your primary job of maintaining boundaries:

Take the heat. Your task is to facilitate the expression of negative feelings about the group experience and encourage their being directed toward you. When members see that you can contain their anger, fear, and paranoia, they are safe to begin engaging each other. Expressing shared frustration about the leader is also a major way of establishing commonality, the first developmental task of the group.

Normalize feelings. We all need to have our feelings recognized and reflected to us. We also need to understand how our feelings fit in the normal (usual) range of human experience, that they are expectable, that others in the group have them, and that we don't have to feel ashamed and alienated because of them. None of the feelings expressed by your members are a bit out of the ordinary for a new group.

Teach members how to find allies. To remain in the group, each member must feel emotionally connected to at least one other person. Anxiety is diminished when we know someone is there whose feelings are similar to our own. Also, one person alone speaking for an issue may be undersupported and in danger of becoming a scapegoat. Members must learn to ask for, and expect, confirmation that others can identify with their point of view or experience. If no other member steps forward, then the leader must find a way to join the individual for the moment. Part of your job in a new group is to teach members how to work in this unfamiliar, asocial situation. They must become familiar with a new process, even a new language that will serve them through their time in the group.

It appears to me that you are working very hard to prevent, or get rid of, uncomfortable feelings in the group. Also, you are considering each member's complaint as a separate problem to solve rather than welcoming them collectively as necessary expressions of the group experience and of the developmental tasks of the moment. Your discomfort is impelling you to consider even more action as you try to create structural solutions rather than attending to the group's process. It would not be wise to add more members until you have been able to settle these members, and yourself, into feeling "we are a group." "Put your thoughts and feelings into words, not into action," applies to the therapist as well as the patients.

In any important relationship, what begins with excitement and promise must inevitably encounter frustration if the system is to do the difficult work of becoming involved enough, dedicated enough, cohesive enough, skilled and practiced enough to handle increasingly complex problems and therefore earn increasingly valuable rewards.

David M. Hawkins, MD, CGP, DFAGPA

Dear Therapist:

The fact that you are concerned about issues of combined individual and group therapy offers cause for optimism about the outcome. In today's "on demand" therapy climate, many therapists unfortunately "throw" groups together without seriously thinking about the "whys and wherefores" of group formation and boundaries. As one who has long maintained an interest in the evolving interactive perspective within psychoanalysis—that is, object relations theory, self psychology, and relational-intersubjective viewpoints, all of which emphasize how the "margins" and "frame" impact on the therapeutic relationship—I am gratified that you are sensitive to these issues and how they impact on your patients.

First of all, I would assure you that it is rare, if not impossible, to establish a perfect frame (Langs, 1976) for psychotherapy, especially group therapy. In my view, a perfect world is not necessary or even desirable for psychotherapy and for self-transformation. Just as Winnicott (1960) spoke of "good enough mothering," so the inevitable variations and fluctuations in therapy boundaries and settings provide windows of opportunity for learning and growth. Indeed, good evidence exists that, although not without its difficulties, a combination of individual and group psychotherapy works well, or even best, for many patients (Porter, 1993). The choice of whether to include one's own individual patients in one's groups has to be made on a practical basis, and—especially in private practice—it is often pragmatic for us to include our own patients in our groups.

As I will try to show, when a need exists to deviate from "ideal" boundary conditions in treatment, one must be aware of the effect. When such a deviation is reasonable and in the patients' and group's best interest, the crucial matter is to consistently address the impact of such deviation on the patients and the process. The object relations–self–intersubjective-relational spectrum of psychoanalysis gives us many clues and guidelines for attending to such "transference/countertransference problems" (Racker, 1968), "deviations from the frame" (Langs, 1976), "empathic failures" (Livingston, 1999, 2001; Wolf, 1988), or relational dilemmas (Mitchell & Aron, 1999) that are both the cause and effect of boundary changes in psychotherapy. In addition, I use a "living systems" (Agazarian, 1997; von Bertalanffy, 1968; Durkin, 1981) perspective to help me think about the relationship between the individual, the group, and the context. Thus, I think I can help you by looking in detail at your own ideas and reactions from such perspectives.

Your note, to begin with, states that "I've had a few dropouts along the way, even before the first group meeting because some people either didn't want to wait or have lost confidence in me because I hadn't been able to get the group mobilized. I was beginning to lose confidence myself, so I actually did something that may have been a mistake." Do you perceive your own anxiety here? If I were your supervisor, I would invite you to look, in a nonpathologizing way, at what may have been the sources of your anxiety: (a) in the group process; (b) in supervision; and (c) in your own life. I would wonder, for example, what those dropouts left with you (and your group); in other words, what they "projectively identified" into you (and conversely, what you and the remaining members may have projected into them), that led you to feel insecure about your role. Untended, your anxiety could have a more negative impact on the group than simply the act of bringing in your own patients. So, the first order of business in establishing proper boundaries is "Clinician, heal thyself."

You next describe the situation that arose as a result of your "countertransference" and your "forgetting" to inform the group members:

> I now have a seven person group with four members who are in individual therapy with me, and three who have other individual therapists . . . Unfortunately, I had failed to inform everyone prior to the group's start that some of them were in treatment with me . . . .

Here we see a boundary violation that is a direct consequence of your countertransference anxiety. Feathers have been ruffled and boundaries have been disturbed, but every crisis is also an opportunity. I see the potential here for a powerful growth experience for everyone in the group. Keep in mind that the initial "cohesion" of the beginning group relies to a great extent on the idealization and trust the members have in the therapist and his or her professionalism. Thus you need to handle this situation sensitively. You need to acknowledge your error of omission, but you also need to acknowledge your error with a sense of inner security reflecting your ability to introspect about your own issues, and in such a way that the members have a full opportunity to work through their feelings and reactions. If you do that consistently, not only will the proper boundaries be restored, but the members will begin to deal with some of their narcissistic vulnerabilities, as well as some of the failed relationships that led to therapy in the first place. Genuine group treatment will have begun.

Next, you appropriately focus on individuals who were especially vulnerable in this situation: " . . . one of the people not in individual therapy with me has expressed a concern that her needs might be short shrifted. . . . A second member, also not in therapy with me, asked whether I ever spoke about him in my individual sessions with the others, and didn't seem to believe me when I said I worked hard to protect everyone's confidentiality."

These members are "voices" for the entire subgroup (cf. Agazarian & Peters, 1981) of patients "not in individual therapy with you." Throughout the early life of this group, you're going to have these subgroups in a dialectical movement of conflict versus concordance, and you're going to need to sustain this dialogue. The "shy" member raises the "sibling rivalry" issue of "entitlement," implying that your one-to-one patients are a privileged lot (She is wondering anxiously whether she will be able to make a place for herself in the group and with you. This is undoubtedly true not only in this group, but in her life in general, and the group experience provides an ideal setting to work out her issues of inclusion.)

Further, the member who worries about a "confidentiality leak" is not just expressing a trust issue. He or she is also seductively challenging your own boundaries, because it might indeed be therapeutic at times to bring examples from group into individual sessions. To deal with these "seducers" (Gibbard, 1974) who challenge the boundaries (in both positive and negative ways), you're going to need to not be diverted by them but rather assiduously stick to the tasks of observing the group process and sorting out each members' particular vulnerabilities within it. Otherwise, your leadership function will be compromised and you'll be placed in a position of joining one or the other subgroup, thus undoing your neutral, empathic stance.

This brings into focus your next concern:

> To complicate matters even more, it's evident that two of my individual therapy patients are disappointed that I seem to have warm personal relationships with both of them . . . and watching me be empathic to obvious competitors has brought out aggressive comments toward me in the individual therapies of each.

Which patient has not experienced the surreal disillusionment of finding out that his or her therapist has other patients? This is, of course, about the loss of symbiotic bliss (Mahler, Pine, & Bergman, 1975) or "mirror transference" (Kohut, 1971, 1977) vis-à-vis the primal mother. It's an inevitable loss, but your patients' aggression is telling you that they are experiencing a profound narcissistic injury, probably exacerbated by the boundary difficulty that arose so early in the life of the group. You're going to have the difficult task of empathically interpreting the hurt they feel, yet not being perceived by their "competitors" as taking sides.

You ponder the following: "The group has spaces for nine people, and I'm wondering if I dare bring in any more of my own patients." My answer to you is firm: *Do not* bring in more patients until you've fully resolved the boundary issues with the current membership. If you bring in new members prematurely, the boundary problems will "cascade" (Rubenfeld, 2001) as the new members become confused by what is currently unresolved. You should bring in new members only when your present group is relatively stable, cohesive, and a "work group" (Bion, 1960/1974).

Finally, you—my "doubting Thomas" (or Thomasina)—query: "I'm even wondering whether I should have mixed my individual patients with the others in the first place. What is a good boundary here?" Very importantly, the boundary question requires a more sophisticated analysis of the individual in the group than just its overt rules and structure. The "implicit" (psychological) boundaries are ultimately more important than the "explicit" overtly stated ones. That is, for example, one can have both one's own individual patients and others in the group—admittedly not a perfect solution—as long as one attends to the issues of safety, security, and entitlement it brings up. This has to do with the internalized boundaries in each member (which, by the way, contributes to their relational difficulties and symptoms), as well as the maintenance and task needs of the group-as-a-whole. This is the "invisible" group (Agazarian & Peters, 1981) whose boundaries will ultimately determine the therapeutic usefulness of the group experience for all the members.

I'm glad you're not going to disband this group—they really need you! It is a real challenge to articulate one's position on confidentiality and separation of material from one therapy to another. This is, indeed, a lifetime process for any clinician! In general, what I would say is that, (a) anything that comes up in group may be discussed in individual sessions (no confidentiality is being violated, although one must be wary of the tendency to avoid or sequester group issues by over-discussing them "privately," which could cause appropriate resentment in the membership); (b) if something comes up in individual therapy it should only be disclosed in group by that member or by you with the member's prior permission; and (c) one cannot ultimately keep separate material from individual and group therapy, except where one-to-one disclosures might jeopardize the patient or others (e.g., a disclosure about a legal matter, and so on).

Essentially, patients need to trust the total therapy process as a multimodal combination of approaches. This means that the "system" and "institutional setting" need tending as well! Living systems boundaries (von Bertalanffy, 1968) are semi-permeable: they both separate and allow for flow among systems, and what counts at all times is not "purity" of boundaries but that life-enhancing needs (in systems terms, the tendencies toward negative entropy and creative evolution) are being met at individual and group levels.

Victor L. Schermer, MA, LPC, CAC, CGP

References

Agazarian, Y. (1997). *Systems centered therapy for groups*. New York: Guilford Press.

Agazarian, Y., & Peters, R. (1981). *The visible and invisible group*. London: Routledge.

Bertalanffy, L. von (1968). *General system theory: Foundations, development, applications*. New York: Braziller.

Bion, W. R. (1974). *Experiences in groups*. New York: Ballantine Books. (Original work published 1959)

Durkin, J. E. (Ed). (1981). *Living groups: Group psychotherapy and general system theory*. New York: Brunner/Mazel.

Gibbard, G. (1974). Individuation, fusion, and role specialization. In G. Gibbard, J. Hartman, & R. Mann (Eds.), *Analysis of groups* (pp. 247–266). San Francisco: Jossey-Bass.

Kohut, H. (1971). *Analysis of the self*. New York: International Universities Press.

Kohut, H. (1977). *Restoration of the self*. New York: International Universities Press.

Langs, R. (1976). *The bipersonal field*. New York: Jason Aronson.

Livingston, M. (1999). Vulnerability, tenderness, and the experience of selfobject relationship: A self-psychological view of deepening curative process in group psychotherapy. *International Journal of Group Psychotherapy. 49*, 1–21.

Livingston, M. (2001). *Vulnerable moments: Deepening the therapeutic process with individuals, couples and groups*. Northvale, NJ: Jason Aronson.

Mahler, M., Pine, F., & Bergman, A. (1975). *The psychological birth of the human infant*. New York: Basic Books.

Mitchell, S. A., & Aron, L. (1999). Preface. In S. A. Mitchell & L. Aron (Eds.), *Relational psychoanalysis: The emergence of a tradition* (pp. ix–xx). Hillsdale, NJ: Analytic Press.

Porter, K. (1993). Combined individual and group psychotherapy. In H. I. Kaplan & B. J. Sadock (Eds.), *Comprehensive group psychotherapy* (3rd ed.). Baltimore: Williams and Wilkins.

Racker, H. (1968). *Transference and countertransference*. New York: International Universities Press.

Rubenfeld, S. (2001). On complexity theory in group psychotherapy. *International Journal of Group Psychotherapy, 51*, 449–472.

Winnicott, D. W. (1960). Theory of the parent-infant relationship. In *The maturational processes and the facilitating environment: Studies in the theory of emotional development* (1965), (pp. 37–55). New York: International Universities Press.

Wolf, E. S. (1988). *Treating the self: Elements of clinical self psychology*. New York: Guilford Press.

Section II
Difficult Patients

Overview

In the movie *Fatal Attraction*, Michael Douglas, a successful lawyer and married man, has a one-night stand with Glenn Close. When he abandons her, Glenn Close, lonely and disturbed, stalks him and his family. Some therapists view Glenn Close as the classic borderline who cannot tolerate the loss of the previously idealized other. Others view Michael Douglas as the classic narcissist who, out of his own insecurity, thinks only of his own needs. Either of them in a group would stir complex feelings in the therapist and possibly wreak havoc in the group as well.

In *Treating Difficult Patients in Groups,* Scott Rutan begins with a provocative question: are there really difficult patients or are these just people in pain who are trying to connect with others the best way they can? Through case examples, he explores why and how patients are complicated: because of specific diagnostic issues, improper referral to the group, countertransference issues for the group therapist, and more.

The therapist in *Angry Angela and Controlling Connie* is faced with the demise of her group after she adds an enraged group member to a long-standing mature group. She asks the consultants whether she should have removed this patient after she first exploded in a rage. Anne Alonso wonders whether the new member is functioning at a different ego level than the other group members but, now that she is a member, suggests the therapist "stay the course" so that the group members have an opportunity to re-own intolerable aspects of themselves. Hillel Swiller encourages the therapist to go back to basics and ask the group if they are getting what they want from the group and if not, why not?

In *All About Adam*, a narcissistic patient has been monopolizing the group and a number of members have or are considering dropping out. The therapist, out of his own frustration, finds himself allowing the group to attack the patient. Arnold Cohen, writing from an object relations perspective, advises the therapist to help Adam and the group see the problem as a group issue, not Adam's issue, while at the same time helping Adam to own his envy and rage. Elizabeth Shapiro suggests that the dropout is the result of patients' angry feelings toward the therapist "gone underground" and that Adam is a "gift to the group" who brings the possibility of strong feelings and a deepening of their relationships with one another.

In the next dilemma, *Getting Our Affairs in Order*, the therapist suspects that two of her group patients are having an affair, which both vehemently deny. Our consultants respond with two very different responses. Earl Hopper sees an affair between two group members as destructive to the culture of safety and honesty in the group and believes the therapist must insist the two patients end their sexual relationship or leave the group. In contrast, Suzanne Cohen encourages the therapist to reiterate the group agreement to bring outside contact back into the group, but also recommends that the therapist not become too invested in whether or not the two patients are actually having an affair.

Treating Difficult Patients in Groups

J. SCOTT RUTAN, PHD, CGP, DFAGPA

I am not sure any "difficult" patients exist. I am equally not sure any "easy" patients exist. "Complicated" patients certainly exist. All the patients I have seen were doing their best and were trying to be *in* relationships rather than trying *not* to be in them. They were not *trying* to be difficult, even when they were. So, when asked to contribute a chapter on treating the difficult patient, I was immediately confronted with several questions. What constitutes a difficult patient? Are such patients difficult to *treat*, difficult to *sit with*, difficult to *help*, or difficult to *like*? Are they difficult for the therapist, for the group, or both? Are they difficult in life or just in the group? Is the degree to which a patient is considered difficult correlated to *diagnosis*, *defenses*, or *countertransference*? Would there be consensus among therapists as to who are the difficult patients? Is that description highly variable, contingent on specific patient–therapist–group factors? Perhaps a difficult patient is one who has few life-saving options beyond being needy, whining, threatening, and the like. Or is it one who invites difficult countertransference from the therapist, a patient who forces us to face difficult aspects of ourselves? If the latter is the case, it is not the patient who is difficult, but rather unresolved or not accepted aspects of the self. Finally, do these patients experience *themselves* as difficult, or are they utterly confounded by the reactions they evoke in others?

The difficult patient

Difficult patients are not necessarily correlated to the seriousness of their diagnoses. Chronically ill patients have been defined by Goldman, Gattozzi, and Taube (1981) as "persons who suffer severe and persistent mental or emotional disorders that interfere with their functional capacities in relation to such primary aspects of daily life as self-care, interpersonal relationships, and work or schooling and that often necessitate prolonged hospital care" (p. 22). Many of these patients are delightful and rather easy to treat (though not easy to cure).

That said, specific *types* of diagnoses, such as borderline and narcissistic personalities, may contribute more difficult patients than other diagnoses, but what is it about those patients that makes them *difficult*?

Yalom (1975) refers to specific types of roles that patients demonstrate in groups that make them "problem patients" (p. 376). They are the monopolist, the schizoid patient, the silent patient, the psychotic patient, the narcissistic patient, the boring patient, the help-rejecting complainer, and the self-righteous moralist.

These are dated concepts. We now understand that each of those roles are actually in part created by and rewarded by the group because they provide group functions. For example, I have never known an individual who can "monopolize" a group without the group's cooperation. Often the purpose of this role is to regulate the time in the group that is used for hard, vulnerable work in therapy. One might say the same of the boring patient —an individual who anesthetizes the group against more painful affects. Gans and Alonso (1998) have added the important notion that difficult patients are created by a variety of factors. They write, "Difficult patients, to some extent, are co-constructions, the results of interactions among the leader, the group members, and the group as a whole" (p. 312). Stone (1996), for example, suggests that difficult patients may involve situations where an individual is "apparently grossly interfering with group developmental processes" (p. 173). Stone goes on to suggest that in these instances one should look to group-as-a-whole issues such as scapegoating rather than focus on the specific "difficult" individual.

Billow (2003) added to this understanding of the difficult patient in a recent article entitled "Rebellion in group." Billow notes that rebelliousness often serves a function in group development—testing leadership, testing group safety, and perhaps acting out an unspoken aspect of group dynamics. This, in part, echoes Nitsun's (1996) concept of the anti-group, a destructive aspect in all groups.

Gans and Alonso (1998) cite four factors contributing to a difficult patient, the personal dynamics of a specific patient, mistakes made by leaders, the influence of intersubjectivity in the group, and whole-group dynamics (p. 312).

The difficult patient in group

In treating difficult patients in a group, we need to distinguish between the patient who is difficult because of (a) specific diagnostic issues, (b) an improper referral to the group, (c) a countertransference issue for the group therapist, or (d) because the patient is taking on a group-as-a-whole function and speaking or acting out the unspeakable for the rest of the group.

Specific diagnostic issues

Some character issues represent unique problems in group therapy (as in life). Two of the most obvious diagnostic categories would be borderline and narcissistic personalities. Rutan and Stone (2001) state, "A majority of patients who are viewed as 'difficult' carry a borderline or narcissistic diagnosis" (p. 290). This does not imply that these patients are not helped in group therapy. Quite the contrary, McCallum and Piper's (1999) research led them to conclude: "The finding supports the relevance of intensive dynamically oriented group therapy for treating patients with personality disorder" (p. 13). They continue, "The outcome results cited in the present study are encouraging for the clinicians who work with the challenging population in intensive group-oriented programs" (p. 13).

According to the fourth edition of the American Psychiatric Association's *Diagnostic and Statistical Manual of Mental Disorders* (DSM-IV) (1994), borderline personalities are characterized by "a pervasive pattern of instability of interpersonal relationships, self-image, and affects, and marked impulsivity . . ." (p. 280). Obviously, an individual carrying this diagnosis may be as disruptive in a group as in all other aspects of his or her life.

Clinical Example—Betty the Borderline

Betty always arrived early for her group and always took "her" chair. She routinely began meetings and evidenced intolerance if someone else began. She was unapologetic for wanting (needing?) the attention of the group and especially the leader. She was extremely volatile emotionally, moving instantly to tears or screaming anger.

This particular evening a new member, Barbara, joined the group. She walked in while Betty was using the bathroom and unknowingly sat in the seat typically occupied by Betty. When Betty re-entered the group room her face darkened as she saw that "her" chair was occupied. The rest of the group watched with anticipation, knowing that there would be fireworks, but Betty did not speak, she simply stood and glowered. Barbara got more and more uncomfortable and asked, "What is going on?" Betty said, "Didn't the others tell you that you are sitting in my seat?" Barbara responded, "No, I'm sorry. I didn't know there were assigned seats."

With that the expected uproar occurred. Betty raged at her old group colleagues, "Why did you do this to me? You say you like me, but I know you hate me. You set me up!" With that, she picked up a box of tissues and began shredding them and throwing the pieces around the group.

This represented a "difficult moment" for the group therapist. The group room now resembled a snow storm, with pieces of tissues floating down on everyone and everything. Betty was screaming at the top of her lungs, and the poor new member was terrified. The older members, familiar with Betty's behavior, were rather amused.

What distinguishes borderline patients is that they are *too* aware of the importance of others. Their skin is too thin and they are too easily wounded. In groups they are often useful to others in reminding everyone of their yearnings and their needs for interpersonal contact.

In this meeting, for example, we can assume the context is the introduction of a new member. This is difficult for everyone concerned. In a real way this is a brand new group. Betty, via the metaphor of "her" chair, demonstrates the group concern with being replaced. Furthermore, she is correct —the group *did* set her up. They did not tell Barbara that Betty was particularly wedded to that chair. This allowed them to act on their sadistic wishes that their "new baby sister" be stillborn and not disrupt the family while not having to own or be responsible for those wishes. That job was deeded over to Betty.

As Betty stopped ranting and the tissues stopped falling, there was an awkward silence. Then various group members looked around and began to smile, then to laugh out loud. Before long everyone was laughing at the absurdity of the situation. Barbara meekly asked, "Betty, would you like me to move?" Betty responded, "No, I guess you're already here now."

At this point the leader made her first comment. "The entrance of our new member seems to have brought about a storm of feelings." The group was able to focus on the various emotional responses members had to the advent of a new member.

At the end of the meeting Betty began carefully picking up all the tissues and her group colleagues, including Barbara, joined in to help. This demonstrated that at some level all the members understood this was a whole-group issue.

In this case, as is usually the case, there was not so much a difficult *patient* as a difficult *situation* (the entrance of a stranger into an ongoing group). A particular patient, because of her specific character issues, "volunteered" for the role of bringing those issues into vivid relief. However, Betty's difficult uncontained behaviors lent themselves to the occasion, and so she was indeed difficult by character as well as by context.

If borderline patients are *underprotected* from how important others are, narcissistic patients are *overprotected*. They attempt to act as if others are not important at all, but it is essential that we recognize this is a defense.

Clinical Example—Neal the Narcissist

Neal would look distracted and bored when any other member spoke in group. Occasionally he would accentuate this behavior by dramatically looking at his watch, as if measuring how much time a particular member was taking. He also had a remarkable ability to "associate" to whatever was being said in such a way as to end up talking about himself. If others did not come to a meeting, he did not miss them. Rather, he felt there was more "air time" for him. He would often come a little early in the hope that the group therapist would also enter the room early and give him some individual time.

Donna, a long time member of the group, was engaged to be married. This was the result of hard work in the group and the rest of the group (save only Neal) was very pleased for her and thrilled that the date of her wedding was approaching. In the group meeting just prior to her wedding (and her upcoming absence for several weeks because of her honeymoon), there was a festive air in the group. One of the members had purchased a congratulatory card for her and had secretly gotten all the members (and the therapist) to sign it. Each of the members, except Neal, had written short statements wishing Donna well in her marriage. Neal had simply signed his name—and he alone had signed only his first name.

As the group spoke of the hope they had gained from watching Donna succeed in her work to attain an intimate relationship, Neal checked his watch. When he finally spoke it was to state, "So I guess you will be leaving group now, Donna." Then he turned to the leader and said, "I hope you don't add anyone else. This group is too big." Then he launched into a prolonged monologue about how unsuccessful he has been in trying to find a wife through computer dating.

This behavior, even from Neal, was too much for the group to bear and they confronted (attacked?) him. One member captured the group's feeling: "Donna has not said she is leaving. Why would you wish her gone? How can you just ramble on about your lack of success when we were all enjoying Donna's success? You are just so damned oblivious!"

In this example, the narcissistic patient, through his own character pathology, highlights affects that others share but of which they are either unaware or are too "polite" to reveal. Neal is up-front in his jealousy that Donna has what he would like. He is all too willing to call for more and more attention.

In response to the confrontation above, Neal was stunned. He said, "How can you be happy for Donna when she is getting what we don't have?" He was genuinely confused.

Improper referral

Sometimes the difficult patient is the result of putting someone in a group who is not an apt candidate for group therapy at this time or is placed in the wrong group. Often the latter occurs when a patient is placed in a group where his or her developmental level is not a good match with the other patients. If the new patient is much more primitive, then he or she might feel overwhelmed and the other patients might be frightened by the aspects of self that are more repressed in them.

Occasionally a therapist will not foresee how easily wounded an individual can be and is surprised by how devastated the individual is when confronted in a group. Likewise, sometimes in an individual evaluation interview it is impossible to ascertain the depth of social phobia that appears instantly when an individual enters a group. These errors of referral can usually be corrected by helping the patient leave the group quickly and without shame, and these individuals do not necessarily become difficult patients for the group. Often they can use their brief exposure to a group in a very productive manner in their individual therapy.

It is important that we also take responsibility for the fact that on occasion therapists just make mistakes and put individuals in groups where they do not belong. If the therapist does not own this error, he or she contributes to the making of a "difficult" patient. Indeed, if the therapist does not own his or her error, the *therapist* becomes the difficult member of the group.

Mature groups can tolerate and profit from much more diversity among members than newly formed groups. Newly forming groups or groups in crisis have much more trouble accepting wide differences. Neal, from the example above, might have been an inappropriate referral to the group if it had been a new group. His unbridled narcissism and neediness would have made it difficult for others to empathize with him.

Likewise, Betty's emotional volatility was helpful to her mature (but somewhat affectively stifled) group. However, had she entered the same group at a much earlier time in the group's development, she likely would not have been accepted or would have frightened some others away.

Countertransference

At times it is not the *patient* who is difficult, but rather the *therapist* who cannot contain the real as well as the countertransference reactions that specific patients arouse. This is a situation that will be covered in depth by Dr. Counselman in the fifth chapter of this book. For our purposes, it is important to note that the leader's antipathy can and probably will induce increasingly difficult reactions in the vulnerable patient. It is a two-way street on impact and influence.

Group-as-a-whole function

Often the difficult patient is acting out or speaking group-as-a-whole feelings that others dare not know or show. Again using Neal as an example, it may be that he is speaking for the whole group the unacceptable narcissistic wish to get all of the leader's attention. Similarly, Betty, by her dramatic reactions, often helped individuals in the group recognize just how affected they were by the reactions of others.

The difficult patient as asset

Gans and Alonso (1998) point out that the difficult patient is often an asset in a therapy group. This is subjectively verifiable by noting how often troublesome patients who have left the group are referred to by their groups long after their departure, often with a fondness that was not apparent when the patient was a member. These patients stir affect and make groups passionate.

The earlier examples are obvious—Betty and Neal helped others in the group by speaking the unspeakable and by introducing deeper levels of affect into the group. Here is another example of a difficult patient as an asset.

Clinical Example—Albert the Alcoholic

Albert was referred to group therapy because he sabotaged his interpersonal and work life through alcoholism and obstreperous behaviors. True to his character, Albert was very difficult in his group. He would often arrive late, smelling of alcohol (though professing not to have drunk any), and would proceed to demand immediate attention no matter what might have been occurring when he walked in.

The group moved quickly from trying to empathize with Albert, to being furious with him, to being furious with the group therapist for having introduced Albert into their midst. The group was often punctuated by screaming, loud confrontations, and intense affect.

At the same time, the group was evidencing high cohesion by regular and timely attendance (even by Albert after a while). They would also rail against the therapist if he canceled a session. (A variant of the old axiom, "The food in this place is terrible and the portions are too small!")

Ultimately Albert fled the group. A case could easily be made that he represented an inappropriate referral to group therapy. The group expressed enormous relief and no sadness whatsoever when it was announced that Albert would not be returning. Indeed, when a subsequent new member was announced, the group demanded reassurance that it would *not* be Albert rejoining the group.

However, precisely one year after Albert's departure, members began bemoaning the lack of emotion and "fire" in the group. They began remembering Albert with fondness, commenting "those were the good old days when this group was really working!"

At about the same time, Albert reconnected with the group therapist and said he had learned a great deal while in the group (This surprised the therapist.) He requested and was granted admission into a different group. He often spoke of his inappropriate behavior in his prior group, but having learned from his prior group he never demonstrated it in his new group.

Difficult patients can be assets to groups in a variety of ways: (a) they can speak the unspeakable; (b) they can stir emotions and invite more reticent members to experience things more deeply; and (c) they can carry unacceptable aspects of others until such time that the others are able to own and explore them. They can also function as the classic scapegoat.

The term "scapegoat" comes from the Bible (Leviticus 16:5–10). It has to do with Aaron confessing the sins of Israel over the head of a goat, which was then sent into the wilderness carrying the sins of the people with it. So the fundamental role of a scapegoat is to *protect* the tribe, the family, the group. The scapegoat does this by containing all the "sins" that others do not want to, or cannot, bear themselves.

Summary

Let us return to the questions raised in the introduction. Are there difficult patients? Of course, but most of the time what makes them difficult is either their character or their unconscious role in and for the group.

Are these patients difficult to *treat*, *sit with*, *help*, or *like*? This is dependent on many factors, including the personal preferences of the therapist. Usually patients who seem to interfere with the smooth functioning of our groups tend to annoy us, even if we understand that at some level they are assisting the group. The projective identification aspects of this are such that we are often being trained to respond in familiar ways for those patients. On the other hand, some of these feisty, rambunctious patients are utterly delightful, like a mischievous child who makes us laugh.

Are these patients difficult in life or just in group? It is almost inconceivable to me that someone would be so very different in a therapy group from how they are in life outside the group. When the difficulties these patients pose in a group are confronted and reflected back to them, rarely are the patients surprised.

Often our difficult patients are a gift to the group, moving the process from the superficial to the more affective. Even in those cases when a difficult patient appears to be confounding or interfering with the progress of the group, it is usually the case that something productive will ultimately result.

References

American Psychiatric Association (1994). *Diagnostic and Statistical Manual of Mental Disorders* (4th ed.). Washington, DC: Author.

Billow, R. M. (2003). Rebellion in group. *International Journal of Group Psychotherapy*, 53, 331–351.

Bion, W. (1959). *Experiences in groups.* New York: Basic Books.

Gans, J. S., & Alonso, A. (1998). Difficult patients: Their construction in group therapy. *International Journal of Group Psychotherapy*, 48, 311–326.

Goldman, H. H., Gattozzi, A. A., & Taube, C. (1981). Defining and counting the chronically mentally ill. *Hospital and Community Psychiatry*, 32, 21–27.

McCallum, M., & Piper, W. E. (1999). Personality disorders and response to group-oriented evening treatment. *Group Dynamics*, 3, 3–14.

Nitsun, M. (1996). *The Anti-Group: Destructive forces in the group and their creative potential.* London: Routledge.

Rutan, J. S., & Stone, W. N. (2001). *Psychodynamic group psychotherapy* (3rd ed.). New York: Guilford Press.

Stone, W. N. (1996). *Group psychotherapy for people with chronic mental illness.* New York: Guilford.

Yalom, I. D. (1975). *The theory and practice of group psychotherapy* (2nd ed.). New York: Basic Books.

Angry Angela and Controlling Connie

Dear Consultant:

I run an ongoing psychodynamic women's group. The group has six patients aged 25 to 55 who have been in the group for at least 2 years. Three months ago I added a patient, Angela, whom I thought would be a good match. Like the other patients in the group, Angela has a history of dysthymia and trauma. In the intake, she was quiet, depressed, and shut down emotionally. Like many trauma survivors, she told me a lot about herself during the intake. She reported that she has conflict with her siblings, difficulties with her parents, and no close friends. I went over the group agreements about showing up each week on time, working on the problems that brought her to group, putting her feelings into words and not actions, and discussing with the group any intention to terminate.

The group has been going through a difficult time of transition. One patient abruptly left the group in the fall. I took an extended vacation about the same time. One patient, Connie, has a conflictual marriage. She spends a portion of each session talking about the details of each argument she and her husband have. When Connie has been absent, other patients have said they feel conflicted about sharing positive aspects of their lives when Connie is going through such a painful time, but they also feel Connie uses too much time.

Although I met with Angela several times before she entered group, I did not see the extent of her rage. On her first night, she angrily announced that she was only in the group because her individual therapist told her she needed it. The group was taken aback and left her alone after that. I occasionally have asked Angela what she is thinking or feeling, but for 3 months since she has said almost nothing in group.

My dilemma has to do with both Angela and Connie, who have a con-flictual relationship. Several times Angela confronted Connie aggressively because she feels Connie dominates and controls the group. When Angela has confronted Connie, Connie threatens to leave the group, saying she can't deal with her bad marriage and Angela at the same time. When Angela was absent one night, the group members told me they thought I had made a terrible mistake bringing her in.

The problem is that five of the seven members are now planning to ter-minate. Connie has decided that she needs individual treatment instead of group because she feels so needy. Another patient who has confronted Angela is leaving because she wants to be in a group for eating disorders. Two others are planning to leave to go to graduate school out-of-state. I think some of the terminations are legitimate and others are not. Interestingly, in the last couple of weeks, Connie has begun to work in the group and the group members have encouraged her. She has acknowledged to the group that she doesn't know how to connect and on one occasion shared that her style is to create chaos and then sit back and watch.

I feel like I blew it. I never saw Angela's anger in the intake and I feel like I've destroyed my group. What should I have done differently in the intake? Should I have removed Angela from the group after the first night? Maybe I shouldn't have brought her in when the group was dealing with Connie's marriage. Should I take her out now? I'm afraid my group is going to fall apart. How do I get the group to look at why they are thinking of leaving now? And what about Connie? She seems to be holding the group hostage with her constant talking and her threats and now is planning to leave.

Dear Therapist:
The situation you describe here is a painful and familiar one, all too common in the sometimes vexing work of group therapy. I know what it feels like to be anxious and uncertain about proficiency at a time of crisis in any group.

My own position bridges object relations theory and systems theory, and it is from this lens that I offer the following exploration of your case. With that in mind, I would consider the situation from the point of view of the group-as-a-whole, the individuals in the group, and the position of the leader of the group. Once we have laid out the case, I will offer suggestions —although gingerly, because one person's group is idiosyncratic to that person, given the cocreation of the transferences, but more about that later.

You describe the group as a psychodynamic women's group consisting of trauma survivors. It's not clear to me what the goal of the group may be. Is it a group for dealing with life constraints and the need to resolve neurotic conflicts, or is it specifically aimed at working with Post Traumatic Stress Disorder? If I assume the former, then I would wonder about the homogeneity of population. To my thinking, the ideal group is homogeneous at the level of ego development, and heterogeneous in every other way. The problem arises when a group is put together around a symptom (trauma?) and will often consist of people at a broad range of ego development. If these women are indeed at a very disparate level of ego strength, then they will lose some of the capacity for empathy that comes with a differently chosen group membership. It may also mean that the problem absorbing Angela may be simply that she is more disturbed and thus the group would move to extrude her because they cannot easily empathize with her.

Other factors are operating simultaneously. If we think in terms of systems, then we might assume that each member is speaking some aspect of the whole group's unconscious needs. Is Angela, in her rage, serving as a carrier for the unacknowledged rage of the rest of the members? Are they suspiciously sweet and "supportive" at the risk of unduly muting their aggression or confronting it? This is a fairly common dilemma for women's groups (Alonso & Rutan, 1979). Thus Angela may be hitting at a vulnerable resistance in the group-as-a-whole, and they will want to extrude her, or abandon her, in a classic scapegoating situation. As always, the scapegoat is a ready volunteer for the job, and Angela's provocative manner is such an example.

A compelling message always appears whenever two antagonists seem only to have eyes for each other. We usually suspect that a bond forged by a strong projective identification is at work. Is Angela speaking Connie's rage at her husband? Is Connie's wish to flee an enactment of her flight from her marriage? The group may be aware of Connie's disowned rage because they can only criticize her behind her back. Do you, the leader, make sure their criticism is aired when she comes back? Why not?

You also ask about timing. Did your vacation precede Angela's arrival, or follow it? In either case, is Angela taking the heat for the leader who leaves and then comes back, leaving them holding their rage toward the leader and directing *it* at the new "baby" instead?

I would suggest that Angela is a gift to the group: she has brought in the denied dark side of the members and insisted it be acknowledged. It seems they are quite a disparate group of women. The two graduate students are, for better or worse, gone for reasons that may seem unimpeachable, but their data about the group as they have experienced it remains very valuable. Given that they are leaving, it may be easier for them to look at the whole range of interactions in the group, beyond the new member's impact.

The woman who is looking for an eating disorders group is very interesting. Is she saying she can't eat here or that there is no room for her hunger? Can this disappointment in the group be addressed as a whole-group message? Greed, primitive oral aggression, and a distorted sense of self may be problematic for all these women. The expressed wish of this woman to find an eating disorder group may be heard a symbolic and useful fantasy for all of them to look differently at one another's ravenous hungers.

Although I fully sympathize with the feeling of doom and disaster in the group, I would encourage you to stay the course. Most assuredly, I would not ask anyone to leave, least of all the new arrival. Nor would I collude with the wishes of the other women to put feelings into action. They may all want to "get out of Dodge," and you may also; this is a worthy wish to explore. It is always tempting to hear strongly expressed insistence on taking action as inevitable. Over the many years of practicing group therapy, I have learned to take a deep breath and remember that after all, I did invite them to speak from the heart, and here they are doing just that! However, as we know in cooler moments, the best work of therapy occurs especially around moments of crisis and resistance. This is the "crunch" that Paul Russell (Fishman, 1998) described, and it leads down into the deeper levels of the work.

It's hard not to feel guilty as a leader. The guilt of the woman who is leaving her marriage may not be able to be openly acknowledged, yet it must be there unless she is a saint. She and the others have to cope with the losses of past loves and present losses, such as you leaving on vacation and the two leaving for graduate school. She is concretely expressing a universal reality in your group, namely that it's easier to rant than to grieve, and bringing it in may help her to be in the moment with her colleagues and with you. It may also be that as a group leader you want to clarify to yourself what the contract you have offered is explicitly about, and how much time is spent in preparing the new patient for joining the group.

I like to describe the group as a hall of mirrors, with people in the room reflecting a sometimes disowned aspect of the self (the tenderness for Angela, the fury for Connie, and so on). I also ask people to stay until they have finished what they came to do. Then, when premature departure is threatened, I am able to say something like, "How fortunate we have this agreement that you will stay, so that it lets us look respectfully at the power of your impulse to break that good-faith agreement."

The contract then becomes the superego, leaving the leader and others free to serve as auxiliary egos for the person who is driven by id impulses at any point in time. In other words, symptoms are not ever the problem in this model; rather they are compromise solutions to deeper and less conscious conflicts. In this sense, they are welcome harbingers for the direction the work must take.

If you can avoid participating in the enactment wishes of some of the members, I imagine you will move to a far more fruitful exploration of the balance between tenderness and destructiveness, between attachment and aggression, and between merger and abandonment. The goal of all dynamic groups, as I understand them, is to allow for a healthy interdependence, for a resolution of old grief, and toward a greater capacity for intimacy. It may be time to forcefully remind everyone that the ingredients are all in the room, and it remains for the group to use them well.

Anne Alonso, PhD, CGP, DFAGPA

References

Alonso, A., & Rutan, J. S. (1979). Women in group therapy. *International Journal of Group Psychotherapy, 24,* 481–491.

Fishman, G. (1998). Paul Russell's "The crunch." *Psychotherapy Forum, 5,* 3.

Dear Therapist:

When the going gets tough the tough are well advised to go back to basics. This is group therapy—use the group!

Did you possibly make a mistake in the intake of Angela? Sure, it is possible, but that is nothing about which to berate yourself. I feel that if a therapist never makes a mistake in putting a high risk patient into group, that therapist is playing it too safe. We all know patients who will do well in any nonmalignant therapy. If we choose to treat only such patients, we are failing in our obligation to help those who need our help the most. Of course, every failure of a member in group deserves our careful reflection (and, if possible, a discussion with a respected colleague), but we owe it to those who are the most trouble to risk making an error in our attempt to be helpful.

The full amount of a patient's anger rarely surfaces within the intake sessions, even in an extended evaluation. The patient is receiving focused, thoughtful, nonjudgmental attention from a trained and highly motivated professional. What is there to get angry about? A careful and detailed history of familial, romantic, and professional relationships may disclose excessive anger, but not always. Every one of us has had the experience of adding to group a patient we have treated extensively in individual therapy and then been dazzled by the sudden appearance of an utter stranger. The first point that I think deserves to be made in all this discussion is: Do not be harshly self-blaming for an error in screening. I say this not simply to help you feel better about yourself, but also because excessive self-blame often leads, and does in this instance, to therapeutic paralysis. Because you felt guilty about your "mistake," you held back from making sufficiently forceful interventions.

This problem may have preceded Angela's joining the group. Connie had been dominating the group with her marital woes for some time. Such monopolization is never useful. Here, as well, the group should have been used to move the discussion into more productive areas. How can that be done? Back to basics! Remind the group that what happens in the group sessions is up to them. Ask if they are satisfied with the ongoing discussion. If they are not, why not and why do they tolerate it? Will this upset Connie, and later Angela? Of course it will. That's the point. They, and the other members of the group, have sought in the group to recreate familiar ways of being with people, but those ways don't work all that well or they wouldn't be in therapy. So by all means, get them upset enough to try new ways of being. Do that by directing the group to examine its responsibility for an unsatisfactory situation and encouraging—and, when necessary, guiding— them toward new behaviors.

Is it too late for this group? Possibly, but not necessarily. Connie may have begun to move her attention to her behavior in the group and that is an excellent development. Should Angela be removed by the therapist? Not on the basis of the information currently available. The group should be encouraged to confront and moderate her self-indulgent behavior. She may not be able to tolerate that and may leave of her own accord. Should she choose to stay and work on the issue of her anger in the here-and-now of group, she can have a wonderfully successful therapeutic experience. It is quite possible that with a move toward more productive group discussions several of the threats of premature termination will evaporate.

Good luck!

Hillel I. Swiller, MD, CGP, FAGPA, DLFAPA

All About Adam

Dear Consultant:

I need help! Adam, one of eight members of my psychodynamic group, has been monopolizing a number of the sessions and it has been very hard to get him to stop. The frustration of several of the other group members has been expressed in eye rolls, obvious lack of attention, even direct comments to Adam that he is taking up more than his share of time. In addition, when Adam is momentarily chastened to the point of refraining from speaking, he then barely listens to the other group members, and when he does respond, his comments are typically self-referential, tangential to the point being made, and never responsive to the affect being expressed. Once, a female group member shouted at him, "Adam, you're unbelievable. You're such a narcissist!" Adam turned to me to ask whether I allowed name-calling in the group, to which I responded, I am ashamed to say, that "narcissist" was a diagnostic category rather than a name.

Adam, 34, has been in the group for a year, and the group turnover, which had been limited prior to his arrival, has escalated since he came. He was referred to my co-ed group by his therapist who described him as a narcissistic personality disorder who needed to get feedback about the effects of his egocentricity on others, and the therapist was operating from a Kohutian model, and therefore was more supportive and affirming than confrontational. During the screening interviews, Adam reported an awareness that he was having little success in making friends, and especially in finding a woman good enough to marry. He had one male friend, another Internet programmer, with whom he watched sports. He was currently romantically unattached, and described several previous women he dated as "high maintenance." He agreed that he must be contributing something to his lack of success at relationships, but he wasn't sure what.

He thought that listening to others talk about relationships in group therapy might give him some ideas, and he said he was willing to hear others share their impressions of him because "I like hearing what people think about me, whatever it is." Consequently, he seemed like a decent group member for this particular group because he was in the right age range, several of the members were single and struggling with developing successful relationships, and several of them were also gentle in giving feedback, especially when the recipient was not too defensive about receiving it.

During the year Adam has been in the group however, he has rarely seemed open to hearing or utilizing the feedback the group has given him. I have come to wonder whether narcissistic patients are treatable in psychodynamic group therapy. I have only been practicing group therapy for 3 years, so I am eager to hear from someone who has seen it all. Is Adam treatable in group therapy or should I find a way to ask him to leave, which he shows no signs of doing on his own? What might I have done differently in either the screening process or in the early months of treatment? What can I do now to try to improve the situation for Adam or the group? Also, what can I do with my own feelings that are, frankly, feelings of anger at Adam, frustration with his lack of willingness to hear from the others, and also intermittent anxiety that the group—which generally has an idealizing transference toward me—will turn on me?

═══════════════════════════════════════

Dear Therapist:
You have your hands full. Adam is quite a challenge. Even the most experienced group leader would be tested by his entrance into a group. To make sense out of the material we need to have some road map in our heads to follow. My own bias is to work from an object relations point of view. I view patients' behaviors as their solutions to early childhood difficulties and their best attempt to connect with the world of people. Group therapy offers a variety of opportunities for these connections to take place, which is why it is such a useful treatment modality.

You state that your colleague who referred Adam worked from a Kohutian model and described Adam as a narcissistic personality. Severely narcissistic patients are especially difficult to work with in group therapy because of their inability to differentiate between themselves and others and their insatiable need to be the center of attention. Kohut (1971, 1977), who had a great influence on our understanding of narcissism, contends that all people require a caretaker who serves as a selfobject solely to satisfy the needs of the child. Without a selfobject, narcissistic pathology results.

In an effort to get the mirroring they missed, narcissists attempt to have others fill the void of their unmet needs by being admired (i.e., mirrored) by or admiring (i.e., idealizing) someone else. Kohut believes that separate, independent, and parallel lines of development of narcissism and object relations exist in childhood. This is where object relations theory differs from self psychology. Kohut implies that the person's relationship to himself can be studied independently from his relationships with others.

Object relations theorists such as Kernberg (1975) assert that the development and study of narcissism and object relations cannot be separated. He believes that the narcissistic person has underlying issues of primitive rage and envy. The major defenses center on splitting and projective identification. How does this help us understand how to treat Adam?

Adam's attempts to have others fill the void of his unmet needs by being the center of attention have been met with little or no success to date, which is clearly frustrating for everyone in the group. The leader must use his skill to help Adam and the group reconceptualize the issue as a group problem, not just as Adam's problem.

Gans and Alonso (1998) suggest that individual behavior in the group must be viewed as a co-construction between the group and the patient. Viewed through this lens, many ways appear of addressing this dynamic in the group. You can address the whole group, any individual, or an interpersonal dynamic. For instance, when addressing Adam's monopolizing behavior it might be helpful to say something like: "I wonder why the group is allowing Adam to do all the work tonight?" By addressing the issue as a group problem, it takes the spotlight off Adam, places it on the whole group, and allows Adam to recede into the background. It also helps mobilize others in the group to address their own passivity in dealing with Adam. You will have to make this type of comment many times over the course of many sessions. Working through takes a long time.

In addition to working with his monopolizing behavior, you clearly need to help Adam own his internal experience, such as his envy and rage. We can assume that these feelings are not consciously available to him. They are split off and projected on others in the group. Your challenge as a leader is to get him to reown those projected feelings while encouraging other group members not to collude with his behavior. This pattern of projective identification is extremely prevalent in group therapy.

A group can be described as a hall of mirrors. Any behavior in another member can be seen as a reflection of a part of ourselves. The opportunity to experience ourselves and observe others engaged in these projective identifications is truly a gift, as long as the leader can help the group members observe the process and help people own their own projections. If we view

Adam's behavior as a reflection of parts of each of the other members, it is hoped that we can get Adam to contain his feelings and get other members to own their feelings.

The leader has three types of interventions he or she can make in a group session. He or she can intervene at the whole-group level, at the interpersonal level, or at the intrapsychic level. In the case of Adam, as I mentioned before, the group-as-a-whole level is important to keep the focus off Adam and to make the group a safe place. However, over time it will be necessary to intervene on an interpersonal and an intrapsychic level. The type of pathology that Adam brings to the group requires him to explore his interpersonal world and his internal world. It may be necessary for Adam to enter individual therapy. His ability to use the group effectively may require a place outside of group to deal with the feelings that come up in the group that he will not have adequate time to explore because of the need to share the time.

The countertransference reactions of the group therapist to these types of patients are often problematic and require an enormous amount of restraint and skill. I noticed in the dilemma that a female member called Adam a narcissist. This name-calling is extremely hostile. Adam turned to you for support and your response was to agree with the patient that she had not done anything wrong. The fact that narcissism is a diagnostic category doesn't mean that one does not use the word to be hurtful and I suspect your own emotional reaction got in the way of recognizing her hostility. Your countertransference may reflect that part of you that would like to kill Adam off (i.e., get him to leave the group). Your response is understandable, considering Adam has interfered with the successful integration of new members into the group. In fact, my sense is that it feels like he is destroying the group.

To figure out how to respond to Adam, pay attention to your internal reaction. Recognizing your desire to kill him off should clue you in that you are caught in a transference-countertransference bind. Once understood, you can help Adam and the group to own their hostility, which will help the group to become unstuck. You might encourage the patient who called Adam a narcissist to describe what she was feeling instead of calling him a name, which could lead to a fruitful dialogue between Adam and the group. You could even verbalize your own internal experience. You would have to self-disclose in a thoughtful and careful way because of Adam's susceptibility to narcissistic injury.

It is your responsibility to make the group a safe place for all of the members. You must not allow an incident like this to occur without intervention, or the sense of safety will be eroded. If Adam can be called a name, so can any other member of the group.

Finally, considering all the difficulties a narcissistic patient like Adam presents, one of the main things you must do when referred a patient is a thorough pregroup screening. You need to determine the appropriateness of the patient for your group. Does he have the capacity to share the time with others? Is he capable of tolerating narcissistic injury? You should place him in your group only after considering these questions carefully. Adam may not have been ready to join your group, considering his behavior thus far. However, now that he is a member, your challenge is to find a way to help him sit back and not monopolize the sessions. With some of these suggestions above, I think it is possible to help him and the group accomplish this. Good luck!

Arnold Cohen, Ph.D

References

Gans, J. S., & Alonso, A. (1998). Difficult patients: Their construction in group therapy. *International Journal of Group Psychotherapy, 48,* 311–326.

Kernberg, O. (1975). *Borderline conditions and pathological narcissism.* New York: Jason Aronson.

Kohut, H. (1971). *The analysis of the self.* New York: International Universities Press.

Kohut, H. (1977). *The restoration of the self.* New York: International Universities Press.

Dear Therapist:

I have good news and bad news for you. The *good* news is that I think Adam can, in fact, be treated in group therapy. The *bad* news is that I think Adam can, in fact, be treated in group therapy. Psychodynamic theory would suggest that if you can learn to tolerate and work with the very primitive affect that is stirred up in both you and the other group members, you are off to the races. Well, "races" does not quite describe the pace at which change is likely to happen for Adam. The pace could probably be better described as "glacial."

Your anxiety about the group turning on you for bringing Adam into it is right on target. My only argument is that they *already have* turned on you, but the affect has gone underground. This would explain the recent increase in the dropout rate. If you can invite the group's anger at you (and I bet it applies to more than just this situation of inviting Adam to the group), the group would not be left with the choice of ripping Adam to shreds or leaving the group prematurely. Easier said than done, I know. It might help to be reminded that the group's expressing its anger toward you is part of a healthy, working group. Nonetheless, that anger stirs up our sense of incompetence at best and our inner badness at worst. For the beginning therapist, threats to one's sense of competence cut especially deep. Rest assured, however, that even 50 years of experience would not inoculate a therapist to the rage and shame stirred up by working with someone like Adam.

Think of Adam as a gift you brought to the group. This may sound counterintuitive, but he brings something unique to your group. Most groups filled with relatively healthy patients tend toward "tea parties" if not regularly reminded by the leader what their purpose is or if not stirred up so powerfully by a particular patient or situation. A difficult patient such as Adam allows group patients to access deep and terrifying parts of themselves. If we welcome that access, both in ourselves and in our patients, then we give our groups the message that such access is the first step in the process of working toward living a fuller, richer life. In Adam's case, the terrifying parts of themselves that he gives the group members access to are probably entitlement, envy, shame, and rage. Naturally, members are resistant to acknowledging these painful affects.

It is easier to be angry with Adam than it is to help him uncover the wounds that lie beneath the surface of his annoying behaviors in the group. Witness your response that "narcissist" was a diagnostic category, not a name. You were probably enacting something very powerful, straight from Adam's unconscious. (I am basing this on your being appalled at your own comment, which suggests that this is behavior far out of the ordinary for you.) The shame you felt at having blurted this out probably reflects the unconscious shame to which Adam currently has no access. The rage in response to what I would assume is your feeling of impotence similarly reflects the unconscious rage to which Adam currently has no access. We can understand these experiences as examples of projective identification where the patient projects intolerable aspects of his own unconscious on to another so that the other begins to feel what it is that the patient cannot feel. The therapist is then unconsciously prodded to behave toward the patient in ways very familiar to the patient. We do not have the historical data to back this up, but we do have the group experience on which to base this supposition. Of course Adam shows no signs of leaving group: he has created a very familiar home for himself.

Some would say that a narcissistic patient such as Adam belongs in a group with similarly character disordered patients and that it is only a setup for him to be scapegoated if he is placed with group members who are more on the neurotic end of the spectrum. I suspect this has less to do with any theoretical position and more to do with the comfort level of the group therapist in dealing with the likelihood of the rage toward—and scapegoating of—the more compromised patient. My belief that your group can prosper together is rooted in the conviction that we all have an "Adam" within us.

Hindsight is 20/20, of course, but it always helps to be prepared, and I am guessing that your assessment sessions did not include an exploration of his relationships to important others that may have tipped you off that Adam would be the very difficult patient he has turned out to be. Often I let the "here-and-now" experience dominate the group process but it can be very helpful at crisis points to have a patient reflect on what part of his or her history is being enacted at a particular moment. This helps both the patient and the group take a step out of primary process into secondary process in order not to simply replay but to learn from these inevitable enactments.

I also try in the assessment sessions to explore with new referrals what their troubles in the group are likely to be. That way we—and soon the group, too—have a language to recognize and talk about the "crises" that ensue when they have their problems in the group. I often solicit answers to such disturbing questions as, "What kind of group member would be your worst nightmare?" or "For whom would you be the worst nightmare?" Following that, I suggest we can only hope that they find these people in the group so that they have an opportunity to understand these nightmare parts of themselves. In this way, I am inviting group patients to bring their ugliest, most unappealing selves forward.

In sum, I leave you with the following recommendations: (a) invite the group members' anger toward you so that they need not extrude Adam or themselves (e.g., "The group must be furious at me for bringing Adam in here when his presence reminds us of our own rage and envy and deep sense of inadequacy."); (b) encourage group members to bring their own pain into group to stop making Adam the container for their disowned selves (e.g., "John, what inside you is making you so willing to give Adam the spotlight?"); (c) interpret the underlying meaning of Adam's behavior for the group in a way that maintains his dignity so that the group is not simply caught up in the projective identification but can create a new scenario (e.g., "How intently must Adam ignore the comments of the group before everyone is willing to see how vulnerable he feels?"); (d) make comments that connect Adam's behavior to behavior exhibited by other group members in the past so as to promote subgrouping and counteract the tendency to scapegoat (e.g., "This reminds me of the time when Jane was trying to get our attention by repeatedly coming late to group."); and, (e) appreciate Adam's role as the difficult patient (Gans & Alonso, 1998) that allows the group to find out useful information about you as a group leader (e.g., "The group owes Adam its gratitude for attempting to size up just how well I can handle its most offensive behavior.").

Elizabeth L. Shapiro, Ph.D

References

Gans, J. S., & Alonso, A. (1998). Difficult patients: Their construction in group therapy. *International Journal of Group Psychotherapy, 48,* 311–326.

Getting Our Affairs in Order

Dear Consultant:

I have a coed group that includes four men and four women aged 35 to 55. The group has been ongoing for about 5 years, and several of the members have been in the group for at least 2 years. My group contract includes the agreement that patients put their feelings into words and not actions and that no social contact outside the group will occur. Recently, I noticed that two of the members, Jack and Paula, have been paying a lot of attention to each other and even flirt occasionally in the group. I think they may be having an affair, but I have no proof—only a gut feeling.

What leads me to believe this is that they often catch each other's eye and smile coyly. Other group members have mentioned that they seem to have an attraction to each other, but they deny it and just say they like each other. Several members seem to enjoy the flirtation, and often a great deal of laughter and sexual innuendos appear in the group. I admit I enjoy their lightheartedness, but I also wonder whether anything is going on and whether the group is colluding with it.

A month ago, Jack and Paula were seen coming out of a coffee shop together just before group. When revealed by Susan, who has had a crush on Jack for about 4 months, Jack and Paula said that they had inadvertently run into each other, rather than having planned to meet there. Bill, a single 48-year-old who has not had a relationship in his 3 years in group, fantasized about Jack and Paula, saying that he wished Jack and Paula would have a relationship because it would give him hope that he might meet someone in the group at some point, too. When I pointed out that outside contact was a violation of the contract, Bill said that if he met someone he liked in the group he would drop out of the group to go out with her.

Two weeks ago, sexual tension mounted in the group when Linda, a somewhat histrionic 35-year-old, said that she was attracted to Leon, a successful CEO who is married. She said that she'd love to go on vacation with him to some place "really hot." Leon blushed and said that he is happily married. This led the group to focus again on Jack and Paula. The group imagines that they meet regularly after group (they, in fact, ride the same subway together on their way home) and that they probably talk about the other group members. Jack and Paula continue to vehemently deny any outside contact.

My guess is that the group's fantasies are not just fantasies and that Jack and Paula are having an illicit affair. How should I address their relationship? How does one encourage the group members to tell "secrets and lies?" If it does come out that they are having an affair, do I ask them to leave the group? I'm afraid if I don't contain these intense feelings in the group that it will explode. Worse yet, I'm worried that if Paula and Jack are having an affair and it breaks up, there will be a lot of dropout in the group.

Dear Therapist:

The basic question, "How does one encourage group members to tell 'secrets and lies?'" is not only specific to your dilemma, but appropriate to psychoanalytical therapy in general. The inclination to keep secrets and tell lies is a function of the tendency of the members of the group to feel shame and guilt about the subject matter, and of the degree to which they feel safe, held, and contained in the group. The inability to talk openly about sexual matters is often a function of shame and guilt, but so too is the inability to talk openly about other matters, usually those involving a sense of vulnerability, humiliation, and low self-esteem. This must be addressed from time to time in all groups.

Our first obligation is to help provide and maintain a culture of safety and honesty, although getting the optimal balance between these two group virtues is easier said than done. To do so, it is important to interpret a variety of defenses against fantasies and impulses within the context of holding and containing. It is also important to ask questions about a possible absence of a sense of safety, and the way that members of the group perceive the therapist's contribution to this. Nowadays we are concerned with issues of narcissistic vulnerability as much if not more than with more traditional issues of sexuality and aggression, and we are inclined to address early vulnerability much sooner in treatment than we used to.

Whether or not Jack and Paula are having an affair, you imagine that they are, as do other members of the group. Moreover, other members of the group have acknowledged that they would like to have sexual relationships with one another of one kind or another. Therefore, I would say to the group, directly and simply, that I imagine that Jack and Paula are having an affair, not an "illicit affair," because in this context the phrase is redundant. I would remind the group about the therapeutic contract and the reasons for it.

I would then try to analyze these real and imaginary relationships in terms of group processes and individual contributions to it, addressing Oedipal wishes and anxieties and their repetition in the group, as well as the dynamics of sibling incest in terms of whole and part object relationships, that is, in terms of pre-Oedipal dynamics.

Especially important would be the interpretation of basic assumption pairing, which I understand to be a function of sexuality as a manic defense against depressive anxieties. I do not have enough information about the various members of the group to enable me to make precise suggestions about how they are each personifying the pairing processes. Jack's denial and anger as such are hardly a problem. However, being sensitive to the use of anger as a way of avoiding sadness, I would wonder aloud what members of the group might be feeling sad about. These confrontations and inter-pretations and working with responses to them are likely to take several weeks, if not months, before the current impasse is modified.

If my suppositions were confirmed by the group, then in parallel with confrontation, clarification, and interpretation, I would insist that Jack and Paula stop their relationship. If they did not do so, I would ask them to leave the group. If others also left the group, then so be it, but I doubt that they would. The group might continue at a less than optimal size, but eventually it would be reconstituted. Or not, as the case may be, because it would be better to close the group entirely than to support these perverse processes. New patients should not be brought into the group until problems about trusting and believing the members of the group were resolved. Also, if I did not have a sufficient number of referrals to enable proper selection and the maintenance of numbers, I would terminate the group. This would be preferable to conducting a group under false pretenses, that is, as though it were a social club or a dating agency, which is not to say that such activities are not necessary and desirable in modern urban life, but they are not ther-apy as I attempt to provide it.

Before making the final decision about their termination, I would be pre-pared to see Jack and Paula individually and as a couple. I might even see every member of the group individually, or offer to do so, for a short while, while continuing to hold sessions of the group. I might also offer to refer Jack and Paula as a couple to a senior colleague, or as individuals to two dif-ferent senior colleagues.

I would consult a colleague about my own countertransference to the group and the various participants in it, because I would assume that their behavior was a response to my being unable to understand and to verbalize their "material." However, a problem would arise if my suppositions about pairing in and out of the group were not confirmed, but I continued to have them, in which case I would consult a colleague sooner rather than later.

On what grounds or principles do I offer these recommendations? I have described my own clinical technique in group analysis elsewhere (Hopper, 2003a, 2003b). Winnicott (1975) distinguished between "management" and "therapy." An interface always exists between management and therapy, but they remain different realms of clinical endeavor. Sometimes, the differences between management and therapy are not clear cut until boundaries are tested. If management is poor, it is difficult to provide a good therapeutic experience, although it must be acknowledged that good management does not guarantee a good therapeutic experience. An essential element of good management is the maintenance of boundaries.

Fundamental to group analysis, as to all psychoanalytically informed treatments, is the rule that although all fantasies, thoughts, and feelings can be expressed verbally, they should not be enacted outside the time and space of the group. (Actually, in an ideal world, fantasies, thoughts, and feelings should not be enacted inside the group either, whether in the form of subtle nonverbal communications or in the form of poor impulse control.) I recognize, of course, that verbalization and nonverbal communications can be very powerful, perhaps more powerful than other forms of action or enactments. It is important to make this edict clear at the outset. It is also important to explain the reasons for it, although in my experience most people do not really understand this until boundaries are tested, in one way or another, as they usually are, sooner or later. After all, infants and children are told that they cannot have their parents entirely to themselves, and this is expressed and enforced with authority and power long before they understand and accept the reasons why—if, in fact, they ever do. Civilized life is based on edicts concerning enactment generally and enactment of sexual and aggressive fantasies and impulses toward particular people specifically.

In this sense, the therapist and other members of the group are taboo— that is, sexual and other kinds of relationships with them are not allowed. The problem is that in regression many people some of the time, and some people virtually all the time, are unable to stop themselves from enacting their fantasy life and, in this connection, are unable to use insight and other features of talking cures. When insight based on communication fails, taboos must be maintained through management. Such management may lead to the termination of therapy, primarily for those who are simply unable to use what is offered. However, much more often it leads to the maintenance of therapy and to a sustained period of maturation, both for the group-as-a-whole and for particular patients.

Nonetheless, at least one question remains: What do we do about those who cannot form the requisite therapeutic alliance? Over the years I have formed the view that they are not suitable cases for the treatments that I am offering, and they cannot be in therapy with me. I no longer believe that if I cannot help and understand then no one can, and, therefore, that I must keep leaning against the boundaries of the contract with the utmost zeal to cure and rescue everyone—which is based on an omnipotent and grandiose fantasy, and which ultimately may be more harmful than helpful. (In saying this I do not wish to imply that in such cases countertransference issues never appear or that colleagues might not do better.) In the context of group analysis, those patients who remain in the group are better able to form and to maintain a culture that sustains the talking cure, and to make therapeutic use of this, primarily because they feel safer and more trusting.

Earl Hopper, PhD

References

Hopper, E. (2003a). *The social unconscious: Selected papers*. London: Jessica Kingsley.

Hopper, E. (2003b). *Traumatic experience in the unconscious life of groups*. London: Jessica Kingsley.

Winnicott, D. W. (1975). *Collected papers: Through paediatrics to psycho-analysis*. London: Hogarth Press.

Dear Therapist:

The first order of business is for you to have confidence that you and your group will work out this period of instability and distress. Toward this end, I would encourage you to look at the group-as-a-whole. What is occurring is serving the entire group. Your job is to help the group members figure out what is going on internally and interpersonally.

Your dilemma raises many complex issues for the group therapist. Before I respond, let me tell you a bit about my background. I have been a group therapist for over 30 years and have also taught group therapy theory and practice for 25 years. My orientation is psychodynamic, interpersonal, and systems based. A basic principle of my perspective is the use of permissive curiosity and inquiry into the meanings of thoughts, feelings, and behaviors. I try to create a milieu where group members believe that anything can be talked about because we will look at the material together with non-judgmental curiosity. I am very attuned to feelings and emotions in group therapy. Patients often resist experiencing and expressing emotions so I work with my groups to explore these resistances, to understand them, and to nourish the experience and expression of emotions (Cohen, 1997). In recent years, I have also become attuned to the body and bodily experiences as they relate to thoughts and feelings. I ask about sensations and comment on body language when I think this will lead to more awareness.

I come to group therapy from a systems perspective. I listen for and comment on whole-group interactions, especially when I suspect that unconscious processes are at work to keep material from being talked about. I try to bring these forces to light when I become aware of them, because group members cannot see the whole group in the same way that the leader can. When groups reach an impasse, I find that most often anti-therapeutic forces are at work.

Four major areas appear that I will address in my response to your dilemma: (a) the impact of the developmental stage of the group on the members and leader; (b) your contract and its effect on the group; (c) Bion's (1959) notion of pairing as a basic assumption in this group; and, (d) the definition of the "difficult" patient.

This group is relatively new, with many members having been in the group for 2 years or less. Active conflict exists in the group, suggesting that your group is in the fight–flight stage of development. If you are aware of the developmental stage of the group and the impact of the stage on you and the members, you will be able to put the material that is emerging into the proper context and can normalize what the group is struggling with and why.

Jack is clearly challenging your authority by telling you implicity that you had no right to tell him or anyone else in the group what they could do outside the group. As I understand it, your group members have agreed that outside contact is a violation of the contract. The use of the term "contract," which is a legal term, may be stimulating defiance in the fight–flight stage of group development, and in those, like Jack, who have conflict over autonomy and individuation. You may wish to consider the impact of the wording and meaning of your contract. I prefer to use the term "Group Agreements." I ask group members to agree "to discuss in the group any relevant interactions between group members occurring outside the group, and to use the group for therapeutic purposes."

For now, Jack is correct because you, in fact, do not have a right to tell him or anyone else in the group what they can do outside the group. You can remind the group that group agreements are guidelines for the group to follow. Of course people will have contact outside the group. The important thing is for people to be able to talk in the group setting about whatever occurs between and among group members. I sometimes do some didactic explaining when the group agreements are challenged. In this case, I would explain that subgroups of members that have contact outside the group—and don't discuss it in group—can interfere with and compromise the group's cohesiveness.

To address the pairing basic assumption (Bion, 1959), I would encourage other members to talk about their fantasies about Jack and Paula, and the purpose of those fantasies. I might say something like: "It is much easier to imagine Jack and Paula having illicit fun than to face your own inner struggles and emotional pain." I would not get too invested in whether Jack and Paula are actually having an affair. If they are, it will come to light in due time. The group needs to feel that you are confident in their ability to figure this out. There is no urgency here. This is a wonderful group of people who are struggling to work together to find out more about themselves and their relationships with others.

It is tempting to locate or label a "difficult patient" in your group. I agree with Gans and Alonso (1998) that the "difficult" group member is co-constructed by the group members and leader. In addition, Shields (2000) suggests that the "inclination to be troublesome" is an invitation for hope and creativity in the group. Behavior is appearing in your group that is not being addressed by the group with curiosity. Some group members would rather act out their feelings than feel their feelings. This is often characteristic of group members whom we experience as difficult. I suggest that you view your group members as people with problems who are demonstrating those problems in the group. They are fulfilling their agreement to bring into the group the problems that have brought them to treatment.

You may need to encourage Jack to challenge you and express his anger toward you directly. How comfortable are you when group members are angry with you? If you are not comfortable, or if your group members seldom express anger directly toward you, I suggest you seek supervision to work on this. It is very important for your group members, and especially Jack, to feel safe in expressing anger directly toward you. The other group members can observe his angry retorts and you can ask them about what they make of him. They may know about his family history and may be able to help him understand what his transference enactment means. Focusing on understanding and looking at the meaning of behaviors in the group is what you can offer. I prefer this stance to "containing" emotional expression.

Ultimately, if you explore meaning you will contain. Group members become more curious about themselves and more interested in understanding their feelings than in acting them out in the group.

I encourage you to find enjoyment in working with this evocative and challenging material. My goal as a group therapist is to find pleasure in helping people to learn about themselves, others, and relationships.

Suzanne L. Cohen, EdD, CGP, FAGPA

References

Bion, W. (1959). *Experiences in groups.* New York: Basic Books.

Cohen, S. L. (1997). Working with resistance to experiencing and expressing emotions in group therapy. *International Journal of Group Psychotherapy, 47,* 443–458.

Gans, J. S., & Alonso, A. (1998). Difficult patients: Their construction in group therapy. *International Journal of Group Psychotherapy, 48,* 311–326.

Shields, W. S. (2000). Hope and the inclination to be troublesome: Winnicott and the treatment of character disorder in group therapy. *International Journal of Group Psychotherapy, 50,* 87–103.

Section III
Complex Defenses

Overview

On her way to Oz, Dorothy meets the Tin Man, the Cowardly Lion, and the Scarecrow, all of whom feel they are missing an aspect of themselves. One can view their adventure as a journey to reincorporate disowned aspects of the self—in a group! Group therapy is a place where patients try to reintegrate parts of themselves. This process of accepting intolerable aspects of oneself can be painful, however, so patients often defend themselves by projecting those aspects of themselves on other members or the leader. If the other member or leader accepts the projection, he or she may feel or behave in a way that feels like a "not me" experience. This process of projective identification is one of the most complex in group psychotherapy.

In his chapter *Unraveling Projective Identification and Enactment*, Robert Weber reviews the history of these defenses, explores the confusion around them, and tries to elucidate their meaning and role in group therapy.

In the first dilemma, *Axis II Had Me Spinning,* the group therapist is paralyzed when members verbally attack a different member each week, but refuse to accept the therapist's interpretations about what is going on. Consultant Hylene Dublin argues for good pre-group preparation, "benign tolerance of the group's anger and projection," and engagement of the group members in a reflective process about their behavior. Kathy Ulman uses the lens of object relations to understand the scapegoating behavior and she advises the therapist to maintain good boundaries and encourage nonjudgmental curiosity as a remedy.

The therapist in *Will the Real Expert Please Stand Up?* feels compelled to provide advice to his group members as they become increasingly passive. Both Allan Gelber and Marsha Vannicelli note in their responses that projective identification is at play. Gelber tracks affect rather than associations, and focuses on self and mutual regulation because he believes that patient-therapist interactions are co-constructed. In contrast, Vannicelli focuses on the countertransference evoked and suggests analyzing the countertransference first, followed by interpretations to the group about the projective identification process.

In *Serial Scapegoating*, the therapist, who has inherited a group of chronically depressed patients from a therapist on maternity leave, wants to add new patients to her group but finds the group "firing" each new arrival. Consultant David Altfeld highlights the feelings and insecurities evoked by the loss of a therapist and suggests that these be articulated and worked through before the group can feel safe with a new therapist. Bonnie Buchele observes the paradox for these patients that to become healthy would result in the loss of the very community—the group—to which they are so attached.

Unraveling Projective
Identification and Enactment

ROBERT WEBER, PHD, CGP, FAGPA

Introduction

The concept of projective identification (PI) is one of the most useful, confused, and confusing ideas in the psychoanalytic literature: useful, because it cogently describes a phenomenon that is ubiquitously familiar and troubling to clinicians; confused, because it has been transplanted from its original theoretical context and applied at times as a "catch-phrase for all interpersonal phenomena" (Hinshelwood, 1991, p. 196); confusing, because it is unclear whether it is a uniquely distinguishable clinical phenomenon or merely a whole that is not greater than its parts, which are splitting, projection, and identification (Crisp, 1986; Finell, 1986; Goldstein, 1991; Meissner, 1980, 1987). Nonetheless, its widespread application by clinicians to identify, understand, and manage crucial and important clinical conundrums attests to its conceptual utility and empirical validity in individual (Grotstein, 1981; Ogden, 1979, 1982), couples (Morrison, 1986; Rutan & Smith, 1985; Zinner, 1976; Zinner & Shapiro, 1972), family (Dicks, 1967; Zinner & Shapiro, 1972), and group therapy (Grinberg, 1973; Grinberg, Gear, & Liendo, 1976; Horwitz, 1983; Malcus, 1995; Masler, 1969).

As with all psychoanalytic ideas, PI is a work in progress since it was first identified and named by Klein (Klein, 1946, 1955) and emerged as the "cornerstone" of Kleinian theory (Hinshelwood, 1991) and Bion's theory of group (Bion, 1961). This chapter will examine the concept of PI as it has evolved historically, with emphasis on its translation to group therapy. In this chapter I will: (a) sketch a brief history of the concept of PI; (b) articulate theoretical confusions and conflicts; (c) trace the translation to the group therapy context; and, (d) discuss practice elements of PI in group therapy.

A brief history of the concept of projective identification

The concept of PI was first developed by Melanie Klein in the context of child analysis as she developed her thinking about the paranoid-schizoid position. During this early period of development, the infant must experience "fantasies of personal fragmentation and disintegration, of persecution by 'bad' breasts and penises as well as their poisonous substances, of tantalization by unstable 'good' objects, of unbounded greed and envy—in short, that terrifying, phantasmagoric world infancy that Klein has described, without order or security" (Eishold, 1985, p. 330).

Klein's work was "a major turning point in one of the modern developments of psychoanalysis" (Ganzarain, 1977, pp. 442–443). Her main point of departure from the Freudian trajectory was the concept of the superego in which she saw enshrined "the child's earliest 'whole-object' relationships with mother and father, by identification and introjection (Ibid.)." From this starting point evolved Klein's theories of "internal objects" and the "inner world" that became the foundation for an object relations theory.

Freud's work on projection and Karl Abraham's further development of the concept formed the basis for Klein's formulation of PI. For Freud, projection was a defense that described "how one person's ideas may be attributed to someone else, thus creating a state of paranoia" (Freud, 1895/1966, p. 209). Abraham (1927) observed that there were "cycles of projection followed by recuperative introjection of objects" (Hinshelwood, 1991, p. 180). For Abraham, projection meant "the projection into the world of an internal object," or "the externalization of the superego" (pp. 180–181). Klein struggled to integrate the concepts of Freud and Abraham with her own, but her clinical observations led her to conclude that "both the object and part of the self were being projected" (Hinshelwood, 1991, p. 181).

Klein viewed PI as emerging during the period of the paranoid-schizoid position as the child begins to grapple with his or her own aggression in relationship to the maternal figure. The child experiences a dilemma. On the one hand, anxious about these aggressive drives that represent the bad parts of the self, the child attempts to segregate them from the good parts of self (i.e., the "splitting" aspect of PI). Then the child tries to get rid of them by putting them into the (m)other (i.e., the "projective" aspect of PI). On the other hand, the child, having put these bad, aggressive parts into the (m)other, is fearful and paranoid that the (m)other's own aggression threatens the child with the prospect of danger or destruction. If the (m)other is able to contain this projection (i.e., the identification aspect of PI) and metabolize it, then the dilemma resolves for the child who can gradually take back and integrate these bad, aggressive parts.

Bion (1957) advanced the concept of PI by distinguishing normal from pathological PI. He emphasized PI's two alternative aims: first, to rid one of painful, unwanted internal experiences, thoughts, and feelings by projecting them into someone else, thereby gaining a sense of control over them; and second, to create a state of mind and feeling in the other person that enables communication about what may otherwise be an unbearable and unspeakable internal experience.

The following example illustrates the emergence of such paranoid-schizoid fantasies in group therapy.

Case 1. His first night in group, a reluctant new group member reported a dream in which he dove into what appeared to be an inviting tropical pond only to discover that, as he hit the surface of the water, it was covered with "pond scum." Despite his disgust he kept swimming only to find himself bumping into floating objects, which he discovered to be "turds." The implications were not lost on either the therapist or the group, and a profound discomfort and deep silence ensued until another member responded, "He is one of us!" The new member's unconscious had pinpointed a central therapeutic issue for himself and other group members, the inability to form intimate, loving relationships because of a mistrust and paranoia that resulted in self-protective disdain of others.

Conflicting theories of projective identification

As the study of PI has grown, theorists have developed conflicting theories as to its meaning and operation. Horwitz (1983) has called PI "more elusive and confusing than any other psychodynamic concept I have encountered" (pp. 260–261). Central to the confusion are two questions: first, are one or two bodies involved in PI, and, second, what is the nature of the identification that occurs? In the one body view, one perspective is that the projector, not the recipient of the projection, is the one who identifies (Grotstein, 1981; Segal, 1964). Essential contact with that which is projected is maintained via the identification with that which is projected. A contrasting one body notion is that of Wolberg (1977), in which the projector is projecting an identification. For example, the child feels aggressive, having identified with the aggressor parent, but cannot tolerate this aggression, so projects it onto someone else, and then may even retaliate against the other for being aggressive.

Within the two body conceptualization, two ideas predominate. First, that the projector projects and the recipient identifies with the projection. In other words, "the recipient of the projected, split-off aspect of the personality 'becomes' the person of the attributes of the projection" (Rutan & Smith, 1985, p. 198). Second, the emphasis falls on the mutual relationship in which the projector and recipient are involved (Grotstein, 1981; Ogden, 1982; Shapiro & Carr, 1991; Zinner & Shapiro, 1972). Shapiro and Carr (1991, p. 24) identify a number of stages to the process of this dynamic:

1. The projection or disavowal of an uncomfortable aspect of ourselves
2. The discovery (through empathic resonance) of another person who has an attribute that corresponds to that aspect of ourselves that we are attempting to disavow
3. The willingness, conscious or not, of the other person to accept the projected attribute as part of himself
4. The development of an enduring relationship between ourselves and the other in which the projections are sustained by unconscious collusion
5. The other (now seen as possessing the disavowed characteristics) is consciously identified as unlike the self, whereas an unconscious relationship is sustained in which the projected attribute can be experienced vicariously
6. The use of manipulative behavior that is unconsciously designed to elicit feelings or behavior from the other to support the idea that the projected attribute belongs to him
7. Selective inattention to any of the real aspects of the other person that may contradict or invalidate the projection
8. A complementarity of projections—both participants project

Shay (2002) presents a straightforward definition of the concept. An *intrapsychic* tension becomes an *interpersonal* conflict (or, more precisely, an interpersonal interaction). Using a baggage metaphor, Shay expresses the PI process as follows: "This baggage is *not mine*! I don't identify it as mine. But I can see that *you're carrying the baggage.* It's yours! I identify it as yours and you are carrying it like you own it. And I think it's ugly. What do you have to say about that?" Elsewhere, Shay (2001) argues for replacing the concept of PI entirely, because its meaning has been so confusing, coining the substitute term "projective recruitment."

Projective identification in the context of group therapy
In his book, *Experiences in Groups,* Bion (1961) translated Kleinian theory and applied the concept of PI to the group context. He observed that sig-

nificant and important regressions that pose threats similar to those confronting the infant during the paranoid-schizoid stage occur in a group for members and leader alike. He termed this threat "psychotic-like anxiety." Horwitz (1983, p. 277) identifies a number of these threatening group forces: the contagion effect of group emotion; threats to one's individuality and autonomy; revival of early familial conflicts; and the prevalence of envy, rivalry, and competition.

In an attempt to allay this anxiety and structure the group world, groups, Bion observed, employ the defensive functions of the basic assumption (BA) groups (Bion, 1955, 1961; Eishold, 1985; Rioch, 1970). The job of the group leader is to address these BA defenses (dependency, fight–flight, and pairing) in order to keep the group focused on its task; that is, to maintain the group's function as a "work group."

Bion (1959, 1970) formulated the model of container-contained in working with groups and indicated the importance of the containing function in the resolution of projective identification. It is the leader and the group-as-a-whole that provide the container for processing and "metabolizing" the PIs (Ogden, 1982) such that they become the basis for therapeutic progress. Thought and emotion are made tolerable to the members as the group therapist and other members gradually present them repeatedly to the members "in the forms of words, silence, and nonverbal and paraverbal behaviors" (Billow, 2003, pp. 114–115).

Billow (2003) summarizes Bion's theory as follows: "The cornerstone of Bion's theory of individual and group development is that . . . thinking . . . matures in the context of social communication. To grow and mature the individual needs a communicative containment by self, pair and group . . . . [In other words,] to develop emotions and learn from experience, one must exercise a social capacity and interact reciprocally with the containing minds of other human beings. The social container of the other . . . actively participates to make emotions and thoughts meaningful" (pp. 111–115). The result is that new understanding and meaning emerges "from the discovery of isolated, split-off, or undeveloped aspects of the self linked to recurring, developmentally early, emotional experience—all meaning-making requires container-contained processes" (Billow, 2003, p. 129).

Morrison (1986) offers a succinct statement of containment's functions: (a) to impose delay in responding to the attacks, accusations, and idealizations in a projective process; (b) to reflect on the meaning of the projection (both to the initiator and to the recipient); (c) to alter the intended response by the recipient; and (d) to communicate this alteration in a way that it can be understood and reinternalized by the initiator (p. 71).

A case example of two beginning group therapists provides a dramatic instance of the "numbing" impact of the BA fight–flight dynamic, the successful containment of the attendant PIs, and their metabolization by the leaders and group-as-a-whole.

> Case 2. Two neophyte coleaders were given a therapy group as part of their training. During meetings with their supervisor they expressed feelings of ineffectiveness and invisibility in the eyes of the group members who had a lengthy history with a succession of trainee group leaders. The two leaders were rendered "mute" during the meetings with no idea what to do or say. As they spoke about this with the supervisor they began to understand and appreciate that the group members were experiencing very similar feelings. In subsequent sessions the members began to make it clear to the leaders how powerless they felt in having no say about the transition of leadership each and every year. They too felt that what they felt, did, or said did not matter and that they, like the leaders, were invisible and powerless within the hospital system of which they were a part. The containment and analysis of the PIs that were occurring enabled the coleaders to resolve this impasse and gradually establish a therapeutic alliance.

Projective identification and group practice

Since Bion (1955) first translated the Kleinian perspective into the context of group dynamics, various authors have discussed the application of Kleinian PI to group therapy. Masler (1969) observed this dynamic in a group member who "first projects on the group a certain structural element of his own psyche, either portions of his id, ego, or his superego. He then reacts to the group as if the group represented that projected intrapsychic structure" (p. 442). During the 1970s, several other articles appeared that emphasized Kleinian theory and PI in groups (Ganzarain, 1977; Grinberg, 1973; Grinberg, Gear, & Liendo, 1976; Wolberg, 1977).

Despite the apparent importance of PI, Horwitz (1983) puzzled over the relative lack of articles on PI in group therapy. Since the 1980s, many more authors have addressed the concept, working to understand it and make better therapeutic use of it in group therapy (Billow, 2003; Clark, 1997; Eishold, 1985; Ganzarain, 1992; James, 1984; Malcus, 1995; Morrison, 1986; Rogers, 1987; Schain, 1980; Zender, 1991). The remainder of this chapter will draw out the implications of these contributions to group practice especially insofar as they result in important enactments.

Enactment and PI in the group process In 1973, Grinberg wrote: "From the moment of his birth the individual functions as a member of a group. The primary group, his family, conditions in him reaction patterns that will affect his links with all later groups including therapeutic groups in which he may become a member. One of the dynamisms of family interaction, indeed the foundation for communication, is dependent on projective identification . . . Knowledge that identification mechanisms are constantly operating in the group can be extremely helpful to the therapist in understanding the group dynamics and movement. . . . [Within] the regressive atmosphere of a therapeutic group . . . there is an emergence of roles assumed by different members. These are either accepted or, where repudiated, assigned to others through projective identification" (p. 145), and, thereby, enactments occur.

"Enactment" entered the therapeutic lexicon in the 1970s and 1980s (Eagle, 1984; Kohut, 1977; McLaughlin, 1987) and refers to "events occurring within the dyad that both parties experience as being the consequence of behavior in the other" (McLaughlin, 1998, p. 80). Eagle (1984) suggested that enactments could be understood as "unconscious attempts to deal with, in the relative safety of the therapeutic situation, material related to early conflict and trauma, for the purpose of mastering such material" (p. 103). Eagle's conceptualization includes the notion of purposefulness (i.e., an effort at mastery). This idea echoed earlier observations by Kohut (1977): "such activities ['action-thought'] are not . . . regressive steps, but constitute a not-quite-but-almost completed forward movement . . . 'pioneering experiments.' These experiments, in other words, are *enactments*—concretizations—of thought processes of a pioneering mind" (pp. 36–37, italics added).

Enactments, like PIs, involve mutual, reciprocal influence and purposefulness that serve defensive and communicative functions, and, with effective understanding and management, also therapeutic purposes. Group therapists should expect them to occur and to make use of them. In effect, the enactments are the external manifestation of the unconscious dynamics, the fruit of the PI. The group therapist must be aware of his own emotional responses and use them to manage the PIs and their enactments.

Manifestations of PI in groups   Although the manifestations of PI through enactments are myriad, two occur with particular regularity: the "spokesperson" phenomenon (Ganzarain, 1977; Rutan & Stone, 2001b); and "scapegoating" (Gadlin, 1991; Ganzarain, 1977; Kahn, 1980; Malcus, 1995; Scheidlinger, 1982; Rutan & Stone, 2001a; Toker, 1972). The assumption of these roles is the consequence of the interacting, psychodynamic needs of the group, group therapist, and individual members (i.e., their mutual, emotional influence that serves to protect the self and the group from dangerous drives and emotions by avoiding them through the process of PI). Put simply, the "spokesperson" speaks for the group the thoughts and feelings the group cannot express for itself because of anxiety and fear. An example of the spokesperson role follows.

> Case 3. Susan was a bright, successful professional who was given to lengthy self-pitying stories about her life. She quickly became the group's container for neediness and the "spokesperson" for weakness and vulnerability that was shamefully avoided by the other members despite its obvious presence in them. Another woman, Joan, felt increasingly contemptuous toward her each week. In individual sessions Joan complained to the group leader about the needy Susan, wishing that Susan were not in the group, without awareness of her own intense longings to have her own needs met. For Joan, these yearnings had been supplanted years before by a self-reliant self-sufficiency required because of the family's dynamics. Finally, an opportunity occurred to interpret the dynamics of this PI and mitigate the potential "role lock." Both women became closer and more respectful and appreciative of each other's very similar life experiences.

The "scapegoat," as in the Biblical concept, is burdened with unwanted thoughts and feelings and driven off into the wilderness, unless the group therapist assists the group and its members to re-own these split off and projected aspects. If unresolved, at least two undesirable consequences occur. First, those assuming these roles may be asked to bear a disproportionate burden and, ultimately, be driven from the group. Second, other members, because of their PIs and the consequent depletion of their drives and emotions, may no longer have "full use of (their) total personality endowment" (Ganzarain, 1977, p. 443).

These dynamics are potentiated by the increased permeability of boundaries and by the emotional contagion of the group (Redl, 1980/1942) and by the "valencies" of the group leader and members—that is, their proclivity and predisposition to assume certain roles. The needs of the individuals to replicate their object worlds produce what Redl (1963) called "role suction." Ganzarain (1992) points out that, Redl's role suction is "mediated by projective identification. . . . It is a microscopic variety of the emotional contagion. . . . By contrast, however, projective identification 'catches' these emotions that are not expressed or conscious but are instead denied, projected and split" (p. 17). He goes on to describe this dynamic as "the group members' internal objects performing as characters searching for actors to represent them . . . (an) assembly of the group's internal objects, floating in the group's atmosphere, searching which member can incarnate them, represent them in actual group interactions" (p. 17).

Case 4. George was destined to become the "scapegoat" in the training group he joined to advance his learning as a group therapist. His primary clinical work was with women who had been abused in various ways, including sexually, and his ethnic background spoke "machismo," though his personality and demeanor were not manifestly so. The large training group was predominantly women, many of whom had been sexually abused. The group lasted for several days and it did not take long for George to become the major interlocutor with the women in the group. Rapidly, the projections of the kind of man he was—hostile, misogynistic, hypermasculine—were heaped on him, and, for the early going, he managed the situation quite well, given the depth of his knowledge and experience in handling such projections on a daily basis. However, in this context, the burden of projections turned projective identifications became too much and he finally said, in a direct and forthright way, that he could no longer bear to be the recipient of and container for the hostility-laden projections. The women were able to respond to his plea and reabsorb their projections, thereby working through trauma-induced feelings, avoiding scapegoating him, and allowing both him and themselves to integrate that complex array of thoughts and feelings they all contained.

Klein, Bion, and therapeutic change in groups

"Communication through projective identification is a vital part of group life and often provides an effective pathway for psychological growth" (Rogers, 1987, p. 99). One important goal of group therapy is the integration of all aspects of the self: "The end result, when successful, is the transformation of the defensive projective identification into communicative projective identification" (Ganzarain, 1977, pp. 442–443).

The group setting is a context in which to make a connection with "the most feared parts of the personality," those aspects that contaminate relationships by interfering with "loving feelings towards one's objects and oneself" (Schain, 1980, p. 329). It is essential to interpret PI in order to "help the patients protect their relationships from their own pathological projections" (Schain, 1980, p. 327). As these are then worked through, group members can feel relief "from their feelings of persecution (and) repair the damage that they have done, in fact or in fantasy, to have their intimate relationships" (Schain, 1980, p. 327). If the group leader does not facilitate this process, therapy is undermined and progress thwarted, PI continues unabated, and "thinking and emotional awareness do not occur" (James 1984, p. 209).

Malcus provides a cogent, overall description of this process in relation to PI. The goal of group therapy is to:

> ... help members develop more temperate, balanced, realistic, object and interpersonal relations. In progressing toward this goal, members reclaim projected material, integrate intrapsychic splits, and develop a more balanced view of self and others, one less governed by primitive devaluation and idealization. The therapy group is a rich stimulus for evoking and containing members' splits, projections, fantasies, and primitive modes of mental functioning. The evocation and availability of these primitive operations are prerequisites for learning and growth. To these ends, the therapist must explore and interpret whole-group maternal transference, splitting, projective identification, and resultant indirect scapegoating when it arises. The therapist must also help the mother group perform the essential functions of containment, holding, good-enough mothering, and optimal frustration. (1995, p. 62)

References

Abraham, K. (1927). A short study of the development of the libido. In K. Abraham (Ed.), *Selected papers on psycho-analysis* (pp. 418–501). London: Hogarth. (Original work published 1924)

Billow, R. M. (2003). *International Library of Group Analysis. Vol. 26: Relational group psychotherapy: From basic assumptions to passion* (M. Pines, Ed.). New York: Jessica Kingsley.

Bion, W. R. (1955). Group dynamics: A re-view. In M. Klein, P. Heimann, & R. Money-Kyrle (Eds.), *New directions in psycho-analysis* (pp. 440–477). New York: Basic Books.

Bion, W. R. (1957). Differentiation of the psychotic from the non-psychotic personalities. *International Journal of Psycho-Analysis, 38,* 266–275.

Bion, W. R. (1959). Attacks on linking. *International Journal of Psycho-Analysis, 40,* 308–315.

Bion, W. R. (1961). *Experiences in groups and other papers.* New York: Basic Books.

Bion, W. R. (1962). A theory of thinking. *International Journal of Psycho-Analysis, 43,* 306–310.

Bion, W. R. (1970). *Attention and interpretation.* London: Tavistock.

Clark, A. J. (1997). Projective identification as a defense mechanism in group counseling and therapy. *Journal for Specialists in Group Work, 22,* 85–96.

Crisp, P. (1986). Projective identification: An attempt at clarification. *Journal of the Melanie Klein Society, 4,* 47–76.

Dicks, H. V. (1967). *Marital tensions.* New York: Basic Books.

Eagle, M. N. (1984). A reformulation of the psychoanalytic theory of therapy: The work of Weiss, Sampson, and their colleagues. In M. N. Eagle (Ed.), *Recent developments in psychoanalysis: A critical evaluation* (pp. 95–106). New York: McGraw-Hill.

Eisold, K. (1985). Recovering Bion's contributions to group analysis. *American Journal of Psychoanalysis, 45,* 327–340.

Finell, J. (1984). Projective identification: Mystery and fragmentation. *Current Issues in Psychoanalytic Practice, 1,* 47–62.

Finell, J. (1986). The merits and problems with the concept of projective identification. *Psychoanalytic Review, 73,* 104–120.

Freud, S. (1966). Draft H—paranoia. In J. Strachey (Ed. and Trans.), *Standard edition of the complete psychological works of Sigmund Freud* (vol. 1, pp. 206–212). London: Hogarth Press. (Original work published 1895)

Gadlin, W. I. (1991). On scapegoating: Biblical-classical sources, group psychotherapy, and world affairs. In S. Tuttmann (Ed.), *Psychoanalytic group theory and therapy: Essays in honor of Saul Scheidlinger* (pp. 27–44). Madison, CT: International Universities Press.

Ganzarain, R. (1977). General systems and object-relations theories: The usefulness in group psychotherapy. *International Journal of Group Psychotherapy, 27*, 441–456.

Ganzarain, R. (1992). Effects of projective identification on therapists and group mates. *Group Analysis, 25*, 15–18.

Goldstein, W. N. (1991). Clarification of projective identification. *American Journal of Psychiatry, 148*, 153–161.

Grinberg, L. (1973). Projective identification and projective counter-identification in the dynamics of groups. In L. Wolberg & E. Schwartz (Eds.), *Group Therapy: 1973* (pp. 145–153). New York: Intercontinental Medical Book Corporation.

Grinberg, L., Gear, M. C., & Liendo, E. C. (1976). Group dynamics according to a semiotic model based on projective identification and counteridentification. In L. R. Wolberg & M. Aronson (Eds.), *Group Therapy: 1976* (pp. 167–179). New York: Stratton Intercontinental.

Grotstein, J. S. (1981). *Splitting and projective identification.* New York: Jason Aronson.

Hinshelwood, R. D. (1991). Projective identification. In R. D. Hinshelwood (Ed.), *A dictionary of Kleinian thought* (pp. 179–208). London: Free Association Books.

Horwitz, L. (1983). Projective identification in dyads and groups. *International Journal of Group Psychotherapy, 33*, 259–279.

James, C. (1984). Bion's "containing" and Winnicott's "holding" in the context of the group matrix. *International Journal of Group Psychotherapy, 34*, 201–214.

Kahn, L. S. (1980). The dynamics of scapegoating: The expulsion of evil. *Psychotherapy: Theory, Research and Practice, 17*, 79–84.

Klein, M. (1946). Notes on some schizoid mechanisms. *International Journal of Psycho-Analysis, 27*, 99–110.

Klein, M. (1955). On identification. In M. Klein, P. Heimann, & R. Money-Kyrle (Eds.), *New directions in psychoanalysis* (pp. 309–345). New York: Basic Books.

Kohut, H. (1977). *The restoration of the self.* New York: International Universities Press.

Malcus, L. (1995). Indirect scapegoating via projective identification and the mother group. *International Journal of Group Psychotherapy, 45*, 55–71.

Masler, E.G., (1969). The interpretation of projective identification in group psychotherapy. *International Journal of Group Psychotherapy, 19*, 441–447.

McLaughlin, J. T. (1987). The play of transference: Some reflections on enactment in the psychoanalytic situation. *Journal of the American Psychoanalytic Association, 35*, 557–582.

McLaughlin, J. T. (1998). Clinical and theoretical aspects of enactment. In S. J. Ellman & M. Moskowitz (Eds.), *Enactment: Toward a new approach to the therapeutic relationship* (pp. 77–91). Northvale, NJ: Jason Aronson.

Meissner, W. W. (1980). A note on projective identification. *Journal of the American Psychoanalytic Association, 28*, 43–68.

Meissner, W. W. (1987). Projection and projective identification. In J. Sandler (Ed.), *Projection, identification, projective identification* (pp. 27–49). Madison, CT: International Universities Press.

Morrison, A. P. (1986). On projective identification in couples' groups. *International Journal of Group Psychotherapy, 36*, 55–73.

Ogden, T. H. (1979). On projective identification. *International Journal of Psycho-Analysis, 60*, 357–373.

Ogden, T. H. (1982). *Projective identification and psychotherapeutic technique.* Northvale, NJ: Jason Aronson.

Redl, F. (1980). Group emotion and leadership. In S. Scheidlinger (Ed.), *Psychoanalytic group dynamics: Basic readings* (pp. 15–68). New York: International Universities Press. (Original work published 1942)

Redl, F. (1963). Psychoanalysis and group psychotherapy: A developmental point of view. *American Journal of Orthopsychiatry, 33*, 135–147.

Rioch, M. J. (1970). The work of Wilfred Bion on groups. *Psychiatry, 33*, 56–66.

Rogers, C. (1987). On putting it into words: The balance between projective identification and dialogue in the group. *Group Analysis, 20*, 99–107.

Rutan, J. S., & Smith, J. W. (1985). Building therapeutic relationships with couples. *Psychotherapy: Theory, Research, Practice, 22,* 194–200.

Rutan, J. S., & Stone, W. N. (2001a). Expressions of affect in group psychotherapy. In J. S. Rutan & W. N. Stone (Eds.), *Psychodynamic group psychotherapy* (3rd ed., pp. 229–258). New York: Guilford Press.

Rutan, J. S., & Stone, W. N. (2001b). Mechanisms and processes of change. In J. S. Rutan & W. N. Stone (Eds.), *Psychodynamic group psychotherapy* (3rd ed., pp. 74–100). New York: Guilford Press.

Schain, J. (1980). The application of Kleinian theory to group psychotherapy. *International Journal of Group Psychotherapy, 30,* 319–330.

Scheidlinger, S. (1982). Presidential address: On scapegoating in group psychotherapy. *International Journal of Group Psychotherapy, 32,* 131–143.

Segal, H. (1973). *Introduction to the work of Melanie Klein.* New York: Basic Books. (Original work published 1964)

Shapiro, E. R., & Carr, A. W. (1991). *Lost in familiar places.* New Haven, CT: Yale University Press.

Shay, J. (2001). My problem with projective identification. *Northeastern Society for Group Psychotherapy Newsletter, 23,* 1–2.

Shay, J. (2002, June). *Projective identification goes to the movies.* Presented at the Northeastern Society for Group Psychotherapy. Wellesley, MA.

Toker, E. (1972). The scapegoat as an essential group phenomenon. *International Journal of Group Psychotherapy, 22,* 320–332.

Wolberg, A. R. (1977). Group therapy and the dynamics of projective identification. In W. R. Wolberg & M. L. Aronson (Eds.), *Group Therapy: 1977.* New York: Stratton Intercontinental Medical Book Corporation.

Zender, J. F. (1991). Projective identification in group psychotherapy. *Group Analysis, 24,* 117–132.

Zinner, J. (1976). The implications of projective identification for marital interaction. In H. Grunebaum & J. Christ (Eds.), *Contemporary marriage: Structure, dynamics and therapy* (pp. 293–308). Boston: Little, Brown.

Zinner, J., & Shapiro, R. (1972). Projective identification as a mode of perception and behavior in families of adolescents. *International Journal of Psycho-Analysis, 53,* 523–530.

Axis II Had Me Spinning

Dear Consultant:

The more group therapy I do, the more I realize that my understanding of defenses from my individual psychotherapy practice has only limited applicability to my group work. Like many of my colleagues, I began as a group therapist in a clinic setting and then took my group private when I left the clinic. In the clinic however, and even after, I had no real training in group therapy, with the operative assumption in the clinic being that my individual therapy experience would suffice. From my individual work, largely with healthier patients, I am familiar with such higher-level defenses as repression, sublimation, and projection. In my group work, however, especially with the more primitive patients I now treat, many from Axis II, cluster B (the "dramatic–erratic" personality disorder cluster), I often feel in over my head. The intense conflict between members and the fluidity of what members experience at any one time have been puzzling to me. It's a lot different from having an individual patient in the office whose affects are predictable from week to week.

I could use some help in formulating what occurred in a group I ran several years ago, which I never fully understood. I often felt like an observer at a Ping-Pong match, but with several balls in play at one time. Here's the background.

This co-ed group of eight members lasted for 2 years with members coming and going over its life, although three members were there from start to finish. I saw none of the members in individual therapy, but most of them were in individual therapy elsewhere. Ages varied from 20 to 38, and diagnoses were typically in the personality disorder spectrum, with many patients having co-morbid depression or anxiety. The women especially, over the years of the group, were diagnosed with borderline, histrionic, or dependent personality disorder, whereas the men more typically carried a narcissistic or obsessional diagnosis. As a woman, I was attuned to the way gender can affect diagnostic practices, but the diagnoses did seem accurate to me. Few of the group members had healthy social or romantic relationships outside the group.

In almost every meeting, a process occurred in which one of the members—often a different one from week to week—was placed in the hot seat and accused of having said something mean-spirited, selfish, or insensitive in a prior session. When the group explored whatever offense the member in question had committed, it was as though the complaining members had little recollection that they themselves had been in a similar position just weeks before. For example, Anna and Becky might accuse Bill of obnoxious sexism in his commentary, as they tittered about finding Mr. Right who would also be Mr. Well-Endowed. The rest of the group, including the men, would take sides with Anna and Becky leaving Bill feeling he alone was sexist in the room. My commentary that the group might be repressing their own sexism and projecting this on Bill was met with vehement disagreement that I was not only denying an obvious reality about Bill, but that I was in fact accusing them unfairly just to protect Bill, perhaps because I was attracted to Bill. In fact, I did find him attractive, but I never said so, nor do I think I demonstrated it.

After my repression-projection interpretations were rejected, I often sat silently, feeling intimidated and impotent. This seems to have led some group members to feel sufficiently unsafe in the group, fearing attack, so that they terminated early. This resulted in even less of a feeling of safety, but I was often unable to comment on this either, fearing that my comments would give it such reality that the group would lose confidence in me. Gradually, this may well have occurred, because after I took a pregnancy leave, during which time the group was in hiatus, the group never really got off the ground again, and the membership dwindled to two members, at which point I ended the group. I'm not exactly sure what happened, but I certainly didn't feel very effective, from week to week or overall. Any thoughts would be welcome.

Dear Therapist:
Let's begin by recognizing what a frustrating, disappointing group therapy experience you had, the type of experience that often leads the neophyte group practitioner to conclude that groups don't work. Perhaps by understanding your experience, however, we can come to a different conclusion. Let us first examine the complex elements contributing to your dilemma,

including your sense of intimidation and impotence, factors stimulating your inhibited stance.

To place my comments in context, I will describe my theoretical orientation to group treatment, which has evolved considerably. My earliest experiences included psychoanalytic group training and supervision in a psychiatric outpatient clinic. Milieu therapy and inpatient group experiences followed. Object relations, self psychology, and intersubjectivity theory have further contributed. In addition, I am influenced by the interpersonal orientation heralded by Yalom (1995). Not to be excluded are group-as-a-whole concepts, which inform actions to be taken when whole-group phenomena such as you describe occur.

Notably, your intimidation and powerlessness must have contributed significantly to the group's difficulty in establishing a healthy bonding and sense of safety. Bonding involves a sense of connection between individuals "in which the individual feels satisfactorily recognized, cared for, and understood, and thus safe" (Billow, 2003a, p. 83). Without issues of connectedness and safety being addressed early in the life of the group, little progress can be made. The group stays superficial or avoidant with few members assuming responsibility for their affects or actions.

Your feelings of anxiety and powerlessness may be elements of projective identification induced within you by the group. Ziskind and Zasa (2003) describe "times when the members of the group are unconsciously compelled to put into us parts of themselves they are not yet able to contain and want us to hold." All of this, as a group phenomenon, ultimately required examination within the group. With the therapeutic alliance and sense of safety not yet established, group members were not receptive to the too early individual interpretations. Dies (1994) suggests that inexperienced therapists often offer "interpretations that discourage further elaboration" and are "hesitant about following through if members do not immediately pick up on their comments" (p. 69). Probably your interpretations were perceived as criticisms and narcissistic injuries. MacKenzie (1994) states, "A critical approach that implies lack of good will or personal shortcomings will unnecessarily antagonize the membership or shut down the process" (p. 53).

You note that most of the group members were in individual therapy elsewhere but say nothing about the basis of referral to group, whether individual therapy was begun before group, or the nature of your communication with individual therapists. Yalom (1995) suggests that individual patients are often referred to groups when transference is too intense or when the patient becomes defensively isolated. It is important to know about the patients' individual treatment relationships and how these affect their involvement in the group. Sometimes splitting between group and individual therapists occurs, making the work much more difficult, particularly if this isn't within the therapists' conscious awareness. Naturally, informed consent for communication must be obtained at the outset.

Another consideration is how well potential members were prepared for inclusion in a therapy group. Increasingly, the importance of forming a beginning therapeutic alliance with individuals has become clear. Dealing with anxieties about joining the group and enabling potential members to understand how the group might be useful to them (i.e., how to translate their own problems and goals into operational terms vis-à-vis their participation in the group) are crucial. There is not always sufficient opportunity within group to learn about the treatment process. Entering into an unstructured, ambiguous situation full of strangers heightens anxiety and stimulates regression. This intensifies transference reactions, but the resulting level of anxiety tends to "obstruct one's ability to cope with stress" (Yalom, 1995, p. 290). Growing awareness of prospective group members' anxieties and their need for adequate preparation has resulted in fewer dropouts and group casualties.

Also important in preparatory interviews is the necessity of involving members in maintaining shared responsibility for examining the processes of the group. A key element in joining a psychotherapy group is assuming responsibility for expressing thoughts and feelings about the here-and-now process. Having clarified this expectation at the outset, you would have felt more able to stop action and engage the group in describing and understanding what was taking place.

It would be important to note during which phase of the group's development the blaming and finger pointing began. Bernard (1994) cautions that how one handles a dilemma is dependent on the group's level of development. I would suggest your group was struggling with the competitive issues that emerge during what has been variously labeled the "storming," "differentiation," or "conflict, dominance, rebellion" phase.

Members highlighted the "bad" aspects of each other in an attempt to demonstrate superiority, attain a higher place in the pecking order, and win high regard. This suspicion is further substantiated by their accusation that you protected Bill from sexist accusations because you were attracted to him, a clear indication of envious, competitive feelings regarding your investment in them. What may also have stimulated these sexist and sexual concerns was the issue of your pregnancy, a discussion of which is not mentioned. The fact of your pregnancy and subsequent leave of absence potentially heightened feelings of competition and concern about your investment in group members.

What was needed (difficult for any neophyte group therapist) was benign tolerance of the group's anger and projection, realization that it was not personal, and exploration of their differing viewpoints and conflicts—

to affirm that it is alright and necessary to disagree. Also, you needed to engage the group in examining the processes you were witnessing. For example, you might have said, "It seems to me we've been locked into a pattern of looking at each other's faults in an angry and unhelpful way. I wonder if we can try together to understand this pattern so that we might be more helpful to each other as a group." Bernard (1994) suggests that whereas overt conflict can lead to a good deal of interpersonal learning, some conflicts can be threatening to the group's continued existence, sometimes leading to hopelessness and despair. A difference exists between needing to express anger hurtfully and the goal of having all parties learn from it.

Consequently, in regard to the group's concern vis-à-vis Bill, you might have said, "It sounds as if people feel I'm more protective of Bill. I wonder what I'm doing or not doing to promote this feeling." This conveys an acceptance of negative affect directed toward you and reduces the need to have anger displaced onto other group members.

With the group's emotionally stimulating interactions, "in an effort to wall off turbulent experience," members often "project the disturbance outward, where it is attacked or otherwise controlled," promoting "crises of miscommunication, misunderstanding, and confusion; stimulating the very anarchy they fearfully and unsuccessfully defend against" (Billow, 2003b, p. 340). A pattern of spiraling anxiety resulted which, in your reluctance to address it, only became more frightening. The group experienced as increasingly dangerous those issues to which you yourself could not give voice. The challenge with a rebellious patient or group is to maintain empathic attunement and find a way to "explore the interpersonal dynamic while maintaining a positive therapeutic alliance" (Bernard, 1994, p. 133).

As you acknowledge, practicing effective group psychotherapy requires specialized knowledge, perspective, and self-awareness not available solely through training in individual work. Unfortunately, many clinicians are unaware that adequate preparation for dealing with such a complex group requires didactic instruction, ongoing group supervision or consultation, and, ideally, a group experience. These elements are necessary for successful development as a qualified group psychotherapist.

Hylene S. Dublin, MSW, LCSW, CGP, FAGPA

References

Bernard, H. S. (1994). Difficult patients and challenging situations. In H.S. Bernard & K. R. MacKenzie (Eds.), *Basics of group psychotherapy* (pp. 123–156). New York: Guilford Press.

Billow, R. M. (2003a). Bonding in group: The therapist's contribution. *International Journal of Group Psychotherapy, 53,* 83–110.

Billow, R. M. (2003b). Rebellion in group. *International Journal of Group Psychotherapy, 53,* 331–351.

Dies, R. R. (1994). The therapist's role in group treatments. In H. S. Bernard & K. R. MacKenzie (Eds.), *Basics of group psychotherapy* (pp. 60–99). New York: Guilford Press.

MacKenzie, K. R. (1994). The developing structure of the therapy group system. In H. S. Bernard & K. R. MacKenzie (Eds.), *Basics of group psychotherapy* (pp. 35–59). New York: Guilford Press.

Rosenthall, L. (1993). Resistance and working through in group psychotherapy. In H. I. Kaplan & B. J. Sadock (Eds.), *Comprehensive group psychotherapy* (3rd ed., pp. 105–115). Baltimore: Williams & Wilkins.

Yalom, I. D. (1995). *The theory and practice of group psychotherapy* (4th ed.). New York: Basic Books.

Ziskind, E., & Zasa, M. (2003). The therapist's wish to be liked. *The Group Circle, August/September, 2003,* 1 & 8.

Dear Therapist:

I am not surprised that with only minimal training in group psychotherapy, you felt "in over your head" doing group treatment. Regardless of the level of functioning of the members, leading a psychotherapy group involves understanding not only individual psychopathology but also group dynamics. Numerous theorists have observed the potential for groups to influence individual behavior (see Rutan & Stone, 2001). LeBon (1895/1920) and McDougall (1920) noted the potential for groups to promote regression and, at times, destructive and mob-like behavior. However, McDougall also recognized the possibility that groups could positively affect behavior when they were organized and had clearly defined goals.

It is this power that groups have to influence individual behavior that makes group therapy such an effective and unique therapeutic modality. All therapy and, as noted, especially group therapy, promotes regression. In setting up a therapy group, the leader creates an artificial environment that seduces the members to reveal themselves in new ways. This regression and exposure allows for change and growth, but also leaves the members open to humiliation and shame. It is the therapist's obligation to protect each member from harm and excessive exposure as much as possible. Without training, it is extremely difficult for the group therapist to provide the organization, structure, and interventions that will channel the regressive group energy in a direction that promotes curiosity and learning. This is even more difficult for a leader of a group of individuals with Axis II personality disorders in the "dramatic–erratic" cluster who generally have a poorly integrated defense structure, tend to act easily on strong and regressive affects, and often are highly suggestible.

I will respond to your request for help in formulating what occurred in your group using an object relations perspective. From this perspective, "the group task is to make conscious the inner object relations of the members both as they are played out in the members' relationships with each other and with the therapist and as they are reflected in the problems that brought the members into the group" (Rice, 1992, p. 38). Using the lens of object relations theory, I believe that groups need structure, cohesion, and norms in order to create an atmosphere of predictability and safety in which group members can regress and reenact in the group the most troubled relationships from the past that have been internalized and have become the basis for their current experience of others. It is the leader's role to create this "holding environment" (Winnicott, 1989) for the group.

The leader provides the structure through the development of guidelines that define the parameters of the group. Group cohesion is the positive valence the group has for the members. The leader promotes the development of group cohesion by referring frequently to the group in positive terms as an existing entity. The leader also helps the group develop productive norms by modeling the desired behavior and by his or her reactions to behavior that challenges the group guidelines. For example, the leader promotes a stance of curiosity, rather than blame, about an unexplained absence by the questions he or she asks and the way he or she encourages the group to explore the absence.

Using these theoretical constructs to examine the repetitive dynamic in your group, I see a group stuck in a pattern of scapegoating. As group members regress, they split the internalized good and bad objects in themselves and project the unacceptable parts on the group, the leader, and each other. The aggression that inevitably is stirred up in group has been acted on in the form of blaming others rather than being examined. Often, members will engage in projective identification, with one member accepting the projection of another member and reflecting back the behavior or feeling or attitude expected by the other member.

At times, the leader will also participate in the group's projective identification by responding to a projection from a group member or members and feeling pulled to behave in uncharacteristic ways. You may have felt immobilized in the group because you had been pulled into the projective identification of the group and have accepted the projection of their feelings of ineffectiveness on you. Your sense of incompetence and difficulty in containing the aggression has led the group to feel unsafe and out of control. Some members have left to protect themselves from this confusion and loss of safety. The members have, most likely, replicated their early object relations without having an opportunity to explore and understand what has happened and what could be different.

My first reaction to your vignette is to wonder what guidelines were established for the group. I consider guidelines to be the backbone of the group. They define the frame within which the group functions. As stated earlier, without clear guidelines, group members feel at sea and their regressive energy can become destructive. During the pre-group interview, I review with each prospective group member a set of guidelines that I ask him or her to agree to follow. The guidelines include agreements to come each week, come on time, stay the whole session, put feelings into words not actions, pay the bill on time, keep the relationships therapeutic not social, and keep the identities of the members confidential. The guideline that seems most relevant for your dilemma is the expectation that members will put their feelings into words not actions. In accusing and criticizing others, the group members have projected the negative parts of themselves on others and acted on their aggression rather than putting their hostile feelings into words that could be examined and understood.

The second thing I react to in your dilemma is the apparent lack of development of group norms of curiosity and exploration. I try from the outset to encourage the development of group norms that foster curiosity about everything that happens in group. I do this even in the pre-group interview by stating that all behavior in group has meaning and one of our goals will be to understand the feelings behind the behavior we observe in group. I give examples such as, "If you are angry with me, do not put it into action by staying away but come to group and talk about it." In the case of your group, I would have responded to the group's devaluing reactions to my interpretations with curiosity. I would have pointed out the pattern of repetitive rejection and criticism of my ideas and then invited the group to wonder with me what unspoken feelings were behind the behavior.

Third, I notice in your vignette that nothing is mentioned of negative transference to you, the leader. According to object relations theorists, one of the major functions of the leader is to contain the aggression and splitting that the group will be drawn to as it regresses (Rice, 1992). I would expect a group whose members tend toward Axis II personality disorders to regress into splitting and negative projections earlier and more intensely than other groups. Although over the course of the group the leader and members will serve as transference objects, early on in the group, before a sense of safety is established, I try to protect the weaker members of the group by pulling all negative feelings to myself. Additionally, I assume that scapegoating represents displaced anger from negatively introjected objects. In order to prevent one member from receiving all the negative projections, I pull the critical and devaluing feelings toward myself.

In your group I would do this by observing that each week the group singles out one member to accuse of being mean-spirited, selfish, or insensitive, when, in fact, it is more likely that they might feel that about me. After all, I left them to go on maternity leave in order to satisfy my own needs. I would look for frequent opportunities in the derivative material to bring the anger and disappointment back to me. The societal inhibition of expressing anger toward a pregnant woman makes it very difficult for groups to express directly their negative transference toward the pregnant therapist. I suspect that a pregnant therapist may stir up intense feelings of competition and envy in these group members who need so much attention and for whom feelings of abandonment are prevalent.

The fourth aspect of your dilemma that is worthy of note is the persistence of your feelings of incompetence. If I were feeling as you did, I would have discussed my feelings of incompetence with a supervisor or colleague. It is hoped that they would have helped me to recognize the projective identification and regain access to my usual therapeutic skills. I then would have used another technique I find helpful in managing scapegoating: I would have asked the group to stop the action and to sit back and think about what they were feeling at the moment. I would have invited them to wonder why they were having such a strong reaction to this particular person. In spite of the difficulty individuals with Axis II personality disorders may have, by stepping back and reflecting on the connections between their conscious and unconscious feelings and behavior, I have found that when I am clear and persistent in my interventions they are able to become more introspective and develop some insight about their behavior.

Kathleen Hubbs Ulman, PhD

References

LeBon, G. (1920). *The crowd: A study of the popular mind.* New York: Fisher, Unwin. (Original work published 1895).

McDougall, W. (1920). *The group mind.* New York: Putnam.

Rice, C. A. (1992). Contributions from object relations theory. In R. H. Klein, H. S. Bernard, & D. L. Singer (Eds.), *Handbook of contemporary group psychotherapy: Contributions from object relations, self psychology, and social systems theories.* Madison, CT: International Universities Press.

Rutan, J. S., & Stone, W. N. (2001). *Psychodynamic group psychotherapy* (3rd ed.). New York: Guilford Press.

Winnicott, D. W. (1989). *Playing and reality.* New York: Routledge.

Will the Real Expert Please Stand Up?

Dear Consultant:

So, am I the expert or not? I've become increasingly confused about my leadership position in one of my therapy groups. Although I endorse the idea that the agent of change in group therapy is the group and the group process, I'm in a situation in which the group members all turn to me for the "answer." To my embarrassment, I often feel compelled to give it to them, even, at times, when I'm not completely confident in what I am saying. What troubles me is that I have not been able to reconstruct exactly how I got here. More to the point, I can describe the process but don't really understand this. Can you be my expert?

This group of seven men and women, ages 19 to 35, is for young people who have had difficulty succeeding, whether in completing college, sustaining a job, or maintaining a romantic relationship or intimate friendship. I am 58 years old, with some gray hair, but a youthful attitude. The group has been developing for about 1 year now, with a fairly stable membership until recently. Five of the group members, interestingly, come from families in which the father was abusive or absent, and many of these and the two others also share a history of overly protective mothers. To a person, these group members have fallen behind their age mates in terms of achieving developmentally appropriate milestones. It may not be clear yet, but I feel very warmly toward this group, and have even been called "Mr. Rogers," out of which I get a kick.

Generally, my leadership style is to allow lots of room for group members to comment on and react to one another, although I occasionally make bridging comments, anxiety-reduction comments, or empathic comments of the "it's no wonder, given your history, that you feel this way." For the first month or two, when I stayed more in the background, the group often seemed sluggish and stale, with little energy. Worse still, several members, one in particular, were handing out advice like candy, and much of it was common sense advice that had already been tried or was obviously more than could be done by the recipient of the advice. I had the experience of the blind leading the blind, which was hard to sit still for. So, I didn't.

Here and there, I made an occasional comment that was infused with advice of my own, coming from my more experienced position. I found myself, to my surprise, being impatient with the idea that group members would profit from learning to tolerate the anxiety and pain of failure, and was trying to help them succeed. One evening, near Father's Day, in trying to help several group members reconnect with their fathers, I disclosed that my two sons had gone through periods of estrangement from me, but with persistence, we were able to move beyond this to a more intimate place.

Then, in three consecutive groups, I noticed that whenever a member raised a thorny issue, other group members became very passive, and often gazed at me. This felt like a plea for help, and I answered it. Even I, however, could see, in subsequent weeks, that my advice and support were not being heeded, nor were members reporting improved self-esteem. In fact, absences have begun to increase, even while members have been commenting about how knowledgeable and caring I am. Somehow, my assuming the role of the expert—which I like to believe I am—is backfiring. Can you help me with this?

Dear Therapist:
My hat's off to you for noticing the signals that suggest a consultation might be appropriate. Your confusion is an important signal: It is different from other groups that you lead, and it is out of character for you to be impatient with the group's learning to tolerate pain and anxiety. This tells me that the process of projective identification might be at play.

The projective identification process may be seen here in your pressured reactions to group members' projections of intolerable affect. Your reactions may be experienced by you as intense, unexpected, and sudden, with little clarity about their origins. Your responses (enactments) to these projections are at odds with your view of what promotes change. You feel compelled to provide answers, are embarrassed and angry, and have the sense of being lost ("I had the experience of the blind leading the blind.").

Although your feelings and actions seem unfamiliar to you, you *cannot* eliminate the impact of your subjectivity in the interaction (Maroda, 1999; Orange, Atwood, & Stolorow, 1997). As noted earlier, projective identification and enactment are conceptualized as discrete events, suggesting that moments of interaction occur when they are not present (Aron, 1996). I believe that members and group leader "mutually construct their relationship" (Aron, 1996, p. 213) and "interactiveness is emergent, in a constant process of potential reorganization" (Beebe & Lachmann, 2002, p. 224). Because I practice psychoanalytic group psychotherapy from a relational perspective, I view therapeutic dialogue as constructed by the therapist and the members, and each are affected by it "moment to moment" (Beebe & Lachmann, 2002, p. 207). I primarily track affect rather than associations (as in more traditional psychoanalysis), and explain behavior as an attempt at self- and mutual regulation. I am also influenced by intersubjective theory, which views affect as an organizing factor that provides meaning to one's experience (Stolorow, Atwood, & Orange, 2002).

It is not uncommon to begin a group with a theme or task in mind. I would certainly want to know what your expectations were (e.g., an opportunity to be more of an expert?) and how you prepared the members. Beginning groups generally require that you be more active rather than staying in the background. When these members who have "difficulty succeeding" have difficulty carrying the group on their shoulders, you become frustrated. The members are accustomed to feelings of failure in their lives —dare they hope for more? You act to relieve your frustration rather than using it as a signal to explore the group's affect and your own. Instead, you communicate that painful affect need not be addressed, just as an overly protective mother might try to help her children by protecting them from intolerable feelings.

You are in a position to observe your self- and interactive regulation, make inferences about the members' self- and interactive regulation, and compare the two (Beebe & Lachmann, 2002). Were you the only one experiencing the group as "sluggish and stale?" I would look for verbal and nonverbal expression of this experience in the others. I might ask, "Was I the only one experiencing the group as dull or flat or did you too?"

I would directly challenge any advice-giver to explore what he or she was feeling prior to giving advice. I would use my own feelings as a guide. Was I feeling frustrated, fearful, helpless, or the like? Was he or she? I would be modeling the therapeutic process of learning to recognize, label, tolerate, and express feelings. I would challenge the member receiving advice to speak of its effect. This may open the door for group members to speak of their frustrations, fears, and desires with respect to being rescued. Giving better advice serves to limit rather than to expose affect.

I would wonder what is making you want to stay in the background. I would wonder aloud whether the group is proceeding the way the members anticipated. Were they satisfied? Did they feel helpful to one another? Do these feelings seem familiar? I would wonder aloud if the experiences they brought into group from their daily lives were being re-experienced in the group. If not, why not? I would be attempting to send the message that we can talk about difficult interactions between us. I cannot do this as an absent father.

It seems important for you to be viewed as being the expert, "knowledgeable and caring," like Mr. Rogers. The group seems to be feeding you what you covet (Gabbard, 1995; Shay, 2001) and at the same time increasing their sense of incompetence (Maroda, 1999). This may feel preferable to you than to have the group frustrated, angry, disappointed, or envious. I wonder if you wish to be admired rather than struggle with unresolved narcissism, or wish to be liked, which is "taking precedence over being effective" (Ziskind & Zasa, 2003).

Your gratification is a signal of affect not being expressed by the members (Maroda, 1999). The group needs you to recognize, tolerate, and respond to intense affect with empathy and authenticity (Preston & Shumsky, 2002). You have a wonderful opportunity to explore the members' longings and frustration within the group, and provide hope that it might be otherwise. Your expertise lies in the art of "creating stepping stones" (Gehrie, 2002, p. 20) that will bridge the gap. Interaction with the group has a greater role in change than insight and interpretation (Aron, 1996).

The Father's Day session is another example signaling intense affect and an opportunity for interaction. The members' reaction of becoming very passive and gazing indicates a retreat from strong feelings. Calling the group's attention to these nonverbal communications and inquiring about their meaning would promote a deeper level of understanding. The members might be feeling estranged from you as well as their fathers. As leader, I would suggest to the members that they might be protecting me from their feelings. Then I would ask what I am doing or not doing that might be contributing.

Should you wish to disclose your estrangement from your sons, then you need to be prepared to share your emotional experience in a way that the members can understand (Maroda, 1999). Intentional self-disclosure needs to provide safety for the members (Orange, Atwood, & Stolorow, 1997). By reporting the facts without feelings, your communication indicates that the group is not safe for affect. Subsequent member absences indicate their growing discomfort in the group.

The group members need to know that they are influencing one another and you, and that they are not powerless. This message could be communicated by the following: "Sharing about your estrangement touches me deeply. Does it you?" Or, "My sons are very important to me, and it was painful during that time. I was hurt and angry and it was hard to find a way to constructively share those feelings." If you wish the group to be persistent you must be prepared to share more of yourself.

Group process interventions might suggest that the members are reluctant to challenge your leadership and betray a desire to replace you with one of their own. An absent or abusive father would be a formidable opponent. Projecting unwanted aggressive and assertive feelings on you and reacting as passive and dependent has been their solution. You could interpret the wish and the fear inherent in the transference. You could then explore your countertransference, which, in group process dynamics, is considered independent of the group rather than co-constructed as it is viewed in relational theory.

Then again, I am no expert.

Allan H. Gelber PhD, CGP

References

Aron, L. (1996). *A meeting of minds: Mutuality in psychoanalysis.* Hillsdale, NJ: Analytic Press.

Beebe, B., & Lachmann, F. (2002). *Infant research and adult treatment: Co-constructing interactions.* Hillsdale, NJ: Analytic Press.

Gabbard, G. (1995). Countertransference: The emerging common ground. *International Journal of Psycho-analysis, 76,* 475–485.

Gehrie, M. (2002). Heinz Kohut memorial lecture. In A. Goldberg (Ed.), *Progress in self psychology* (vol. 18, pp. 15–30). Hillsdale, NJ: Analytic Press.

Maroda, K. (1999). *Seduction, surrender, and transformation: Emotional engagement in the analytic process.* Hillsdale, NJ: Analytic Press.

Orange, D., Atwood, G., & Stolorow, R. (1997). *Working intersubjectively: Contextualism in psychoanalytic practice.* Hillsdale, NJ: Analytic Press.

Shay, J. (2001). My problem with projective identification. *Northeastern Society for Group Psychotherapy Newsletter, 23,* 1–2.

Shay, J. (2002, June). *Projective identification goes to the movies.* Presented at the Northeastern Society for Group Psychotherapy. Wellesley, MA.

Stolorow, R., Atwood, G.E., & Orange, D.M. (2002). *Worlds of experience.* New York: Basic Books.

Ziskind, E., & Zasa, M. (2003). The therapist's wish to be liked. *The Group Circle, August/September, 2003,* 1 & 8.

Dear Therapist:

Your dilemma entices me to respond, yet I fear that in agreeing to be your "expert" I may run the risk of setting a poor example by taking on that which I would have you avoid. The real expert is not the therapist, but the patient. The therapist's job is to help patients realize the extent to which they are their own experts and to understand, as well, their resistance to seeing themselves in this way. In this written format, I cannot gradually lead you through an ongoing process to capitalize on what you know, as I would urge you to do with your patients. I am stuck, instead, with a one-shot commentary from the lens of a psychodynamically oriented therapist. That said, here is what I see.

You note that group members turn to you for the answer. Perhaps the problem here is less that they see you as an expert (I assume that in many ways you are), but confusion exists on their parts (and yours) about what kind of an expert. You are an expert in understanding process and in using the many techniques that you have learned through experience and training to help the group inform you, as well as group members, about what is going on. You are not an "expert on life," nor "the master of advice." Although you have had lots of life experience, so have the members of your group and, myths to the contrary (and gray hair not withstanding), age and wisdom are not necessarily correlated.

A group composed of individuals seen as homogeneous for difficulties succeeding in life might be especially eager to induce an expert to try to fix them—especially a group in which several members have histories of overdependence on nurturing mother figures. Through the induction, the group members simultaneously achieve the short-term gratification of receiving nurturing leader behavior, while creating resonating failure experiences in their group leader who is not effectively doing his or her job. That's a mouthful. So let me elaborate.

You mention group members' shared histories of overly protective mothers and the "Mr. Rogers" label out of which you get a kick. This, together with your description of the kinds of interventions that you make in the group (bridging, anxiety reducing interventions, and empathic comments), suggest that you may be enjoying the nurturing (albeit overprotective) mother role into which you have been induced. The comments you make sound like a combination of sweet pabulum and mother's milk to a group who waits dependently to be fed. Tiring of the sluggish, stale state that emerges while they wait, you feed. We might understand this as a countertransference reaction resulting from your response to their maternal transference. In keeping with this, it is not surprising that you found yourself "impatient with the idea that group members would profit from learning to tolerate the anxiety and pain of failure," leading you to "feed" rather than to push group members to see what they were doing.

Another kind of countertransference—projective identification—also seems to be operating. When the group got stalemated at the beginning, with members' passive-dependence and lack of energy, it seems likely that you were being induced to walk in group members' shoes—leaving you to feel, like them, unable to succeed. Perhaps you were similarly induced to be intolerant of delayed gratification and in search of success-too-soon (a strategy of many failure-prone individuals that tends to backfire—leading to further failure). Did this well-worn failure strategy induce your unfortunate Father's Day disclosure? This particular I-am-the-expert move seems, not surprisingly, to have created further helpless dependence on the leader (and also possible anger about your making yourself look good at the group members' expense).

What might have seemed to you as healthy role-modeling to instill hope might have felt to this group of "failures" as one more in a lifetime of comparisons that underscored that others could do what they could not. With increasing commentary about your own skills and talents came members' decreasing involvement in the group, more limited attendance, and decreasing self-esteem. It is as if the group was saying, "If you are so great— obviously we aren't—then *you* can do the work!"

It seems likely that fear of failure (induced early on) led you to defend by assuming an inflated, grandiose position that would temporarily protect you, but in the long run pushed you further into the kinds of feelings that you were trying to short-circuit. As such, your somewhat self congratulatory self-disclosure, as well as other aspects of the active "expert" role you assumed, may have been an attempt to buoy yourself up in the face of your own feelings of failure—feelings that were being projected on you and which you desperately needed to shake off. Not surprisingly, the shaking-off procedure itself, backfiring as it did, further mired you in the projective identification loop, no doubt leading you to feel even less successful.

Let's turn now to some possible interventions to extricate the leader from the projective identification impasses that emerged. As soon as you began to feel that things were not going well, you needed to promptly respond. The first line of response would have been to actively work at understanding what you were feeling and what was being induced. Often this understanding is sufficient to extricate the leader from the projective identification impasse. However, some group leaders, in addition, might be inclined to make a projective identification interpretation to the group (Vannicelli, 1992, p. 225), saying something like, "I have a hunch the group has needed me to understand how painful it feels to have difficulty succeeding and to experience something that I am invested in not going so well —feelings that are plentiful among members of this group."

Short-circuiting might have occurred even earlier had you intervened actively at the first indication of being put in an expert, advice-giving role or when first noticing the group members' tremendous dependency on you. You might have said, "Although I am interested in your questions and might even enjoy answering them, I worry that in so doing I would reinforce the view that I am the one with all the answers—a view which I think does a disservice to the group and underestimates the experience in this room." You might have responded to their questions with further questions of your own such as, "Why do you assume that in a group of eight bright individuals that I am the one most able to answer your question?" or "I wonder what function it might serve for the group to keep me in the expert role, and how the group might rob itself by doing so?"

As the years pass, I find, as my interventions suggest, that I am more direct in offering certain kinds of expertise—in particular, framing questions that will help highlight aspects of the process for the group to think about. I may also provide hypotheses (hunches) about things that may be going on in the room, framed in a way that will hopefully stimulate other hypotheses, as well—with the message that I am one smart observer among many and that I am offering one possible take, but believe that there may be other hypotheses that are equally good. So it is with my comments to you—which hopefully will stimulate other ideas as well.

Marsha Vannicelli, PhD

Reference

Vannicelli, M. (1992). *Removing the roadblocks: Group psychotherapy with substance abusers and family members.* New York: Guilford Press.

Serial Scapegoating

Dear Consultant:

Three years ago I took over a co-ed group from a resident who went on maternity leave. I had no group experience prior to taking over the group, but was excited by the opportunity and got supervision from a senior group therapist. Initially, there were three men and one woman in the group, all of whom had a history of chronic depression and either a narcissistic or dependent personality disorder. They were in their 50s and 60s, and had been chronically unemployed or on disability for many years.

I spent a fair amount of time advertising my group and eventually added two other members, Penelope, a bipolar woman with borderline personality, and Steve, a schizoidal man who experienced depression. All went well until an original member, Janet, left after she was hospitalized for acute suicidality. I invited her to return to the group, but she chose not to. At about the same time, my supervisor got sick and took a leave of absence, so I have been without supervision. I hope you can help me.

For many months the group has been stuck, doing little deep work, and talking superficially about mundane aspects of their lives. I decided to add another woman to the group, hoping that might change the dynamic, but I have been unsuccessful in getting someone to stick. The first woman fled after one group. She talked incessantly throughout that group, and although I tried to interrupt her to interpret what might be going on, I couldn't stop her. After she left, the group talked about her for 3 weeks, certain that I had planted her to "stir things up in the group." The second woman I added lasted for 6 weeks and then left, complaining the group wasn't working for her. She had revealed a trauma history, and although the group listened respectfully, they never again referred to the information she revealed.

The third woman I added, Christina, quickly but subtly got scapegoated and left after about 3 months. When Christina started the group, Penelope said that she didn't feel safe with a new person in the group and proceeded not to talk for 6 weeks. Tony, a narcissistic ex-lawyer now on disability, would offer lengthy, dull monologues about his failed job search. Jesse, whose cat got leukemia during this period, took up where Tony left off and told the gruesome details of hand feeding and giving needles to his cat. Steve listened to all this with his arms crossed and his eyes closed but never said a word. Whenever Christina, the new member, started to talk about her problems the group ignored her and returned to Tony's job search. I tried to intervene by making comments about how difficult it was to share the time, and how little time each felt they were getting now that the group had gotten larger. In frustration, Christina quit and I have now added yet another woman to the group. I am afraid she, too, will be scapegoated and leave.

I'm not sure what is going on although I suspect it has to do with Janet's suicide attempt and my supervisor leaving at the same time. I also wonder about sibling rivalry. Penelope has four brothers and no sisters. Is she keeping women out of the group? How do I address their resistance? How do I talk about the scapegoating without pointing fingers? I'm feeling angry about their passive-aggressive stance toward these women and am feeling exhausted by my search for new members for the group. Can you help?

Dear Therapist:
Group is difficult enough to conduct with considerable experience, and taking on another's group can be that much more difficult. The leader–parent had abandoned this group to care for her baby, producing reverberations on many levels of group experience. The group immediately had a three-fold task, namely (a) to mourn the loss of the therapist who had cared for their inner babies, (b) to express their anger and hurt at the rejection, and only then, feeling safe enough, (c) to express their doubts about your sufficiency and ability to take care of them. When a new therapist enters, lack of safety is paramount. You do not mention these issues, so I assume they were not addressed.

The group, when you enter, therefore, is developmentally stuck, and cannot proceed with its work until the feelings mentioned above are given room to breathe. Parental abandonment, followed by acquisition of an unwanted step-parent inexperienced in group child-rearing, threatens the integrity of the group and produces anxiety and loss of safety.

Individual diagnoses of members show chronic depressions, most are in midlife, unemployed, on disability, and living out marginal life adaptations. Therefore, poor self-esteem, lack of confidence, and feelings of unworthiness pervade the membership. Such feelings would, under stress of abandonment, probably lead to a group fantasy that the rejection was somehow their fault. This needs to be interpreted, understood, articulated, and worked through.

Your attempt to combat the problem was to focus on group size as a root cause of the aimless, deadening, and desultory behaviors evidenced in the group. Your approach was to breathe new life into the group by bringing in new members, new life forms, and the very thing that caused their abandonment. They will have none of it. New members are a disruption, introducing the task of integrating them into, while changing, the ongoing group structure. This group cannot assimilate the new into the old when the group is feeling so fractured and discarded.

Let's examine various events and defensive maneuvers employed by the group to stabilize and protect itself from further damage. The first major event concerned Janet's becoming suicidal, being hospitalized, and refusing to return to group. From a group-as-a-whole perspective, Janet probably expressed for the group the self-destructive feelings experienced in response to the insult and loss that occurred. From this perspective, group members blamed themselves for the loss of the resident therapist. Were they undeserving of her continuing care and attention? Did they kill her off somehow? Even though she was having a child, would she not have taken limited leave and returned if she really cared? Such thoughts remained unexpressed. Suicidal ideation among the chronically depressed is common, and perhaps Janet took on the martyr's role for the group in her enactment. She certainly followed the leader, expelling herself, and refusing to rejoin the group. Perhaps she also had a fantasy of joining the lost leader–mother. Strangely, life delivered a parallel loss and abandonment scenario for you when your supervisor abandoned you. Perhaps the group read your feelings unconsciously, further increasing feelings of lack of safety. It would be interesting to know within the intersubjective field what you were feeling about your supervisor's abandonment and how you were handling it in group.

As for new members: a new member is described as talking incessantly with you unable to stop her while the group let her talk. After she left, they interpret—correctly, I think—that she was brought in "to stir things up." Given her entrance, a better approach would have been to mobilize the group to attend to how her verbosity was aiding the group, what function she was performing for them. Getting the group to do the work rather than assuming responsibility for the task is often a more effective approach, mobilizing the group's resources rather than one's own.

The next series of events illustrates further the group's attempt to deal with their dilemma. Christina's entry brings the scapegoating defense into focus as an attempt to handle the group dilemma. Christina is shown immediately by group members that she is an unwanted addition, symbolizing their own feelings of being unwanted children. This is a good example of projective identification in a group setting. By ignoring Christina, and making her feel irrelevant and unwanted, the group projects their feelings into her. Tony's description of dealing with his sick cat may provide "gruesome details," but he is also portraying what this group really needs and wants, some hand-feeding and special care to keep it alive. Tony's failed job search can be viewed through the same lens as the group's holding up to the therapist the failed search of the therapist to solve their problem.

You raise a number of questions about the nature of the resistances you were facing, and how best to have addressed them without blaming group members. We have discussed a number of these technical issues previously, but your question indirectly raises issues of theoretical orientation—namely, how orientation determines how one intervenes in group. My theoretical bent certainly includes group-as-a-whole conceptualization. I see group as a surviving unit generating both striving and resistant forces, focused on both growth and stability, and these forces gain expression symbolically through individual behaviors, interactions, fantasies, and memories, the many areas of psychic life one focuses on in individual work. Although I attend to individual issues in group, I also try to be aware of the group level of experience. In the final analysis, my concern is that group members have a full emotional life experience with each other, and not only discover transferences and past life events producing their responses. This particular consultation, however, focused me more on group-as-a-whole aspects of events. Also individual diagnosis is not as important to me as the group interaction, where patients can learn to express their concerns with vitality and spontaneity toward each other.

Thus, the approach I have taken here is grounded in both object relations theory and systems work, employing the concepts of projective identification and the group unconscious to understand how this group was coping with its traumatic event. Scapegoating, as seen in the group response to Christina, is the expression, par excellence, of the projective identification concept, where group members select someone to be the container of unwanted feelings, blaming and attacking that person to locate and expel the bad, unwanted, and repressed parts of themselves that, if made conscious, would greatly increase their anxiety.

Although well-meaning, your attempt to find new members could be viewed as a subtle unconscious counter-projective identification into the group. Viewing them as insufficient (in number) could reinforce their feelings of insufficiency as discussed earlier, thus projecting your own understandable feelings of insufficiency about running the group more effectively. This could also be seen as an example of the intersubjective nature of the group field, how projective identification can function within group members, from group members to the therapist, or from the leader to either individual members or to the group-as-a-whole.

Finally, it's important to remember that in running groups, no matter how much we think we know, we are all vulnerable and limited by what we accomplish and miss. We keep trying and growing, building an accretion of experience, and getting help from colleagues when we need it.

David A. Altfeld, PhD, CGP, FAGPA

Dear Therapist:

As a psychoanalyst, I primarily use object relations and group-as-a-whole theories to understand individual and group dynamics. Object relations theory helps me understand the internal workings of each individual while enhancing my understanding of relational patterns. Group-as-a-whole concepts (Horwitz, 1986), including basic assumptions (Rioch, 1970), often help me to discover what unconscious group dynamics might be playing a role and have gotten me out of many a difficult spot like your complex dilemma.

Your group is defending itself against the pain and terror of loss in a fascinating fabric of its group composition and history. The abandonments are many: the loss of the original therapist who went on maternity leave, the frightening and abrupt departure of Janet in the midst of a suicidal crisis, the unplanned indirect loss of the supervisor because of illness, the woman who fled with no warning after one meeting and, to some extent, the second woman and Christina, although by this time the group was playing a role in the action. Fear of abandonment may lead to unwillingness to invest in new members, but there may be other, more complex, ways to conceptualize your dilemma as well.

Three ways of understanding this situation come to mind. All of these events have happened to a group of people who are "chronically unemployed or on disability for many years." Thus, the original group could be viewed as a homogeneous group of persons for whom the ticket of admission— that is, what brings them together and increases cohesion (unemployment or disability status), is the biggest and most difficult resistance to overcome. If they grow beyond the unemployed state they run the risk of having to leave the group, thereby losing what little they have: membership in this community of people hurting in the same way, a source of emotional support, or some protection against suicide. Christina may represent the danger and risk associated with changing the status quo. Thus, the members defend against their fears of abandonment and the potential loss of the group by rejecting new members. The rejections occur by ignoring the new member and through scapegoating and enactment.

I understand scapegoating to be a defense of the whole group in which members project parts of themselves into the most vulnerable member, identify and stay connected with that member (i.e., the projected part of themselves), and attack her or him, unconsciously hoping to eliminate their internal conflicts (Horwitz, 1983). The scapegoat is chosen because he or she is vulnerable in some way, but also has a need to externalize the conflict so participates in the interaction. When Christina joined the group, she may have represented the part of each of them that wants to grow and change, but each may fear the loss of being cared for if they make too much progress. When Penelope said the group felt unsafe and thus refused to speak, she acted as spokesperson for the group, passively attacking Christina. Tony, Jesse, and Steve could all be understood to have joined in scapegoating Christina when they neglected her and did not confront Penelope.

Intervention for scapegoating usually is best begun at the level of the group. For instance, when someone like Christina is talking and no one is responding to her, you could stop her and inquire if any of the others have experienced something similar to what she is revealing. Then, if Penelope says that she does not feel safe with a new member in the room, you could ask if others have some of the same experience. Usually when you start at the level of the group, the scapegoated individual is able to be quiet as the exploration goes on: group members either discover for themselves what they are doing or you can interpret it. If the scapegoat will not allow the group to work, then it is necessary to ask that person to listen for a while.

Another explanation is that the group is displacing their anger and pain at being rejected and abandoned by the original therapist and Janet to new members and rejecting them. We call this an enactment. Acceptance of new women seems more problematic than that of new men, which lends some credence to this hypothesis. Penelope may be the most suitable candidate to be spokesperson because sibling rivalry plays an active role in her history. Thus, she may be more responsive to situations that awaken conflicts related to it.

A third possible explanation is that the group feels threatened and angry with you for failing to protect them against the frightening loss of Janet. They defend themselves against fears of annihilation through fight–flight basic assumption behavior (Bion, 1961). They may be fighting against you and anything representing you (e.g., meaningful work or new members) because their unconscious experience is that you cannot be trusted to keep them or the group alive because you were unable to prevent Janet from attempting suicide and leaving the group. Furthermore, abandoned by your supervisor, you may have felt deskilled, resonating in the countertransference with their experience.

What should you do in this difficult situation? First of all, before adding anyone else I would invite the group to thoroughly explore their feelings about all of the losses. What was it like to lose a therapist because she was pregnant? It is pretty hard to be angry at someone who is having a baby. What did it mean to lose a member because she wanted to kill herself? How do they feel about your repeatedly adding new people? How did they experience the new people? What was it like to hear the second woman's trauma history? Was it too upsetting? (I would also be listening for any indications that the pathologies of the new persons were too "lively" and, therefore, threatening for this group.) How do they feel toward you? What is the state of the transference?

As the exploration goes on, you should be better able to understand which theoretical explanation best fits the situation and then intervene accordingly. Until you get the data from the group, the theoretical explanations I am offering are only speculations. You need to have a concept of why you are stuck and some degree of working it through before adding new members. Even after some working through, adding someone may be difficult because the original members have been together for years.

You do not mention how you prepare prospective new members or the group. I would move slowly and carefully. I would meet with candidates beforehand—a minimum of four sessions—until I have a rudimentary understanding of each individual's difficulties and have established the foundation for building a solid therapeutic alliance. I would tell newcomers that the group will need time to prepare as well. At the point when the group seems ready to hear you, I would say I am meeting with a prospective candidate and, later, announce the person's beginning date (the date should be set so as to have no disruptions before or after it), giving them at least six meetings to process this development. And I would gently inform the new member that the group may take a while to warm up to him or her because they need to adjust to a new person in the room.

Therapist self-disclosure, using an intersubjective model, can be useful in strengthening the therapeutic alliance (Lichtenberg, Lachman, & Fosshage, 1996) with which you are feeling unhappy. Specifically, the group was correct in fantasizing that you were adding a new member to "stir things up" because your experience was that they were stuck, but you were doing it to help, not to sadistically toy with them. At an appropriate moment, such as when they are expressing anger at you, self-disclosure of your subjective experience might be a very useful intervention because they would feel understood and relieved that what they were sensing was correct, but the motives they fantasized about it were not. Then you could invite them to join with you in attempting to understand what is happening. Authenticity builds the therapeutic alliance.

Finally, you imply that you have not had formal group training. If that is true, I suggest that your confidence would grow if you got some. You would then have some protection against the loss of a supervisor. In my experience, which theoretical frame you subscribe to is less important than the fact that you have one. Then, when these difficult times occur, you have a framework to think them through, either alone or with a consultant.

Good luck!

Bonnie Buchele, PhD, CGP, DFAGPA, ABPP

References

Bion, W. R. (1961). *Experiences in groups*. New York: Routledge.

Horwitz, L. (1983). Projective identification in dyads and groups. *International Journal of Group Psychotherapy, 33,* 259–279.

Horwitz, L. (1986). An integrated group centered approach. *Psychotherapist's case book*. San Francisco: Jossey-Bass.

Lichtenberg, J., Lachmann, F., & Fosshage, J. (1996). *The clinical exchange*. Hillsdale, NJ: Analytic Press.

Rioch, M. J. (1970). The work of Wilfred Bion on groups. *Psychiatry, 33,* 56–66.

Section IV
Destructive Forces

Overview

Belonging to a close-knit group can be cozy and gratifying, but even cohesive groups can take a sudden turn. In the disconcerting story *Lord of the Flies*, a group of marooned children bond together for comfort and protection, but are soon challenged by darker group processes that threaten annihilation. Although groups we lead in the consulting room are seldom at risk of literal extinction, damaging and destructive interactions do occur. Such interactions and their attendant affects can gather momentum and quickly move beyond our understanding or control. When destructive forces are at play, the threat of explosion or even annihilation hangs over our groups, sometimes even sparked by our mistakes.

Morris Nitsun, in his chapter, *Destructive Forces in Group Therapy*, explores these "anti-group" forces in persuasive detail, highlighting determinants of these forces and measures to deal with them.

In the first dilemma, *Cuckoo Interrupted*, we see a group composed of very disparate members that is on the doorstep of its demise, with a shaken therapist ready to accept the death. Consultant Yvonne Agazarian analyzes the situation from the systems-centered therapy perspective she developed, focusing on unacknowledged subgrouping of the members and the inadvertent development of confusing communication norms. Walter Stone, utilizing a self psychology model, places the focus not on the patients but on the therapist, and invites the therapist to examine personal anxieties and fears that might have co-constructed the group's difficulties.

Then, in *Does Anyone Want Group?*, we have a clinic—and its patients—resistant to the very idea of groups, protecting clinic therapists against the anxiety of their own inexperience. Undeterred, consultants Nina Fieldsteel and Anthony Joyce both encourage the therapist to use the persuasive power of belief in group therapy as the antidote to these destructive forces. Fieldsteel, from a dynamic and systems point of view, stresses the need to "create a climate of cooperative concern" to alter the dysfunctional system. Joyce, coming from a research perspective, says the robust research findings can speak for themselves if the therapist also attends to understandable anxieties and apprehensions of untrained group therapists.

Finally, in the third dilemma, *A Sinking Depression*, the therapist is held hostage to a member's suicidal depression, and cannot find a way to meet the needs of the other group members. Using Bion's trilogy of passion, consultant Richard Billow highlights techniques to treat such treatment-destructive patients. Jerry Gans, on the other hand, expresses concern that it is not the patient but the therapist who is making the group unsafe, partly because of countertransference blind spots, including angry, perhaps murderous feelings.

Destructive Forces in Group Therapy

MORRIS NITSUN, PHD

This chapter starts from the premise that group psychotherapy is the most complex and possibly the most difficult of all forms of psychotherapy. Destructive processes may be amplified in group therapy in ways that can be very challenging to the group and the therapist. I have given the term "the anti-group" (Nitsun, 1991, 1996) to these phenomena and this paper explores group destructive processes within the framework of this concept. My aim is to legitimize the difficulties that group therapists frequently encounter and to promote a culture of realism and support that strengthens the constructive potentials of this powerful therapeutic medium.

The background

The notion of destructive processes in groups has occupied an ambiguous space in the literature on group psychotherapy. Although problems in the running of groups have certainly been recognized, the full impact of group antagonistic forces and the disruption they could create in the therapeutic undertaking has been minimized and ignored—even denied. Although this could be understood as a consequence of a relatively new psychotherapeutic approach seeking to emphasize its strengths and potentials, the neglect of destructive processes in group psychotherapy is a missed opportunity in several respects: the recognition of group disruptive processes could strengthen group psychotherapy rather than weaken it; the struggle to understand and transform destructive processes occupies a central place in psychotherapy; and the open communication of these difficulties, with a sense of how they might be handled in group, could be empowering to practitioners.

The gradual change in the culture of group psychotherapy toward a more open recognition of these processes was summed up by Schermer in 1994, suggesting that we might now find a consensus that "disorganization, chaos, death, aggression and unknowing are important aspects of groups as of all living systems" (p. 31). In my view, still much exists to be done. Unchecked, destructive processes can create the greatest threat to the survival of the group. It is a responsibility, not a matter of choice, that we engage fully with these processes in our groups and in ourselves.

Historical background   Group psychotherapy has followed somewhat different traditions in the United Kingdom and the United States. Because my background is in the British sphere of group psychotherapy, the focus will be on this tradition, with comparative reference to developments in the United States.

In the United Kingdom, group psychotherapy in the latter half of the twentieth century was dominated by two giants seemingly in opposition: Foulkes and Bion. As has been described in the literature (Brown 1985), these two represented radically different views of the group. Foulkes' vision of the therapy group was optimistic and expansive, to the point of idealization—the group as communicative, healing, and transformative. On the other hand, Bion's dark vision was of the group in the grip of regressive and destructive processes, with the task of the group commonly subverted by the basic assumptions. At their extremes, these two approaches occupy a position akin to the "structure of opposition" (Dews, 1987). In this, the positive and negative potentials of a given phenomenon are subjected to a cultural and institutional split, which makes it difficult to achieve an integration. The split in this instance could be seen as limiting, if not destructive, because it predicates allegiance to one ideology or another and suggests a group fragmenting process of a symbolic sort at the heart of the theoretical debate informing our thinking and practice.

I trained as a group analyst in the 1980s in a culture deeply loyal to Foulkes. Although I encountered much that was valuable, there was a striking omission of serious debate about destructive processes in groups. My concerns about this, and the implications it had for clinical practice, were the source of my later formulating the concept of the anti-group. At the time I was writing, it seemed that other group analysts were experiencing similar concerns. Writers such as Roberts (1991) and Prodgers (1990), both group analysts, were giving voice to the antagonistic and disruptive aspects of groups. In parallel, some of the more rigid edges of Bion-influenced group psychotherapy, as practiced at the Tavistock Clinic, were beginning to soften in the face of evidence suggesting that a group-as-a-whole approach that was conducted in an atmosphere of analytic distance and reduced emphasis on the individual member resulted in poor clinical outcomes (Malan, Balfour, Hood, & Shooter, 1976). The possibilities of integration were emerging.

The approach to group destructive processes in the American literature has been less monolithic, less polarized between opposite extremes, than in the United Kingdom. If anything, as Dies (1992) concluded in a major review of schools of group psychotherapy, there was considerable theoretical confusion in the United States as a result of the myriad of models, generating an overall lack of coherence (perhaps reflecting a different form of intellectual "anti-group" from that in the United Kingdom). Additionally, a perception exists of American group psychotherapy, at least from British shores, as focusing more on the individual in the group than on the group itself. Van Schoor (2000) interprets this as directly attributable to the American cultural emphasis on individuality and self-determination and the relegation of groups to a secondary place in psychological development. Although this view is debatable, its thesis may help to explain the ambivalent view of groups that wove through the positive attempts to establish a new form of psychotherapy. For example, Slavson, one of the pioneers of group psychotherapy, paradoxically considered the group-as-a-whole to be antitherapeutic and Wolf and Schwartz, in the words of Horwitz (1991), "crusaded" to eliminate the "heresy" of considering the group itself as a therapeutic entity.

Later developments in group psychotherapy in the United States tended to adopt an optimistic view of the process, constructively reflected in the contributions of Yalom (1995), although with continuing reservations about the utility of a group-as-a-whole approach. However, increasingly group therapists began to embrace the negative aspects of groups as an integral part of the process that could be understood and constructively handled (e.g., Gans, 1989; Ormont, 1984) and to appreciate the value of the group-as-a-whole approach, particularly if the influence of subgroup formations was recognized (Agazarian, 1997). At the same time, there remained some unease about the destructive potential of groups and the lack of an encompassing theory that could provide a framework within which to view these phenomena.

The anti-group
The concept of the anti-group was formulated in response to the neglect or underemphasis on group destructive processes in the Foulkesian tradition in the United Kingdom but also to the splits and paradoxes inherent in the overall group psychotherapy literature.

My concerns were primarily with theory but clinical experience added fuel to the fire. As the head of a large psychology and psychotherapy department in the National Health Service (NHS) in the United Kingdom between 1974 and 2001, as well as being a practicing group analyst, I had a particular interest in the potentials and problems of developing a comprehensive group psychotherapy service. I became aware of consistent difficulties in setting up and maintaining groups. Fundamentally, patients seeking help wanted individual—not group—therapy. The invitation to join a group was often met with fear and doubt. Here was an anti-group at the outset. This observation has now been confirmed in research on attitudes to group psychotherapy in the NHS. Bowden (2002) demonstrated an overwhelming preference among patients for individual psychotherapy over group linked to widespread negative perceptions of group therapy. In parallel to patients' attitudes, I found that fellow professionals tended to view group psychotherapy with suspicion. Groups run in institutional contexts are often regarded ambivalently and are vulnerable to sabotage. This is a form of anti-group outside the group but is nonetheless potent in undermining the group task in both subtle and blatant ways.

The anti-group was originally formulated as a *critical principle*, a challenge to the conventional optimism of group psychotherapy as a broad discipline and an attempt to recognize the antagonism toward groups in a nondefensive way. I emphasize its status as a critical principle because there has been a tendency to concretize it and to see the concept as denoting a static phenomenon readily identified and categorized. At the same time, the concept provides a *descriptive frame* for group material that concerns group-antagonistic processes, as well as an *explanatory paradigm* that seeks to understand the origins and expressions of seemingly destructive processes in group.

My attempts to define the anti-group have tended to emphasize a complex process in the following way: (a) the process varies considerably from group to group; (b) it has latent and manifest forms; (c) it occurs at individual, subgroup, and group-as-a-whole levels, although these levels are seen to be systemically related; and (d) it concerns aggression *within* the group, but it also refers to aggression *toward* the group. Understanding the anti-group in any particular group must take account of this complexity and consider the phenomenon from both systemic and analytic perspectives.

Determinants of the anti-group

Three fundamental sources of the anti-group exist: the group itself, including the composition of members; the context or setting of the group; and the group therapist. Although each of these dimensions has previously been noted in my writing, I am increasingly impressed by the circular rather than linear nature of these determinants and the reverberations that occur between the different levels. The group is a highly intersubjective field in which these different contexts all feed into the potential creation of an anti-group. For the purposes of explication, however, it is useful to focus on these three sources in turn.

Determinants within the group   To some extent, anti-group processes can be seen to arise in the inevitable conflict between members' individual needs—their hopes, desires, and longings—and the requirements of group membership, in which individual needs may have to be suspended. The dilemma is summed up in Bion's (1961) classic statement that the individual is a "group animal at war with himself for his groupishness" (p. 168). This sense of the frustration of individual needs is frequently superseded in group therapy by a realization of the value of commonality and the learning potential of mirroring and exchange with others (Foulkes, 1964). The frustration is thereby, in part, diminished. However, in some situations the frustration festers and grows and the group is felt to be inimical to personal needs. Common group tensions that can usually be dealt with constructively acquire negative and destructive charge and, if inadequately handled or resolved, escalate and undermine the group and its therapeutic task. Most of the within-group experiences that I have previously noted as elements of the anti-group (Nitsun, 1996) can be seen in this light. Consider, for example, the fear of annihilation and the fear of narcissistic injury, which both express aspects of the individual's anxiety in the group. Also, the frustration of the one-to-one relationship appears, in which the longing for an idealized relationship (which often underlies the preference for individual therapy) is frustrated by the presence of several others competing for time and space.

Several additional processes exist that I have linked to the anti-group.

> *Destructive rivalry and envy*. Although envy and rivalry are common and for the most part natural expressions of group relationships, they may intensify to the point where they cannot be contained and are enacted destructively.
>
> *Failures of communication*. Group therapists tend to set great store by verbal communication. Vital as this may be, it has limitations that can create misunderstandings and misattunements in the group rather than promoting understanding. Words are flawed, are open to misinterpretation, and can separate rather than connect (Stern, 1985). I have referred to a condition called "contaminating communication" (Nitsun, 1996) in which verbal interchange is felt to be damaging and spoiling rather than facilitating.
>
> *Attacks on linking*. This valuable concept of Bion's (1959) refers to the tendency in states of great anxiety and psychological threat to attack

the connections between thoughts, feelings, and actions and to undermine the links that maintain the group.

Projective identification. Apart from the insidious effects projective identification can have on individual members of the group, there can be a more global form of projective identification on the group itself as "bad," unsafe, and unhelpful—the group as object becomes denigrated. The anti-group is created through negative projections on the group.

The expression of desire. A recent development in my thinking concerns the expression of desire in the group. I suggest that groups work well when they enable members to openly express and share personal desire. This includes desire in the broad sense and its more specific sexual sense. How groups deal with the intimacies of desire is not straightforward and if repression or obstruction of its desire exists, there may be an alienation of desire that adds to frustration and disappointment and contributes to the development of the anti-group. In Fairbairn's (1952) terms, the group becomes an antilibidinal object.

Determinants within the context The group takes place within a milieu —institution, clinic, practice—which has its own matrix and which itself can be benign or malignant. In order for the group to progress, it depends on the support of this matrix. Negative attitudes in the milieu can take different forms: suspicion and disbelief in the therapeutic function of the group; curiosity about what goes on behind closed doors; feelings of jealousy at exclusion from the group; and envy of what appears to be a worthwhile task. One way or the other, groups tend to arouse strong feelings not only in those participating but also in those outside the group. Winnicott (1965) postulated that the establishment of a new group is an occasion for hostility and attack.

Anti-group attitudes arising in the external context are likely to have an undermining effect on the group. This can be direct, as in the sabotage of a group in an institution by hostile team members, or indirect, as in a referrer not encouraging a patient who is having a difficult time in the group to persist. Many such examples suggest that the "environmental" anti-group can have a damaging effect, particularly if the group is already in a fragile state.

The identification of anti-group dynamics emerging from the external context may be essential in order to understand and manage what is going on *inside* the group.

Determinants in the therapist It is important to recognize that group therapists may themselves be subject to anti-group reactions and contribute to destructive enactments within the group. In spite of their chosen profession, group therapists may harbor unresolved problems about their own group relationships; they may even have chosen this work as an attempt to resolve their own problems in groups. However, such resolution is seldom complete. A manifest anti-group may trigger the therapist's own internal anti-group. The group as an intersubjective field is constantly influenced by the therapist—not only when she or he consciously intervenes—and the therapist's contribution requires careful consideration.

Among the specific challenges to the therapist as a person in his or her own right are: (a) anxieties about risk and danger in the group; (b) fears for the survival of the group; (c) fears of failure and criticism; (d) narcissistic wishes to be loved; (e) fears of abandonment or engulfment; and (f) fears of losing control and authority. These may all touch on aspects of the therapist's characteristic difficulties with groups.

How exactly the therapist's anti-group enters the group arena will vary, depending on the person of the therapist and the dynamics of the particular group. It could, for example, enter unconsciously into the flawed selection of patients for the group, resulting in difficulties in the group, which then confirm anti-group expectations. It could express itself as a countertransference reaction to disruptive and threatening events in the group: The therapist may come to fear and even hate the group for its behavior. It could be reflected in failure to establish adequate organizational support for the group. It often results in feelings of hopelessness and despair in the therapist. All of this is potentially problematic because groups in states of heightened conflict, rage, or despair need particular containment and this may be difficult for the therapist to provide where struggling with his or her own anti-group.

The impact of the anti-group on the group's development

It is important to recognize that much of what has been subsumed under the rubric of anti-group can be seen as a natural expression of group relationships. Doubt, competition, hostility, envy, and so on are everyday processes in group. Their expression is vital to the life of the group and, as long as the group remains sufficiently cohesive and constructive, they contribute to the therapeutic development of the group. Denial and repression of these processes, if anything, is likely to generate a dysfunctional group, rather than the reverse. If these "ordinary" group processes are to be seen as anti-group at all in the sense that they trigger periods of group tension and disharmony, this can be described as a functional or "natural" anti-group. This, however, is different from what I refer to as a dysfunctional or "pathological" anti-group. Here negative currents in the group, particularly if directed at the group itself, create stasis, rigidity, and insoluble conflict in the group. Fragmentation and disintegration are likely to set in and the group's survival is imperiled.

The hope, however, is that even in extreme states, the group can hold—and deepen and strengthen in the process. This brings me to a particular proposition concerning the therapeutic potential of the anti-group. In line with a dialectical perspective of emotional development (Ogden, 1992), I suggest that the anti-group exists in a complementary and potentiating relationship with the creative properties of the group. Several aspects to this exist. Because the anti-group contains traumatic past experience in relationships, hidden from view but potentially accessible through exploration and understanding, the germ of therapeutic growth exists, contained within the anti-group. Further, the struggle to contain destructive processes *and survive them* is confirming, offsetting fears of repeated trauma and disintegration. This is akin to what Winnicott (1974) called "creative destruction," which is linked in his view to the "use of the object," describing the child's discovery of separateness and interdependence through its aggression toward the primary caregiver.

Dealing with the anti-group

The handling of negative and potentially destructive processes in group taxes many group therapists. This subject is covered extensively in an earlier publication (Nitsun, 1996). Here, it needs first to be said that the task will differ depending on whether the anti-group is what I described earlier as functional or dysfunctional. Although this distinction is, of necessity, simplified, in the case of the functional anti-group, openness to the expression of affect combined with the usual forms of clinical management and containment are usually sufficient, whereas with the dysfunctional or pathological anti-group, more active intervention is required. What form this takes will depend on the circumstances of the group, but the following are some broad guidelines for managing anti-group processes.

Boundary management   The anti-group is often associated with a boundary violation, whether as a cause, consequence, or both. This is sometimes imperceptible, but grows in proportion. The therapist can get caught up unwittingly in the boundary transgression but can also collude without realizing the full implications. Considerable vigilance is required in order to minimize boundary incidents and, where a dysfunctional anti-group is occurring, it is necessary to actively intervene in order to re-establish and strengthen boundaries.

Locating the anti-group I have previously used the term "defensive ag-glomeration" to describe a situation in which the group-as-a-whole is tainted by significant tension and hostility that is occurring within a part of the group that is not recognized or dealt with. This can trigger projections on the overall group of a weak or damaging container and imbue the group with anti-group characteristics. It follows that location of the anti-group at more specific levels is a fundamental requirement. This could be at indi-vidual, pair, or subgroup levels within the group. The location could also be in a noxious contextual influence outside the group or reflect a negative process within the therapist. Each of these levels may have to be clarified—as well as the possible connection with them—in order to deconstruct the anti-group.

Identifying the trauma In line with the hypothesis that the anti-group contains and reveals hidden trauma in the lives of the participants, it is necessary to identify the nature of this trauma. How widespread is past trauma in the group? Are there similarities between members that link the experience of trauma in the group and how do group members resonate to the evocation of trauma? How is this played out in the group in a way that repeats rather than repairs the damage? Identifying and recognizing traumatic experiences, as well as sharing the shame, sadness, despair, and rage consequent to the trauma, is part of the compassionate work of the group and an important part of transforming a dysfunctional anti-group into a therapeutic experience.

Maintaining the connecting function I use the term "connecting func-tion" to describe the overall process of cognitive and affective linking that is essential to the integrity and development of the group. The group is a matrix of connections. Its textures are formed by connections. Typically, the anti-group serves to derail these connections in a way that is similar to Bion's concept of attacks on linking as described previously—a process that is generated by the fear and hatred of connections, borne out of the dread of dependency and closeness. Where a group is unable or unwilling to maintain connections, it is vital that the therapist continues to do so in thinking, words, and gestures.

Support for the therapist Given the disturbing and demoralizing effect a dysfunctional anti-group can have on the therapist, a crucial need exists for the therapist to have professional support. This may take the form of regu-lar supervision, either individual or peer, or at least access to such support

124 • Complex Dilemmas in Group Therapy

at times of difficulty. My impression is that group therapists often lack such support or even avoid it because of the shame associated with feelings of failure, inadequacy, and helplessness. But the alternative, which is to go it alone, can lead to further despair and compound the anti-group constellation that is developing in the group. It is vital to get different perspectives on a stuck and dysfunctional group process and supervision in a group is a particularly effective way of doing this. As suggested earlier, the therapist's negative countertransference is a key consideration in the process.

Conclusion

In this chapter, the anti-group is presented as an approach to destructive processes in group that recognizes the complexities and uncertainties of group life—and the potential for significant disruption and damage—but with the hope of containment and transformation of these processes and the empowerment of group and therapist.

References

Agazarian, Y. M. (1997), *Systems-centered therapy for groups*. New York: Guilford Press.
Bion, W. R. (1959). "Attacks on Linking" in *Second thoughts* (1967). London: Heinemann.
Bion, W. R. (1961). *Experiences in groups*. London: Tavistock.
Bowden, M. (2002). Anti-group attitudes at assessment for psychotherapy. *Psychoanalytic Psychotherapy, 16*, 246–258.
Brown, D. (1985). Bion and Foulkes: Basic assumptions and beyond. In M. Pines (Ed.), *Bion and group psychotherapy*. London: Routledge and Kegan Paul.
Dews, P. (1987). *Logics of disintegration: Post-structuralist thought and the claims of critical theory*. New York: Verso.
Dies, R. R. (1992). Models of group psychotherapy: Sifting through confusion. *International Journal of Group Psychotherapy, 42*, 1–17.
Fairbairn, W. R. D. (1952). *Psychoanalytic studies of the personality*. London: Tavistock.
Foulkes, S. H. (1964). *Therapeutic group analysis*. London: Allen and Unwin.
Gans, J. S. (1989). Hostility in group psychotherapy. *International Journal of Group Psychotherapy, 39*, 499–516.
Horwitz, L. (1991). The evolution of a group-centered approach. In S. Tuttman, (Ed.), *Psychoanalytic group theory and therapy*. Madison, CT: International Universities Press.
Malan, D. H., Balfour, F. H. G., Hood, V. G., & Shooter, A. M. N. (1976). Group psychotherapy: a long-term follow-up study. *Archives of General Psychiatry, 33*, 1303–1315.
Nitsun, M. (1991). The anti-group: Destructive forces in the group and their therapeutic potential. *Group Analysis, 24*, 7–20.
Nitsun, M. (1996). *The Anti-group: Destructive forces in the group and their creative potential*. London: Routledge.
Ogden, T. H. (1992). The dialectically constituted/decentred self of psychoanalysis II. *International Journal of Psycho-Analysis, 73*, 613–626.
Ormont, L. R. (1984). The leader's role in dealing with aggression in groups. *International Journal of Group Psychotherapy, 34*, 553–572.
Prodgers, A. (1990). The dual nature of the group as mother: The uroboric container. *Group Analysis, 23*, 17–30.
Roberts, J. (1991). Destructive phases in groups. In J. Roberts, & M. Pines, (Eds.), *The Practice of Group Analysis*. London: Routledge.
Schermer, V. L. (1994). Between theory and practice, light and heat. In V. L. Schermer & M. Pines, (Eds.), *Ring of fire*. London: Routledge.
Stern, D. (1985). *The interpersonal world of the infant*. New York: Basic Books.

Van Schoor, E. P. (2000). A sociohistorical view of group psychotherapy in the United States. *International Journal of Group Psychotherapy, 50*, 437–454.

Winnicott, D. W. (1965). *The family and individual development*. London: Tavistock.

Winnicott, D. W. (1974). The use of an object and relating through identifications. In D. W. Winnicott, *Playing and reality*. London: Pelican.

Yalom, I. D. (1995). *The theory and practice of group psychotherapy* (4th ed.). New York: Basic Books.

Cuckoo Interrupted

Dear Consultant:

I'm not sure I can save my group from implosion, and I am inviting your thoughts about what I may have done wrong to get to this point, what I might be able to do now to ease the pain of the group's demise, or even whether there is something I can do to keep the group alive. I'm embarrassed to tell this story because I already know several of my mistakes, but you need to know what has transpired.

I've been leading groups for about 5 years, with virtually no supervision or consultation, partly out of my embarrassment about exposing what I'm doing. I began this particular group 2 years ago, starting with six members, two from my private practice, and the other four referred by other clinicians. In the first 3 months, three of the outside four dropped out, and I added one of my own patients, and two others from outside, making six again at that point. It's a coed open-ended, psychodynamic group, and the members, ranging in age from 25 to 55, carry a variety of diagnoses including depression, panic attacks, bipolar disorder, borderline personality disorder with narcissistic features, and antisocial personality disorder. This may be where I first went off the rails.

Because I wanted to get this group off the ground in a short time window, I elected to take in members who I knew were potentially risky, and I expanded my usual 20 year age spread to 30 years. So, I took in Jack, an antisocial 38-year-old man—think of Jack Nicholson in *One Flew Over the Cuckoo's Nest*—who was referred so that he could get interpersonal feedback on how he used people for his own ends. Also in the group at the start was Angelina, 45, with a borderline diagnosis, and one of my own patients —think Angelina Jolie in *Girl, Interrupted*—experiencing as well general unhappiness and an inability to sustain relationships. The oldest group member was Gregory—think Gregory Peck in *To Kill a Mockingbird*—a 55-year-old lawyer referred by his therapist for depression and social isolation. I mention these three because a lot of the action, largely explosive action, occurred among these three with other group members being bystanders. Unhappily, I think I stood by for too long as well.

Beginning in the first weeks of the group, Jack and Angelina often bickered with one another, criticized the other, and exuded disdain. Angelina was also furious with me in individual meetings for have taken Jack into this group because she considered him a destructive force, unaware that she wasn't helping much by taking him on almost every week. Gregory, for his part, reacted to the sparks between Jack and Angelina with withdrawal, although he was too depressed to quit the group—unlike the three members who left early on, each declaring the group a poor fit for them. Angelina and Jack have stayed in the group, with limited progress for either with respect to self-awareness or symptom change, and their chronic conflict has led to a revolving door of new members, who come for the 2 month contracted period, and then routinely flee. My own patients complain to me personally, rarely in the group therapy, about the group being a wrestling ring for Jack and Angelina, and they stay because I essentially persuade them again and again that it's in their best interest.

At this point, four members are in the group, three of mine and Jack, and my former referral sources for this group are drying up. Week after week, vague talk appears in the group of no benefit for the members, and my own confidence has been shaken to the point where I almost agree with them.

How do you understand the destructive forces in this group, and have they become too powerful for the group to survive?

Dear Therapist:

My discussion is from the perspective of Systems-Centered Therapy (SCT). SCT was derived from a theory of living human systems: theory first, practice second! The challenge of a theory-driven system is that when the theory is put into practice, very often, as happened in my case, the methods turn out to be different and unfamiliar (Agazarian, 2000).

As a psychoanalyst and dynamic group therapist, I always *followed* the group, attuning with "the third ear" to the group dynamics. When defensive or maladaptive responses were established in the group, I would address the group-as-a-whole or its members, aiming to bring the underlying dynamics to light. I encouraged group members to use the group process as a context in which they could come, through hindsight, to recognize their compulsion to repeat maladaptive patterns.

In contrast, SCT encourages members simultaneously to explore the impulse to repeat old patterns before they have been acted out and to develop a group system that facilitates this exploration. This shift in perspective required me to use foresight in developing norms in a group that would put the theory into practice. Thus, I began to intervene in the group process before the norms were set. A very difficult change in method (Agazarian, 1997, 2002)!

Communication norms are influenced from the first few minutes of an SCT group. Members are required to give up defensive vagueness, redundancy, and the universally favorite "yes . . . but . . ."! The greatest difference between SCT and psychodynamic groups is that little or no interpretations, no explanations, and no questions appear, three kinds of communication that remove people from themselves and from others. All interpretations are considered projections, mind-reads that need to be checked out with the person whose mind is being read. Explanations are considered to take one to what one knows already instead of exploring what one does not know about the issue. Questions are a way of looking for answers instead of discovering what is fueling the question inside oneself.

Another immediate SCT intervention is to the communication pattern itself. Left on their own, most members talk more to active members and less to passive members, more to members who express the same views as their own and less to members who do not. This rapidly lays down a pattern of people coming together in predictable (stereotypical) subgroups that are not functional. In contrast, the SCT method of functional subgrouping requires members to join in resonance with each other and to explore one side of a group issue, while the other subgroup waits until the first is done before exploring the other side. This way of working contains group conflicts in different subgroups, and in the process of exploration, members are able to build on each other's work, the conflict is understood from different perspectives, and an integration of differences is facilitated in the group-as-a-whole.

From a systems perspective, Jack and Angelina are in the same subgroup, the "fighting" subgroup. The group's work would be to explore both sides of the group phenomenon: the impulse to fight (in the Jack and Angelina subgroup) and the impulse to flee from the fight (in the subgroup of the other members of the group). In containing functional subgroups, members have a better chance to explore their impulses instead of enact them.

The norms of functional subgrouping make it easier for members to bring in difficult issues that they would rather not talk about. For example, in this group, complaints about the group were rerouted to outside the group or into members' own individual therapy sessions. This deprives both the members and the group of surfacing important issues in the group: for example, the dissatisfaction with the repetitive fighting between

Jack and Angelina. Dealing with group business outside the group increases feelings of helplessness and impotence in the members, which may then contribute to members giving up or leaving.

It appears as if this group moved quickly into fight. From an SCT perspective, the liability of a group skipping the flight phase and moving straight into fight is that the members have not yet learned "how" to fight without taking each other's aggression personally, nor have they had the opportunity to modify the flight phase anxieties that are driven by their negative predictions, mind-reading, and the tendency to import war stories from the past (Agazarian, 1999). Thus, fighting too early is liable to increase flight defenses and to lose the experience and information in aggression by discharging it into outrage, blaming, complaining, and other defenses.

Perhaps the most distressing factor in this group is the painful roles that members repeated in themselves and with each other. In SCT, group members learn early the difference between the knee-jerk reactions to each other that come from old roles being repeated in the present, and the authentic relationship to the self, which permits for curiosity, wonder, and exploration of the impulses to react. When all members explore their impulses, no one member becomes a target, an identified patient, or a scapegoat.

Tragically, Jack and Angelina were each other's targets. It's important to note that, from an SCT perspective, Jack and Angelina are actually in the same subgroup! Without the containment that would be necessary for them to explore this issue, it is too difficult for them to recognize that each is repeating some significant past relationship, and each has picked the perfect partner with whom to act it out. SCT calls this a role-lock: a role that reflects the dynamics that individual members have come to group to change locked into a partnership that serves each of them as a repetition. Their role-lock also plays a role for the group. It serves as a container for the group dynamics that the group is too phobic to explore, the group's destructive forces. With such an intense and live potential for insight into the dynamics, it is a tragedy that the two acted out for themselves and the group rather than exploring for insight.

It is probable that Gregory's withdrawal was also a repetition of a typical depressive response to aggression. (If one factor in depression is the defense of turning the retaliatory impulse back on the self, the flight subgroup also had high potential for insight if they were to explore.) The other three members were in Gregory's flight subgroup. When they left the field, we do not know whether they were predominantly acting out, or whether they were using their common sense in leaving a fixated and nonfunctional group, or both.

Another difference between SCT and dynamic therapy is highlighted by the way the issues surrounding membership are framed. The frame seemed to imply that the membership mix was a significant factor in influencing the course of the group. Through SCT eyes, the challenge in establishing a group is not so much in choosing the population as it is in setting communication norms. Thus, the age range and the range of diagnosis would not be considered in itself a problem unless the members were too different to be able to communicate with each other (rather rare, in our experience). This particular population mix does suggest a high potential for acting out. However, addressing the acting-out potential is always important in groups, and particularly with borderlines (and borderlines are particularly responsive to containing norms). The SCT alternative is to encourage members to explore the fork in the road between the impulse to act out on the one hand (the defense) and what impulse, emotion, or conflict the acting out is defending against. This is a potent containment for all, independent of diagnosis.

No information appears in the case illustration to indicate whether the group addressed the issue of some members being private patients of the therapist and others being referred by other therapists. Without working this issue in the group, it is difficult for group members to avoid diverting group tensions into their individual therapy. Failing to surface concern about the different role relationships to the group therapist is a missed opportunity for exploring conflicts about being special or not special, and would almost certainly contribute to the tensions between members that Jack and Angelina expressed for the group.

One final comment: The therapist was reluctant to go for supervision. One wonders what previous supervisory experiences the therapist had that influenced him or her to go through the helplessness, pain, and frustration of leading a group whose survival is at stake. Is it an ethical question when a therapist does not consult with another professional to get insight into a maladaptive therapeutic relationship? An attuned consultant would not be pejorative, and could focus insight into the therapeutic issues in the group struggle and identify the restraining forces in both the therapist and the group that interfere with the innately healthy drive that connects people to their life goals.

Yvonne M. Agazarian, EdD, CGP, FAGPA

References

Agazarian, Y. M. (1997), *Systems-centered therapy for groups*. New York: Guilford Press.

Agazarian, Y. M. (1999). Phases of development in the systems-centered group. *Small Group Research, 30*, 82–107.

Agazarian, Y. M. (2002). A systems-centered approach to individual and group psychotherapy. In L. Vandecreek & T. Jackson (Eds.), *Innovations in clinical practice: A source book* (vol. 20). Sarasota, Florida: Professional Resource Press.

Agazarian, Y., & Gantt, S. (2000). *Autobiography of a theory*. London: Jessica Kingsley.

Dear Therapist:

Indeed, you have serious problems with your group, and I will try to help throw some light on the situation from the self-psychological perspective. Although psychology of the self has been my interest for more than 20 years, I don't think that any single theory is complete. I have a strong predilection for looking at the group focal conflict (Whitman & Stock, 1958), Bion's basic assumption theory, projective mechanisms, and, more recently, intersubjectivity, which focuses sharply on the therapist's contribution to the treatment endeavor. Transactions in the treatment process are co-constructed and are not merely a repetition of the patient's past relationships thrown on a blank screen. The therapist, whether he is interactive or silent, contributes to the therapeutic atmosphere and consequently needs to consider the possibility that unintended results of his stance will emerge in the group (Stone, 2001).

Before considering some of the dilemmas you note, I will comment on my approach to a consultation. Appreciating that you are experienced, I will assume your familiarity with metaphorical communication and aspects of group dynamics and process. I will focus primarily on countertransference, by which I mean the totality of your experience in planning, instituting, and conducting the group.

First, I would like to examine "why now" are you coming for a consultation? I understand your concern about the group's viability, but are other issues contributing to your seeking help at this time? Is something else adding to your long standing distress? Would this be a good time to share concerns you have had about seeking consultation or would you like to wait until later? Next, what kind of help do you have in mind? This addresses the "consultative agreement." Without clarity about the frame, the consultation may be unsatisfactory or ineffective. In an office consultation, we would determine at the end if you wished additional consultation.

In your request for assistance, you perceive the group composition as problematic. Your list includes diagnostic categories, age range, and patients who come from your own practice (combined therapy), whereas others come from other clinicians (conjoint therapy). Is this plethora of concerns a result of pressure to begin the group quickly? Consequently, was careful selection or preparation of applicants neglected? Your description implies that some of those chosen were high risk to either drop out or to become representatives of the anti-group. In self-psychological terms, you feel you included unempathic, insensitive, or manipulative individuals who may interfere with a group formation that could provide satisfactory discourse and serve selfobject needs (e.g., a bipolar patient or an antisocial personality).

You remark about diagnostic labels, so perhaps you have been overly influenced by DSM. What did the diagnoses mean for you? Does this mean that you have neglected exploring the patients' relational styles in the preparatory process? As you noted, "This may be where I first went off the rails." Certainly this suggests you have some affect surrounding your choices. I would then wonder how this has had an impact on your experience of leading the group.

. You also mention concerns that the three decade age span among the members, 10 years greater than your usual practice, may be detrimental to your group. This suggests a fantasy that this expansion constitutes a problem. I wonder what the countertransference is in this regard. You may have interpreted the literature as saying, "don't do it," but your choices may reflect a desire to quickly form your group. Guidelines may become reified and stimulate shame.

Many years ago, while leading a live patient group at an American Group Psychotherapy Association conference, I was asked who, in fantasy, I would like to eliminate from the group and who I would particularly care to keep. This opened the door to examining my countertransference reactions. This might be another avenue to consider in addressing your dilemma in forming the group.

From a different perspective, you are worried about the problem of including individuals seen by other therapists in your group. Clearly you are troubled by the pattern of these patients dropping out. This has meaning for you and the group. Are you worried about your reputation among colleagues? Is it an issue in your other groups? Is conjoint treatment openly discussed? What do the members think? Are they concerned who is the favorite child, who gets the gleam in mother's eye (the mirror transference), or who feels that no one is available with whom to merge or idealize (the idealizing transferences)? Of course it would be helpful if you could reflect on interventions that might be construed to show favoritism or neglect. You would also need the patients' perspectives in addressing these questions. Technically, I would handle this by sharing some of my thinking: for example, "I wonder if you experience me as showing favoritism." You don't have to be "right." Rather, the task is to engage members in a dialogue that will help them reflect on aspects of themselves that they may have been afraid to mention, are only dimly aware of, or know little about.

As an additional question, what is your agreement with patients who are not from your caseload? Do you have permission to discuss their treatment with their individual clinician? Do you think that would help alert you to emerging problems, or is this similar to your reluctance to seek consultation?

You frame part of the process problem as members' responses to the bickering between Jack and Angelina, and you highlight Gregory's behavior as an enactment of his usual responses to aversive situations by withdrawal. I invite you to explore your comment that you, perhaps similar to

Gregory, stayed on the sideline too long. What were your emotional responses to the dyadic conflict when it began and has that changed? Can you describe several specific experiences you had in which you felt you might have been more forthcoming? It might be helpful to compare your "activity" in this group with that in your other groups.

How have you formulated the relationship between Jack and Angelina? On occasion I think that such conflict is a self-protective strategy to keep out of awareness underlying attraction and desire—indeed they are intensely engaged. What might you imagine would happen if you suggested this directly in the group? Of course, pairing dynamics suggest group-as-a-whole (and therapist) contributions to the process. Could you have subtly coconstructed their relationship?

Were this an office consultation, I would now ask for feedback with respect to your consultative experience. What have I said that indicates that I have not understood your dilemma accurately? Can you then help me understand any "misunderstanding" so that we can enrich our collaboration? In this way I am modeling what I believe to be an appropriate and helpful therapeutic stance. To paraphrase Schwaber (1995), however different the perspective held by the supervisor (or therapist), however difficult it may be to grant that our perspective is only that, our own, we have a responsibility to try to understand the supervisee's (patient's) emotional position.

In this response, I focused my interest on your emotions and the possibility of their contributions to your dilemma. I hope that the work you do in clarifying your feelings will enable you to understand what led you to this point and enable you to successfully alter this difficult process.

Walter N. Stone, MD, CGP, FAGPA

References

Schwaber, E. A. (1995). Towards a definition of the term and concept of interaction. *International Journal of Psycho-Analysis, 76,* 557–564.

Stone, W. N. (2001). The role of the therapist's affect in the detection of empathic failures, misunderstandings and injury. *Group, 25,* 3–14.

Whitman, R. M., & Stock, D. (1958). The group focal conflict. *Psychiatry, 21,* 269–276.

The author wishes to thank Esther G. Stone for her helpful comments.

Does Anyone Want Group?

Dear Consultant:

I am a seasoned group therapist who was recently asked by the administration to start a group therapy program at my clinic. I was excited by the prospect because I know how powerful group therapy can be as a form of treatment. The clinic has a long waiting list of clients as a result of the full case loads of our therapists. For the past 6 months, I have talked with these therapists about the effectiveness of group therapy, indications for group therapy, and promoting group therapy to some of their appropriate individual patients. In addition, I recommended to the administration that we start a short-term group for the waiting list patients, where they could be further assessed for individual or group treatment, and then be moved into a longer term group if appropriate.

The problem is that I have met with incredible resistance from both the therapists who might make the referrals and from many of the referred patients as well. One therapist told me directly that she would never refer to group because she deemed it a second class treatment. Because we primarily work with lower income clients, she felt that they should get the same treatment (i.e., individual treatment) as our wealthier clients. Also, our clinicians have productivity requirements, so they don't want to refer their individual clients to group for fear they will lose a billable client hour. We have told them that they could run groups themselves, and get .5 productivity hours for each patient seen in group—that is, they would get twice the productivity hours in half the time with only four members in a group! Still they don't refer and refuse to run a group themselves.

The referred patients are also resistant to the idea of group and argue for being seen individually. Even the administration at this point seems resistant in that they have not supported any group therapy training for clinicians in the program. So far we have only two groups, each struggling to stay viable. Dropouts are common, and the few clinicians who do refer tend to use it as a dumping ground for difficult clients. Many patients referred have severe character disorders, which tends to make the groups chaotic and unstable. The leaders report feeling deskilled by the level of chaos.

I am curious about and frustrated by the lack of cooperation from the clinic staff and administration. How do I deal with their resistance? How can I help them see the importance and effectiveness of group treatment? What is the best way to get the staff to buy in to the program? Should I randomly assign patients and therapists to groups and see what happens? Should all staff have to run a group or even be required to be in a T-group to get a sense of the power of group treatment?

Dear Therapist:

You do indeed have a dilemma. Caught in a web of multiple ambivalences and resistances, the problem becomes where to start. You have been asked to start a group program in a clinic without knowing clearly who wants this and why.

As a psychoanalyst, and as one who does psychoanalytic group therapy, I might be tempted to say you must first confront the resistance. However, being aware of systems theory and the importance of the system in which the individual operates, I would suggest other priorities. You are caught in a dysfunctional system or one that, in this situation, has encouraged dysfunctional behavior. Before you can deal with the resistance, you have to work with the system to effect some basic changes.

The way a new program is introduced to the staff can affect the way in which it is received. Did the administration talk with the staff about starting a group therapy program? Their reasons for this innovation needed to be addressed. Patient needs and the value of group therapy, as well as "productivity" and the financial concerns of the agency, have to be openly discussed.

It is considered unethical to ask a therapist to conduct a form of therapy in which he or she is not adequately trained. The staff appears to be uninformed or misinformed about group therapy. This suggests a lack of adequate training in this important modality. Were you able to discuss training needs with the administration? Did the administration offer the staff opportunities for supplemental training?

The task set before you was made more difficult by having no apparent staff involvement in the decision making and also having no preparation for the proposed changes. It suggests that the administration had some ambivalence about the very program they were suggesting you start. I would also think that their ambivalence was evident in the fact that this clinic had not considered group therapy as a viable treatment modality before this particular crisis.

Before a successful group therapy program can be put into operation at this clinic, two sets of tasks must be undertaken. The first is for the group therapist to work with the total clinic, administrators, and staff, separately and together, to deal with how they feel about what happened in the initial decision to start the group therapy program. It will only be after a full discussion of these matters that you will be able to address the resistances. Then you will be able to create a climate of cooperative concern for the best possible patient care to be developed.

It may seem like a tremendous task but it is essential if these proposed changes will really work well. The staff and the administration have to be able to work cooperatively together, before they can cooperate with you. Their first real group experience will be working with you as you help them become a well functioning group. In the process you will teach them much and demonstrate the effectiveness of groups.

The second task will be to work with the staff, improving their understanding of group therapy and, hopefully, stimulating an interest in learning new skills. Then the therapists may be able to see the need for further information, training, and supervisory instruction in this therapeutic modality. It is not surprising that the patients are not accepting of the assignment to group therapy. Because their therapists see it as "second class" treatment, they must feel that too.

The status of the existing groups speaks to the lack of understanding of group therapy. The questions of who should be in group, when it is most advantageous to the patient to be transferred to group therapy, and how patients should be prepared for group all have to be considered.

Several ways exist to stimulate interest in further training in group therapy. For example, you might encourage attendance at your local group therapy society's conferences. Attendance at an institute or group experience at the conference may be easier than at the workplace initially. You can invite other group therapists to speak at in-house seminars and you might want to start a reading group with your colleagues.

Given the lack of experience and training you describe, you might also start a group supervision for those therapists now working with groups. This could provide them with direct experience with group process and its effectiveness. Although this may seem like a tremendous task for you to undertake, it is important. You will be demonstrating to your colleagues in a very direct way how groups do and can work. This will be their first real group experience.

At the same time you will only be successful in your group therapy program if the administration and the staff are ready to work together with each other and with you in this new way. I would also suggest that because this is a huge undertaking, you might find it useful to get some consultation from someone outside the system. You will need support in this task.

Nina Fieldsteel, PhD, FAGPA

Dear Therapist:

You are clearly in a bind. You have been asked to develop a group therapy program with the apparent backing of the clinic's administrators. At the same time, the administration is not providing leave time or opportunities for clinic staff to receive training in the basics of group therapy. An unfortunate collusion exists between this position and the staff's resistance to the program. It thus appears important that the motivations of the administration first be clarified: Does their stated interest in a group program reflect a belief in the applicability and usefulness of group approaches for the clinic's patients, or does it reflect an interest in simply reducing costs (i.e., using less staff time to provide services for more patients)? If the intent is only to serve "the bottom line," the probability that groups will be used inappropriately, that staff will feel their skills are being devalued, and that patients will feel poorly served increases. Instead, there should be a belief that employing group treatments would be beneficial to the patients presenting to the clinic, and *this belief should be clearly communicated by the administration to the clinical staff.* Achieving a consensus among administrative and clinical staff that a group program would improve services to patients can provide the "developmental substrate" for such a program. Eventually, the practical advantages of integrating group approaches with clinic services would be realized as a bonus.

Developing this staff consensus may require that sufficient time is devoted to a discussion of the *efficacy, applicability,* and *efficiency* of group treatment approaches. In that regard, you might want draw the attention of the administration to the empirical literature. Recent reviews of this literature (Burlingame, MacKenzie, & Strauss, 2004; Folkers & Steefel, 1991; Fuhriman & Burlingame, 1994; Piper & Joyce, 1996; Tillitski, 1990) highlight the evidence for efficacy of group treatments relative to control conditions and for the equivalence of group therapies relative to individual therapies. The literature also underscores the range of patient complaints, conditions, and disorders for which group treatments have proven effective (Burlingame et al., 2004; Piper & Joyce, 1996). A careful consideration of the literature can provide information about which group treatment orientations (e.g., cognitive-behavioral, psychodynamic-interpersonal, psychoeducational-supportive) and formats (e.g., short-term, open-ended) would be most applicable for this particular clinical setting.

With regard to efficiency, you could consider the study by Piper, Debbane, Bienvenu, and Garant (1984). From the therapist's perspective, treatment per patient requires 4.5 hours in a short-term group format (eight members for twenty-four 90-minute sessions) but 21.6 hours in a short-term individual format (twenty-four 50-minute sessions). Thus a considerable savings of time exists for therapists using the group format. From the patient's perspective, individual therapy provides 21.6 hours, whereas group therapy provides 36 hours of treatment. Thus, the group patient can receive a greater "dosage" of treatment than the individual patient. You might suggest that the group patient cannot receive attention from the therapist to the same degree as the individual patient. Although true to a point, the former also benefits from the work of, and feedback from, fellow members (i.e., the group functions as a therapeutic agent).

Even with a clear demonstration of administrative support and a thorough review of the relevant literature, resistance to implementation of a group program may nonetheless be encountered in clinicians and patients. You made reference to the shared perception of group therapy as a "second class" treatment relative to individual therapy, particularly when differentially offered to lower income patients. The findings noted previously (i.e., that group and individual therapies provide equivalent benefits) indicate that no empirical basis exists for this assumption. Moreover, lower income patients may actually do better in group treatments because the modality offers them experiences of peer acceptance, complementarity, universality, and cohesion that can increase feelings of comfort, more so than is the case with a (generally middle-class) individual therapist (Sadock, 1985).

Clinician resistance to the use of group treatments is obviously more of an obstacle to program development than patient resistance (i.e., the latter can more readily be addressed if the former is minimized). As you describe it, your clinic operates with a long waiting list and with individual therapy as the sole treatment of choice, whatever the patient's presenting problem. This may reflect a narrow range of experience on the part of the clinical staff. Consequently, any suggestion to expand their repertoire of interventions may be perceived by them as a threat to their self-image as competent clinicians. They may need sufficient information and time to consider what is required in terms of leading groups, as well as opportunities for observing expert-led groups, coleading groups with more experienced colleagues, and engaging in supervised group practice. Workshops and experiential groups at professional conferences (e.g., American Group Psychotherapy Association) may offer such opportunities. Additionally, the clinic administration can look at contracting or recruiting an experienced group clinician to provide inservice training for staff.

Apart from the need to develop the technical skills associated with leading groups, clinicians may also need to address the anxieties associated with the shift from individual to group therapy:

> There is little doubt that the therapist has less *control* in a group setting. Similarly, a diminished sense of *individuality* and decreased *understanding* are likely experiences for the therapist in group. The therapist is also more exposed in a group (*privacy*) and may also feel more subject to criticism and attack (*safety*). Thus, the therapist may . . . experience greater anxiety and discomfort in the case of group therapy relative to individual therapy. (Piper & Joyce, 1996, p. 323)

These issues are best dealt with in a strongly collaborative supervisory relationship. Additionally, a peer supervision meeting may be ideal for a staff of clinicians embarking on the development of a group program. In addition to providing opportunities for support and understanding, a peer group can serve as a vehicle for strengthening the cohesion and morale of clinicians involved in the treatment program.

Patient resistances to group treatment may arise out of similar apprehensions. Thus, issues related to perceived or actual losses of control, individuality, understanding, privacy, and safety often lead to greater anticipated and experienced anxiety for patients in group therapy when compared to individual therapy. The clinician's sensitivity to and careful management of these issues during the group is therefore critical. Perhaps more important, however, is the clinician's emphasis on carefully *preparing* the patient for group therapy. Preparation should address fears like those listed above, clarify the patient's expectations, provide an outline of the process of group therapy and the patient's responsibilities in that process, and consider the basic ground rules and common pitfalls of the group experience (see Brabender, 2002; Vinogradov & Yalom, 1989). In a new group program, consultation and supervision regarding these issues may be important until such time as the preparation process becomes second nature.

Being specific about how groups can be used is critical in the early stages of developing a group program. This requires a review of the treatment needs of your clinic population and the services you currently offer these patients. The review should help identify the groups that would be most helpful in your setting. For example, homogeneous groups (e.g., young adults in the transition from home to university, depressed elders, and patients dealing with bereavement or eating disorders) might suggest that focused short-term approaches would be appropriate. Alternatively, large numbers of chronic patients needing ongoing monitoring might suggest open-ended support groups with psychiatric backup. Finally, insight-oriented groups might be developed for the well-functioning patients who present with interpersonal problems.

Clinicians will indeed feel "deskilled" if they attempt to implement groups with multiple and incompatible goals. Clarity about the groups to be implemented can decrease these feelings and increase clinicians' sense of mastery. Practically, a cotherapy model may allow staff to share learning and responsibilities with the groups first implemented in the program. Small-scale evaluations of patient change can offer evidence for the effectiveness of these early groups and indications that the new program is moving in the right direction.

Generally speaking, then, if you can help the clinic's administrative and clinical staff to achieve a consensus as *advocates* of group treatment, these attitudes will in turn be communicated to the patients. Attention to preparing patients for group, dealing with therapist concerns associated with leading groups, and continuously monitoring the appropriateness and effectiveness of group approaches vis-à-vis the specifics of the clinical setting can ensure that a group program develops smoothly and eventually becomes self-maintaining.

Anthony S. Joyce, PhD

References

Brabender, V. (2002). *Introduction to group therapy*. New York: Wiley.

Burlingame, G. M., Mackenzie, K. R., & Strauss, B. (2004). Small-group treatment: Evidence for effectiveness and mechanisms of change. In M. J. Lambert (Ed.), *Bergin and Garfield's Handbook of psychotherapy and behavior change* (pp. 647–696). New York, NY: John Wiley & Sons, Inc.

Folkers, C. E., & Steefel, N. M. (1991). Group psychotherapy. In C. S. Audstad & W. H. Berman (Eds.), *Managed health care: The optimal use of time and resources* (pp. 46–64). Washington, DC: American Psychological Association.

Fuhriman, A, & Burlingame G. M. (1994). Group psychotherapy: Research and practice. In A. Fuhriman & G. M. Burlingame (Eds.), *Handbook of group psychotherapy: An empirical and clinical synthesis* (pp. 3–40). New York: Wiley.

Piper, W. E, Debbane, E. G., Bienvenu, J. P., & Garant, J. (1984). A comparative outcome study of four forms of psychotherapy. *Journal of Consulting and Clinical Psychology, 52*, 268–279.

Piper, W. E., & Joyce, A. S. (1996). A consideration of factors influencing the utilization of time-limited, short-term group therapy. *International Journal of Group Psychotherapy, 46*, 311–328.

Sadock B. J. (1985). Group psychotherapy, combined individual and group psychotherapy, and psychodrama. In H. I. Kaplan & B. J. Sadock (Eds.), *Comprehensive textbook of psychiatry IV* (pp. 1403–1426). Baltimore, MD: Williams & Wilkins.

Tillitski, L (1990). A meta-analysis of estimated effect sizes for group versus individual versus control treatments. *International Journal of Group Psychotherapy, 40*, 215–224.

Vinogradov, S, & Yalom I. D. (1989). *A concise guide to group psychotherapy*. Washington, DC: American Psychiatric Association.

A Sinking Depression

Dear Consultant:

Can a severely depressed individual be treated in a group if he or she is the only one who is this depressed? Years ago, I would have argued that group therapy is an excellent treatment for virtually all disorders, including severe depression, but I am now questioning this.

My group met for 5 months and was defined as an open-ended long-term group with places for eight members, men and women. We started with five members, added one shortly thereafter, and added no one since that time. Generally speaking, the members were high-functioning in terms of occupational success and insight-orientation. All group members were referred for difficulties in maximizing their abilities: that is, they were all self-defined underachievers. Three of the members were business executives who had, in adult life, been diagnosed with ADD, which had interrupted their career trajectory.

The first two sessions were of the "hello" variety, with group members sharing stories of mild to moderate impairment in their lives. Humor was common in these groups, and enjoyed by everyone but Elizabeth, an ultrasound therapist, who described herself as shy. In the third session, Elizabeth, on leave from her job while raising her two children, was questioned more about her reserve. After many probes, she revealed she had been experiencing a deep depression for the past 2 months, with frequent thoughts of suicide as her only option. She was unwilling to take antidepressants because she was breast-feeding her 6-month-old, and also had been hiding her depression from her husband. The group offered concern, support, advice, and pressure to seek individual therapy and psychopharmacology. Such extensive attention made Elizabeth feel guilty. She expressed gratitude but insisted that the group move on, which the group did.

In the next several sessions, group members began each group by checking in with Elizabeth who reported no change in her mental state. (I did not deem her committable and she clearly rejected the idea of voluntary hospitalization.) The group's frustration was evident to me, but I did not comment on this for fear of worsening Elizabeth's self-perception of being an unworthy burden. In subsequent sessions, the group found a way to avoid asking Elizabeth for updates, and essentially behaved as though she were not present. What was also clear, however, was that the group's vitality as expressed through humor and sharing of successful situations was muted.

I had the experience of being held hostage to Elizabeth's depression and reasoned that the group must feel this way as well, but again I didn't know how to communicate this without pushing Elizabeth to flee or deteriorate. So, I joined the group in what I later came to see as my collusion in protecting Elizabeth. This failed, however.

Within the next month, one member announced his termination for scheduling reasons, followed in the next session by a termination announcement for financial reasons. My attempts to interpret these decisions as a flight from exposure to difficult and painful experiences of "other group members" and possibly from their own difficult experiences made no impact. Elizabeth said nothing.

Two weeks later, two other members expressed dissatisfaction with the group phrased largely in terms of the group size. After the initial two members left, they argued, there would be only four, which seemed too small to them, so they concluded they should leave. I could not stop them, and the remaining two members, Elizabeth and another woman, commented that people needed to do what they felt was best for them.

Not knowing quite what to do, I disbanded the group or, actually, recommended that the group be on hiatus while I tried to collect a few more members, at which time I would contact the remaining two. I also pushed Elizabeth to contact an individual therapist but she again refused. I never called the two members to restart the group, but did call Elizabeth once after 2 weeks to inquire about her mental state. She reported that she was "fine" but would reveal little else.

In retrospect, I wonder whether this group composition was doomed from the start, or were there other paths I might have taken?

Dear Therapist:

We find a noncommunicative Elizabeth in our midst. The group invites her in; she refuses to link up to their concern, support, and attempts to supply meaning. Is she suicidal, a lethal or depressed character, postpartumly depressed, or is she merely overwhelmed with two young children and without the verbal resources and trust to make herself known? Tellingly, she refuses individual therapy, and an alliance with you, the therapist, and thus, repels the group.

Elizabeth fits the profile described by Freud (1917) as lacking in interest and love, two of the three basic emotions that link human beings to each other and from which meaning may accrue. I am referring to Bion's trilogy of "passion:" an integration of urges for love (L), hate (H), and knowledge (K) (Billow, 1999, 2001, 2002). Elizabeth exhibits a surfeit of disavowed hatred, however, holding the group hostage, scaring all members into silence, retreat, and flight.

Elizabeth proceeds from "a mental constellation of revolt," feeling justified taking revenge and tormenting others (Freud, 1917, p. 248). Although professing guilt and gratitude, she transmits instead a subtle satisfaction in her purposeful mindlessness, unconcerned with her aversive effects on others and "fine" after the group disbands. She behaves as if she did not want to love, and to be loved, to know about others, and to be known. Elizabeth wants to hate, and to be hated, and these wants were satisfied covertly, rather than embraced openly, understood, and dealt with by group process.

Members of a young group, particularly, do not have the conceptual or emotional equipment to deal with the rebellious machinations of a resolutely depressed individual. They are not able to balance an instinctive interest and concern (L and K) in a patient they do not know with a constructive anger (H) toward the same patient who will not be known. Left unchallenged, a patient like Elizabeth may overthrow the members' budding reciprocal allegiances and attachments, such that group process moves to succession, exile, and anarchy (Billow, 2003).

From this example, we may understand that depression is a disorder of disowned but pressing aggression. To reach and relieve the depressed patient, and integrate her into the group, the therapist must link up the patient's dissociated aggression to the here-and-now treatment situation. This first requires recognizing and linking up one's own aggressive feelings and thoughts. You, like other group members, frustrated in your urge to care and be curious, will be overstimulated and possibly frightened by an urge to hate and be hateful. Maltsberger and Buie (1973) have suggested a reciprocal relationship between the therapist's incapacity to tolerate conscious sadistic wishes and the intensity of the therapist's aversive avoidance of the patient. Thus, when the aggressive urge is disavowed in the therapist, as it is in the patient, the group member remains not understood and unreached. Indeed, I believe Elizabeth felt "guilty" when receiving *caring* attention because of her contempt for the group's avoidance of her need for *hating* attention.

In other words, the primary object link Elizabeth seems capable or willing to make is through the emotion of hatred. As her therapist, I expect that sooner rather than later Elizabeth would feel persecuted by my insistence on taking professional responsibility for her care, and would thwart and provoke me. Thus, she provides opportunity for therapeutic "passion" to use anger to link to her with caring interest (LHK).

Imagine how this might be played out:

Initial interventions:

Therapist: Elizabeth, it is important for you tell us what's going on.
Elizabeth (pained by the injunction): No, I said I'm okay . . . .
Therapist: I'm not. I'm concerned about you and about the group as well. If you won't see me individually, which I believe is imperative (Yalom, 1995), you must let me assess whether and how I should be concerned for you.
Elizabeth: I really feel uncomfortable.
Therapist (firmly): I understand, but you are also making other people worried and uncomfortable. I'll give you some time to get it together, but you have to give us some sense of what is going on.

Later in this session or in the following session:

Therapist (concerned by Elizabeth's silence): Elizabeth, you're really working at being unhappy and refusing help. Why would you come to group to do that?
Elizabeth: I don't want to be a burden.
Therapist: You're being a silent burden. Burden us by letting us in.
Elizabeth (annoyed): I'm okay. I appreciate everyone's interest; no one has to worry about me.
Therapist: Let's see if people agree. (Other members most likely will express interest and concern, which Elizabeth will shuck off.) You may not be aware of what you are doing, but you are exerting a tremendous control on the group. You won't let people deal with you, but it is not possible to ignore your pain and function as a group.
Elizabeth: Maybe I should leave.
Therapist: You think you're going to defeat me that easily?
Elizabeth: No, it's not you, it's me; I feel guilty taking so much attention.
Therapist: I'm very egotistical. I take everything personally. I feel you are ignoring the group and I'm part of it. I'm beginning to think you want to hurt us. Who hurt you by ignoring you?

I intervene to interest Elizabeth and the group in making sense of what she is doing and why, not to provoke anger, abreaction, or ventilation, although these may be beneficial secondary effects. Indeed, as Freud (1917, p. 157) implied, it would be prognostically positive should Elizabeth spend her fury, such as by challenging me openly. In my experience, often the group initially takes on this task, functioning as the disturbed patient's auxiliary ego, putting her aggression—and mine—into a knowing, caring context.

Group efforts to modify aggression:

Member: Elizabeth, Richard is asking you what is going on to help you with your problems.
Therapist (frustrated): Elizabeth tells me to get lost.
Member: You shouldn't be impatient and short tempered.
Elizabeth: That's all right.
Therapist: Well, I guess I don't like being dissed.
Member: People have problems. That's why we're here.
Therapist: So what do you think Elizabeth's problems are, and how do they relate to yours?

Some depressed individuals feel relieved of their unconscious guilt and begin to interest themselves in the group when it becomes apparent that the leader is not frightened, wounded, or killed by criticism, disapproval, or direct attack. When patients are dealt with firmly, fairly, and not treated as fragile or fearsome objects, they sometimes reveal social dimensions of their personalities—humor, flirtatiousness, irony, curiosity.

However, such patients as Elizabeth may insist on making others responsible for their survival, act as if they are dead already, and fight therapeutic efforts to be brought back to life (Hendin, 1981). Any patient can defeat any therapist, and the therapist must accept one's own limits in motivation, skill, and strength. After an exhausting series of exchanges—expressed in the patient's silences, verbal or nonverbal rage, contempt, and so on—I might say, "Okay, I give. You win for today. I am a useless piece of shit."

In treating the treatment-destructive patient, the therapist must feel relatively comfortable feeling worthless and useless, guilty for being worthless and useless, and guilty for hating the patient for provoking these feelings. The group therapist's first goal is to preserve oneself, which means preserving a functional, interactional relational consciousness and unconsciousness (Billow, 2003). If the therapist's mentality is sinking, then the depressed member drowns, often taking the group with her.

Richard M. Billow, PhD

References

Billow, R. M. (1999). LHK: The basis of emotion in Bion's theory. *Contemporary Psychoanalysis, 35,* 629–646.

Billow, R. M. (2001). The class that would not read: Utilizing Bion's affect theory in group therapy. *International Journal of Group Psychotherapy, 51,* 309–326.

Billow, R. M. (2002). Passion in group: Thinking about loving, hating, and knowing. *International Journal of Group Psychotherapy, 52,* 355–372.

Billow, R. M. (2003). Rebellion in group. *International Journal of Group Psychotherapy, 53,* 331–351.

Freud, S. (1917). Mourning and melancholia. *Standard Edition, 14,* 239–260.

Hendin, H. (1981). Psychotherapy and suicide. *American Journal of Psychotherapy, 35,* 469–480.

Maltsberger, J. T. & Buie, D. H. (1973). Countertransference hate in the treatment of suicidal patients. *Archives of General Psychiatry, 30,* 625–633.

Yalom, I. D. (1995). *The theory and practice of group psychotherapy* (4th ed.). New York: Basic Books.

Dear Therapist:

In your dilemma, you raise three questions: Can a severely depressed person be treated in a group if he or she is the only one who is this depressed? Was this group composition doomed from the start? Were there other paths that the group leader may have taken?

In answering these questions, just as I do when leading my groups, I assume a pluralistic conceptual stance (Havens, 1987, pp. 328–330) that has two basic premises: (a) I feel more compelled by the needs of my patients than by any particular theory while, at the same time, (b) I place a high valuation on all theories and their methods and apply these methods according to the dictates of a given clinical situation.

Regarding this clinical vignette, I have called on neo-Freudian (Horney, 1950), psychodynamic (Rutan & Stone, 2001), and group dynamic theory (Scheidlinger, 1980) to guide my understanding and possible interventions.

The generic fashion in which the first question is raised makes it difficult to provide a definitive answer. Which group and which severely depressed person? In the group described, Elizabeth may have been too impaired to make good use of the group. Overwhelmed by caring for her new baby and older child, and in a marriage where she hid her depression from her husband, she may have been, at the time of her selection, a better candidate for individual or couples therapy. Did you consider these possibilities or did you suggest group therapy in order to fill a group slot or redress a gender imbalance in its composition? If either of these mistakes was made, Elizabeth's difficulties in the group, and the group's difficulties with her, may have been coconstructed (Gans & Alonso, 1998).

New groups differ considerably from established, stable groups. New groups, like the one described here, are more akin to a small crowd and it is only with the building of trust, safety, and cohesion that the assembled individuals become a group. In a new group, disproportionate pathology in one member—especially if that person's safety is involved—may necessitate the leader's attending to that person before a stable group structure is attained. In the process, the other members may feel sufficiently needy and neglected, as a result of which, destructive forces—the *anti-group*—may emerge (Nitsun, 1996). The fact that a durable group structure does not yet exist may preclude the therapeutic management of these forces, leading to premature terminations or annihilation of the group itself.

In response to the remaining questions posed, I think that the composition of this group did not doom it from the start. I also think that you could have taken other paths that may well have led to a more favorable outcome.

It may be instructive to review how I came to these conclusions. I noticed in reading your account of the group that I felt annoyed at and critical of you. In processing these reactions, I realized that underlying them was a sense that I would not feel safe being a member of this group conducted by you. This realization led me to speculate that members of the group were themselves also not feeling safe with you.

I will offer other ways you may have conceptualized what was transpiring in the group and interventions that you may have made. My comments will address a number of group dynamics including group culture, patient introductions, projective identification, and countertransference.

The group culture, apparently taking the lead from your preferences, appears to value doing more than being. You seem to prefer the group's successes to Elizabeth's depression. Although the word success is mentioned twice, the notion of "painful experiences" is first mentioned in week 18 of the group's 20-week existence. In addition, whereas the group offered Elizabeth "concern, support, advice, and pressure to seek individual therapy and psychopharmacology," no mention appears of the exploration and sharing of her emotional pain.

Other ways exist of understanding Elizabeth's presentation of herself as depressed that you do not help the group consider. Like most introductions, Elizabeth's is most likely not random. For example, it is likely that Elizabeth's depression is related to fundamental aspects of her past history, character, and defenses. Perhaps she learned to get attention in her family of origin by being sick and then rejecting help.

The group's reaction to Elizabeth's introduction could also be conceptualized in a variety of ways. Perhaps she is the "patient" that the other group members wish–fear to be. Although we are not told your gender, it is not uncommon for a group unconsciously to "serve up" a female patient for the male leader to cure. In this way, group members enact their fantasy of ultimately being cured by you as well. The group could also be "using" Elizabeth as a way of indirectly finding out more about the leader.

One thing the group learns is that you are frightened by the (apparent) severity of Elizabeth's depression, which perhaps explains your tendency to focus on Elizabeth as the only patient in the room (notice that we learn next to nothing about anyone else's difficulties). Your countertransference difficulty, and the reactions that result from it in turn, frighten the group. These reactions include your (a) acting as if Elizabeth is spoiling the otherwise "good" group; (b) feeling held hostage by Elizabeth's depression; (c) unconscious anger toward Elizabeth, which, through reaction formation (Gans, 1989), you turn into (necessarily ineffectual) caring; (d) acting out your anger by making Elizabeth the group scapegoat; (e) failing to intervene in ways that truly protect Elizabeth such as finding a subgroup that would join her (Agazarian, 1997); and (f) misjudging the degree of Elizabeth's suicidality.

A group-as-a-whole interpretation (Borriello, 1976) might well have released Elizabeth from the designated patient role and enabled the other group members to own their projections and work on their difficulties. A useful interpretation such as "This group would like to believe that Elizabeth has cornered the market on pathology in the group," would have addressed the primitive projective identifications that so frequently characterize this phase of group development. In the unconscious mechanism of projective identification, group members and, in this case, you as well, project their pathology into the designated "sick member" (Horwitz, 1983). Unlike projection, where the projectors stay away from the object of their projections, in projective identification, the projectors, certain that the pathology exists in the "sick" member and not in them, closely attend to the "sick" member in an attempt to cure that person. It may be the ultimate irony that Elizabeth, who is associated with the image of the nurturing breast, is experienced as the sickest member.

Initially, this new group may have needed to collude in the sacrifice of a fellow member in order to preserve the illusion of your competence. Soon, however, even this maneuver does not sufficiently bind their anxiety and four frightened members rationalize their need to leave (flee) the group. Perhaps their leave-taking is hastened by their ill-understood and guilty complicity in Elizabeth's sacrifice.

What I find most troublesome about this clinical example is the degree to which you have remained out of touch with your angry, perhaps murderous, feelings. Although all of us have our blind spots, I am heartened by the fact of your seeking consultation. I would also encourage you to consider personal therapy. Without active consultation and therapy, a danger exists that harm could inadvertently be done to vulnerable patients.

Jerome S. Gans, MD, CGP, FAGPA, DFAPA

References

Agazarian, Y. M. (1997), *Systems-centered therapy for groups*. New York: Guilford Press.

Borriello, J. F. (1976). Contrasting models of leadership in group psychotherapy: The group-as-a-whole model. *International Journal of Group Psychotherapy, 26*, 149–161.

Gans, J. S. (1989). Hostility in group psychotherapy. *International Journal of Group Psychotherapy, 39*, 499–516.

Gans, J. S., & Alonso, A. (1998). Difficult patients: Their construction in group psychotherapy. *International Journal of Group Psychotherapy, 48*, 311–326.

Havens, L. (1987). *Approaches to the mind*. Cambridge, MA: Harvard University Press.

Horney, K. (1950). *Neurosis and human growth*. New York: Norton.

Horwitz, L. (1983). Projective identification in dyads and groups. *International Journal of Group Psychotherapy, 33*, 259–279.

Nitsun, M. (1996). *The Anti-group: Destructive forces in the group and their creative potential*. London: Routledge.

Rutan, J. S., & Stone, W. N. (2001). *Psychodynamic group psychotherapy* (3rd ed.). New York & London: Guilford Press.

Scheidlinger, S. (Ed.). (1980). *Psychoanalytic group dynamics*. New York: International Universities Press.

Section V
Powerful Therapist Reactions

Overview

In the movie *What About Bob?* Bob becomes the nightmare patient. Initially compliant, he panics when his therapist goes on vacation, so he stalks and harasses him throughout his summer vacation. The therapist, Dr. Marvin, becomes increasingly derailed and enraged by Bob's behavior, and at one point actually contemplates blowing him up. Although the movie is hilarious, most therapists have experienced the intense feelings that patients like Bob can evoke.

In her chapter *Containing and Using Powerful Therapist Reactions*, Eleanor Counselman traces the history of countertransference, enumerates common countertransference reactions, and notes sources of countertransference in group therapy.

In *Legally Incompetent?* the therapist has to grapple with feelings of sadism and murderous rage after he merges two differentially functioning groups into one and a group member challenges him about his competence. Consultants Sally Barlow and Shawn Taylor remind the therapist that research has proven that group therapy works, and what breeds success in group therapy is careful pre-group screening and preparation. Then, using a Lacanian lens and framing his response with a fable, Macario Giraldo argues that it is an intersubjective encounter of analyst and analysand which frees desire.

In *Fear and Loathing*, the therapist, feeling ashamed and humiliated when the group members criticize her, comes to dread the very group she has created. Consultant Barry Helfmann sees the therapist caught in a projective identification with the group where members want her to meet their dependency needs. He encourages the leader to seek ongoing supervision to sort out her countertransference so that she can respond more effectively. Robert Klein acknowledges the therapist's countertransference, but believes she needs to allow the group members to express and explore their rage at her without fear that the group will implode. After all, "No matter how much groups wish to overthrow or destroy us, they also need us and try to protect and preserve us."

The therapist in *Tolerating the Intolerable* wonders whether she should continue working with a patient who openly expresses bigotry in the group and who, thereby, stirs strong countertransference reactions in the therapist. Consultant Allan Elfant argues that the seven previous years of political correctness in the group have been stultifying and that with this group member the group has a golden opportunity for "vigorous group engagement, exchange, and inquiry." Harold Bernard suggests the therapist first consider whether she has lost her empathy toward the patient and, second, whether the patient has irreparably damaged the group climate. He sees either situation as potentially destructive to the patient and to the group.

Containing and Using Powerful Therapist Reactions

ELEANOR F. COUNSELMAN, EDD, CGP, FAGPA, ABPP

Therapists are people. They have feelings and sometimes experience powerful emotional reactions in response to their patients. Group therapy complicates the picture as therapists experience powerful reactions toward a member, a subgroup, or a whole group. Although therapist reactions were once seen as experiences to analyze and get past, current psychodynamic thinking values the therapist's reactions as an instructive and even central aspect of the therapeutic relationship. This chapter will review the development of psychodynamic thinking about therapist reactions, examine the particular effect of group dynamics on them, describe some common therapist reactions in group therapy, and discuss effective containment and utilization.

I will call therapist reactions "countertransference," using the term in its broadest sense as defined by Fromm-Reichmann (1950, cited in Hayes, 1995) and Kernberg (1984): all of the therapist's conscious and unconscious reactions to a client. I include any powerful cognitive, affective, or behavioral reaction that a therapist experiences during or in relation to a therapy group (individual member, dyad, subgroup, or whole group). In other words, I will focus on those reactions created by the intersection of a piece of "group business" (including individual member behavior) and the therapist's personality. Most, although not all, powerful therapist reactions result from the interaction between the individual or group dynamics and the therapist's own self and object relations. Therapist reaction is a huge topic, and I will of necessity omit reactions stimulated by co-leadership, by the therapist's outside life (such as illness, family issues), and by large system events that impact the therapist and members from outside the group (such as hospital or clinic policies or the events of 9/11).

Effective therapists process their reactions constantly. They must be able to be both engaged in an interpersonal dynamic and simultaneously observe it. The emotional reactions I will discuss in this chapter are the ones that stand out, either by their presence or by their absence, that catch a therapist by surprise, or that create a strongly alien ("that's not me") experience in the therapist.

Is countertransference important in psychodynamic group therapy? Although the transference–countertransference relationship between patient and therapist is typically not as intense in group therapy as it is in individual treatment, the multiple transferences and countertransferences in group therapy are all opportunities for important learning. I agree with Roth that "the group therapist can analyze the group only through his ability to analyze the complex individual and group countertransference dynamics" (1990, p. 287).

History of countertransference

Freud viewed countertransference basically as an obstacle to treatment, needing to be overcome. He saw it as the analyst's transference to the patient and wrote to Jung in 1911 that "we must never let our poor neurotics drive us crazy" (Gabbard, 1999). He wrote little on the subject of countertransference throughout his long career. This view of countertransference began to change in the mid-20th century. Winnicott (1949) suggested the idea of an "objective countertransference" in which the therapist reacts to the patient just like everyone else: that is, not as a reaction to the patient's particular transference or the therapist's unanalyzed past. (Winnicott's idea of the objective countertransference seems particularly relevant to group therapy with its "hall of mirrors" opportunities. Although potential for much transference and countertransference work exists, the fact that six or eight people in the room all have the same reaction to a member suggests a certain reality basis for the reaction.) The next year Paula Heimann (1950, cited in Gabbard, 1999) made the revolutionary suggestion that therapists' reactions can be *important* and *useful* for the therapy, rather than an impediment to be overcome.

Racker's (1968) seminal writing on countertransference separated countertransference into "concordant" and "complementary." Concordant countertransference is an empathic identification with the patient. Rutan and Stone (2001) would call this "parallel affect" as the therapist empathically experiences what the patient is not able to articulate. Paying attention to one's reveries, rather than dismissing them as wandering attention, is key to learning about parallel affect. In groups, leaders may experience parallel affect to an individual member or to the group-as-a-whole. For example, a feeling of boredom on the part of the leader may be resonating with a group experience of stagnation that is outside the members' awareness. Parallel affect is an amplification process of what is in the patient or group, not what has been disavowed.

Complementary countertransference occurs when the analyst identifies with a disavowed part of the patient's self that has been projected. In this case, Racker felt, the analyst's own conflicts were activated. Grinberg (1979) distinguished between complementary countertransference (the patient's projection links with the analyst's unconscious conflicts) and "projective counteridentification" (what the analyst introjects comes almost entirely from the patient). The latter concept is hard to imagine without some existing hook in the analyst, unless one sees analysts as empty vessels waiting to be filled.

Kernberg (1984) believed that countertransference could be considered on a temporal basis. He described three types of reactions: short-lived or acute; long-term, gradually built distortions; and finally, those countertransference reactions that are based on the therapist's character pathology. In order to work with the transference, the therapist must be able to sort out the patient's realistic and unrealistic views of him or her. Unanalyzed countertransference limits this process. Kernberg underscored that the therapist's personality is an inevitable part of any treatment, despite efforts at technical neutrality; in fact, "Patients hang the fabric of their transference on protuberances of the analyst's personality" (1984, p. 266).

Gabbard reviewed the psychoanalytic literature on countertransference and concluded that the classical and the Kleinian analytic positions have converged to agree that "countertransference represents a joint creation that involves contributions from both analyst and analysand" (1995, p. 481). Although the analyst is inevitably drawn into a patient-conscripted role, its exact dimensions are also determined by the analyst.

Theory about countertransference in group therapy has developed along similar lines, increasingly emphasizing countertransference as an important ingredient in group work. Bion (1961) was the first analyst to write about a psychodynamic theory of group therapy, with its powerful unconscious life of transferences and countertransferences. Foulkes (1964, cited in Hayes, 1995) subsequently wrote that every group "bears the stamp of its therapist, reflecting his own conflicts and blind spots" indicating the effect of the therapist's own unresolved conflicts. Examples of common conflicts would include need for approval, power and authority struggles, unresolved family issues, separation and individuation concerns, and abandonment fears (Hayes, 1995). Durkin (1975, cited in Tuttman, 1993) applied system theory to group therapy and noted the interaction between group members' individual dynamics and the overall group dynamics. She felt that transference and countertransference operated between each member and the leader, between the members as siblings, and in the group-as-a-whole. Over time, transference and countertransference have come to be seen as always present in group therapy as group therapists receive multiple projections and role conscriptions from the different group members and also from the group-as-a-whole. Effective group therapists work hard to understand the many reactions, and the importance of ongoing self-analysis cannot be overemphasized.

Common countertransference reactions

What are common countertransference reactions? Any human emotion can find its way into countertransference. Because most therapists prefer to think of themselves as kind, competent, and rational people, it is usually the darker emotions such as hate, shame, and envy that cause problems. Winnicott's (1949) classic paper on hate in the countertransference reminded analysts that hate is part of the analytic process. Although his focus was what he called "objective hate" with psychotic patients, he also indicated that hate is part of treating neurotics. In the latter case, he noted that, assuming the analyst has dealt with past personal issues, most hate remains latent but sublimated into the positive aspects of the work as well as "the existence of the end of the hour" (1949, p. 71). Making the argument for motherly hate as well as motherly love, he said that analysts, like mothers, must tolerate their hate without acting on it.

Shame is another powerful countertransference reaction. It is sometimes felt directly and sometimes defended against with anger or with therapist grandiosity and perfectionism. Hahn (1995) felt that shame could be triggered without overt criticism of the leader and argued for more open expression of anger by the leader. MacNab (1995) wrote movingly about his experience of shame as a group leader. His countertransference was that of the group savior, capable of surmounting any obstacle to the therapy. When he could not "save" a particular member, he felt overwhelmed by the shame of the failure. Gans (1989) wrote of the countertherapeutic interaction between therapists' conscious and unconscious needs to "know all and heal all" and the group members' wishes for an omniscient, omnipotent leader. Stark (1995) similarly noted the perils of acceding to patients' relentless hope that the (perfect) therapist will give them what they lacked in their own mothering. The inevitable disappointment that therapy cannot entirely compensate for earlier damage is part of the work. She pointed out that therapists, who often experienced inadequate mothering themselves, are vulnerable to this particular reparative countertransference. Group therapists may express this countertransference by being relentlessly "nice," by allowing groups to run overtime, and by avoiding feelings about ways in which they deprive their groups (e.g., by taking vacations).

Group therapy is particularly suited to stimulate therapist shame. The pull toward being the idealized selfobject is magnified compared to individual treatment. How seductive to be the perfect therapist in front of eight admiring patients; how devastating to fail! Although mistakes and failures in individual treatment usually feel private, the group setting offers more public exposure and potential humiliation. Beginning group therapists typically worry a great deal about this issue. A billing mistake, an incorrect interpretation, a lapse in attention are all fodder for the group, and a sadistic group can make a therapist squirm. Therapist shame is not always just about the therapist, though. It can also be the result of projective identification by a shame-disavowing group or an empathic countertransference resonating with a group struggling with shame.

Countertransference can operate in the area of diversity. Therapists may have unconscious expectations of group members based on ethnicity, gender, or other differences. For instance, gender-related countertransference may create unconscious expectations that are different for men and women (Bernardez, 1996). Group therapists may expect the "feminine" expressions of sadness, inadequacy, and tenderness from the women and the "masculine" expressions of anger, competition, sexual desire, and power from the men. If this expectation is not brought to consciousness, then the group members' compliance to their societal roles will go unexplored. Although therapists like to think of themselves as unbiased, it is probably wise to maintain some uncertainty in this area, as societal training is old and deep.

Trauma groups, or simply treating a traumatized individual in a regular group, can create powerful therapist countertransference. The two major types of countertransference when working with trauma are overidentification and avoidance. Therapists also frequently experience a strong pull into a perpetrator role. Zeigler and McEvoy saw countertransference to trauma survivors in positive terms: as "a primary source of insight and compassion into the victim's past experience and present reality. Thus countertransference responses are route-finding markers that can be used to guide therapeutic interventions in a grounded and timely way" (Zeigler & McEvoy, cited in Klein & Schermer, 2000, p. 117). However, they note the danger of vicarious traumatization, or compassion fatigue, and stress the importance of self-care and personal reflection.

Sources of countertransference in groups

One of the challenges of group therapy is that countertransference can originate from many sources. Roth (1990) summed it up: "Counter-transference in a particular group therapy situation is a function of the particular group therapist, the mix of patients in the group, their particular state at the moment, and the therapist's theory of technique and style of leadership, and what he or she may actually be doing in the group setting" (p. 289). Group therapists must notice and analyze multiple pieces of data on the verbal and nonverbal levels: gestures, nuances, silences, latenesses, and the like, and multiple transferences are embedded in virtually every group event. This complicated mix is the basis for the leader's counter-transference. Vannicelli (1989) has likened it to the resonance that occurs in an orchestra with many instruments, as different from the sound of a single instrument.

Although it is a somewhat artificial distinction and certainly an over-simplification, it seems useful to separate countertransference sources into intrapsychic and group dynamics.

Intrapsychic Intrapsychic therapist reactions occur when the therapist's issues are activated either directly, by triggering unresolved conflicts, or indirectly through projective identification. Rutan and Stone (2001) note that therapists have different personalities and bear different transferences differently. For instance, some need to be loved and idealized, whereas others are more comfortable with hate and aggression. "The first place to look when a therapist experiences powerful affect is to the self . . . . If therapists find themselves preoccupied with powerful feelings, including love, hate, or envy, because the patient is reminiscent of an important and ambivalently held figure from their past, it is their responsibility to work through that feeling" (Rutan & Stone, 2001, p. 184). They note that sometimes it is the group that first alerts a therapist to an unusually powerful and unique reaction.

Projective identification refers to a process in which the patient projects a disavowed aspect of self into the therapist and then places considerable interpersonal pressure on the therapist to accept the projection. The therapist contains and processes the projection, ultimately allowing the patient to take back the projection in a modified form. Group therapists are aware that projective identification can occur between members as well and underlies the phenomenon of scapegoating. It is generally agreed that successful projective identification requires the existence of a "hook" in the recipient. Gabbard (1995) wrote, "Even when the countertransference response is experienced by analysts as an alien force sweeping over them, what is actually happening is that a repressed self- or object-representation has been activated by the interpersonal pressure of the patient. Hence the analyst's usual sense of a familiar, continuous self has been disrupted by the emergence of these repressed aspects of the self" (p. 477).

Sandler (1987, 1993, cited in Gabbard, 1995) cautioned against viewing all intense therapist reactions as projective identification (i.e., induced by the patient). Sandler believed that some intense therapist reactions were role-responsiveness, an empathically based mirroring process that is not the same as projective identification. This concept is particularly salient in group countertransference, as groups recreate family dynamics and members pressure leaders into historically significant roles.

Roth (1990) noted the problem for the group therapist of containing multiple empathic identifications. The therapist must identify with both the wishes and the defenses against them, and with both the reality-based object relations and the infantile-driven ones. He felt that a "bifurcation" is required and that an introspective stance that disallows complete certainty is vital for maintaining the bifurcation. Failure to remain introspective and uncertain leads to countertransference reactions.

Countertransference enactments are those instances when transference and countertransference aspects that are outside of conscious awareness interact. They may be small, perhaps nonverbal, acts of behavior. Current relational and intersubjectivity theories agree on the inevitability and usefulness of countertransference enactments.

Unexplored group contract violations are likely examples of countertransference enactments. Contract breaches are inevitable and examining them is a central part of psychodynamic group work. When a therapist does not point out the violation and invite curiosity about it, one suspects an enactment. Understanding such enactments can provide valuable insight into the therapy.

A final intrapsychic note: Over time, what Rutan and Stone (2001) call a "genuine human relationship" develops between therapist and patient. This does not mean they go out for coffee together but that the relationship itself triggers real feelings in the therapist. When a patient has a triumph, the therapist feels genuinely happy (but scans for anything else lurking there). Far from being a countertransference to resolve, these feelings make a therapist's job rewarding.

Group dynamics Hayes' (1995) review of the group therapy countertransference literature identified group composition and group stage as significant contributors to countertransference. Group composition includes individuals, subgroups, and whole groups. Groups formed around a particular theme (e.g., gender, trauma, substance abuse) have tremendous countertransference material. For example, Vannicelli (1989) wrote of the powerful potential for countertransference in leading ACOA groups, saying that she believes that to some extent all therapists are "adult children," seeking to address dysfunction in their family of origin. Therapists who choose to lead these groups should think carefully about their motivations for doing so and be particularly alert for signs of countertransference.

Group stages, with their different salient issues, can create powerful leader reactions. They may occur in pre-group screening, when a leader with an unfilled group may unconsciously overlook contraindications and may "seduce" a potential member. Competitive issues with other group therapists may create a strong wish to be liked best.

An early form of countertransference is what the group therapist expects for each patient. As Roth (1990) noted, most patients come to group with certain expectations, both conscious and unconscious, usually based on their childhood and unresolved issues. Therapists need to be aware of their corresponding, and possibly induced, expectations for these patients—an early countertransference reaction. Another instance of early expectations would be the potential countertransference involved in taking over an existing group (Counselman & Weber, 2002).

An early stage group, the "dependency" group, could stimulate a therapist's issues around group passivity and being needed. Idealization of leaders is common in early stage groups, and therapists are sorely tempted to believe in it. Also, members at this stage are often ambivalent about becoming involved with each other, and therapist countertransference can allow avoidance of the ambivalence (Brabender, 1987). "Fight or flight" groups often trigger authority reactions in response to the challenges. Groups that are working toward greater autonomy may stimulate fears of not being needed, with a resulting (defensive) increase in leader activity. Groups that have achieved a high degree of intimacy may well create loneliness in the leader (Liebenberg, 2002). Single member or whole group terminations can stir up abandonment issues and defenses against them, as well as real, noncountertransference reactions. Brabender (1987) offered an important reminder that although in individual therapy the therapist's countertransference reaction to a termination does not enter into post-termination treatment, it does in group therapy. A leader may act out a countertransference reaction to a departed member with the remaining group members.

Working with countertransference

The first step in working with countertransference is to become aware of the reaction. What constitutes a "powerful" reaction is of course somewhat subjective and dependent on the therapist's normal way of functioning—and it is important to remember that the *absence* of a reaction can be a powerful reaction as well. Vannicelli (1989) listed the following as indications of possible countertransference: a change of attitude toward the patient that somehow feels sudden or unexplained, preoccupation with a patient or group, feelings of exhaustion or stuckness, a fixed response to the patient or group in spite of new data, inappropriate affective responses, and changes in the therapeutic contract (e.g., therapist lateness or not challenging patients on contract violations).

Hayes (1995) described several countertransference reactions unique to group therapy. Therapists may overly control group interaction because of unconscious fear of conflict, or perform individual therapy in the group setting because of a wish to control, play favorites, not uphold the contract, or participate in scapegoating.

Self-awareness—noticing one's emotions, bodily tension, distractions, associations—is a necessary ingredient for identifying countertransference. Many therapists practice self-awareness enhancing techniques such as meditation, yoga, journal keeping, and, of course, personal psychotherapy. A balanced life and good self-care also increase one's capacities for awareness and containment.

In addition to internal self-awareness, therapists should wonder about any deviations from customary leader behavior. The group contract and challenges to that boundary are a common and important ground for countertransference expression. Therapists who don't raise contract violations for group discussion or who break the contract themselves are probably operating from countertransference. Groups with clear group contracts provide a platform for exploration of the inevitable (and expected) violations, and therapists who avoid these opportunities should ask themselves why. The situation is often murkier in individual treatment where contracts are often less clear.

Other times, the group will point out a therapist's reaction as unusual. Wise group therapists pay attention when a member, or even several members, comment on the therapist's reaction. This "chorus" is a major advantage over individual therapy in checking for countertransference. Groups can also make their point more indirectly through group behavior as in the following brief example:

> A group therapist found herself unavoidably delayed in getting to her group on time. By the time she got there, 10 minutes late, she was quite upset about her lateness. She apologized profusely and explained what had happened. The group assured her that they understood. The group process then ground to a halt, despite some attempts at work. The leader, who had calmed down, realized that her apology had been countertransferentially determined by her wish to avoid the group's disapproval and anger. She wondered

aloud if she had squashed any feelings by apologizing so readily. Many feelings (criticism, anger, abandonment) then emerged, and the group resumed useful work.

The therapist must decide whether the source of the reaction is internal (old issues have been triggered), external (patient- or group-created affect), or (less likely) from the genuine relationship. If external, are the feelings empathic resonance or projective identification? Are they related to group composition, stage, or even a recent group event? This analysis is not easy given how much happens in group. However, the difficulty is balanced by the fact that group is a superb place to work out projective identification because of the opportunities for validation with the members. Rutan and Stone (2001) note that projective identification is very powerful and therefore most group members will be experiencing it, not just the therapist.

The second step in working with countertransference is what to do with the reaction. This step is less important than the first because the crucial work of countertransference is identifying and understanding its sources. It is in this process that new information about the group and its various members emerges. Thus, the best thing to *do* with countertransference is to *be* with it. The greater understanding that results will inform ensuing therapeutic actions.

A discussion of countertransference would be incomplete without mention of self-disclosure (see Section VI in this book). Of course, all therapists inevitably self-disclose in their speech, dress, and office décor. However, disclosure of affect is more complicated. It can be clinically useful (Counselman, 1997) and can model healthy sharing of feelings to patients who have not seen that. Times appear when it would be inappropriate not to disclose feelings—for example, when a patient has experienced a profound loss or great joy—but in general, there is wisdom in restraint, particularly in groups where a therapist's reaction can have a different meaning to each group member. As a rule, in psychodynamic groups more is learned from the transferential projections than from therapist disclosure.

Someone once asked Wilfred Bion how he handled countertransference. It is said that he replied, "When I am aware of it, I try and use it somehow" (Roth, 1990, p. 288). That is good advice for us all.

References

Bernardez, T. (1996). Gender-based countertransference in the group treatment of women. In B. DeChant (Ed.), *Women and group psychotherapy* (pp. 400–424). New York: Guilford Press.

Bion, W. R. (1961). *Experiences in groups.* London: Tavistock.

Brabender, V. M. (1987). Vicissitudes of countertransference in inpatient group psychotherapy. *International Journal of Group Psychotherapy, 37,* 549–567.

Counselman, E. F. (1997). Self-disclosure, tears, and the dying client. *Psychotherapy, 34,* 233–237.

Counselman, E. F., & Weber, R. L. (2002). Changing the guard: New leadership for an established group. *International Journal of Group Psychotherapy, 52,* 373–386.

Epstein, L. (1977). The therapeutic function of hate in the countertransference. *Contemporary Psychoanalysis, 13,* 442–468.

Gabbard, G. O. (1995). Countertransference: The emerging common ground. *International Journal of Psycho-Analysis, 76,* 475–485.

Gabbard, G. O. (Ed.). (1999). *Countertransference issues in psychiatric treatment.* Washington, DC: American Psychiatric Press.

Gans, J. S. (1989). Hostility in group psychotherapy. *International Journal of Group Psychotherapy, 39,* 499–516.

Grinberg, L. (1979). Projective counteridentification and countertransference. In L. Epstein. & A. H. Feiner, (Eds.), *Countertransference* (pp. 169–193). New York: Aronson.

Hahn, K. (1995). Therapist anger in group psychotherapy. *International Journal of Group Psychotherapy, 45,* 339–347.

Hayes, J. A. (1995). Countertransference in group psychotherapy: Waking a sleeping dog. *International Journal of Group Psychotherapy, 45,* 521–535.

Kaplan, H. I., & Sadock, B. J. (1993). *Comprehensive group psychotherapy.* Baltimore: Williams & Wilkins.

Kernberg, O. (1984). *Severe personality disorders.* New Haven: Yale.

Klein, R. H., & Schermer, V. L. (2000*) Group psychotherapy for psychological trauma.* New York: Guilford Press.

Liebenberg, B. (2002). Faded photographs and pressed flowers: Reflections on the institute. *International Journal of Group Psychotherapy, 52,* 131–138.

MacNab, R. T. (1995). Public exposure of shame in the group leader. In M. B. Sussman, (Ed.), *A perilous calling: The hazards of psychotherapy practice* (pp. 110–125). New York: Wiley.

Roth, B. E. (1990). Countertransference and the group therapist's state of mind. In B. E. Roth, W. N. Stone, & H. D. Kibel (Eds.), *The difficult patient in group* (pp. 287–294). Madison, CT: International Universities Press.

Rutan, J. S., & Stone, W. N. (2001). *Psychodynamic group psychotherapy* (3rd ed.). New York: Guilford Press.

Stark, M. (1995). The therapist as recipient of the patient's relentless entitlement. In M. B. Sussman, (Ed.), *A perilous calling: The hazards of psychotherapy practice* (pp. 188–199). New York: Wiley.

Tuttman, S. (1993). Countertransference and transference in groups. In H. I. Kaplan & B. J. Sadock (Eds.), *Comprehensive group psychotherapy* (pp. 98–105). Baltimore: Williams & Wilkins.

Vannicelli, M. (1989*). Group psychotherapy with adult children of alcoholics.* New York: Guilford Press.

Winnicott, D. W. (1949). Hate in the counter-transference. *International Journal of Psychoanalysis, 30,* 69–74.

Legally Incompetent?

Dear Consultant:

I am struggling with a constant feeling of incompetence in one of my groups. This is unusual for me, but at times, I think it is deserved because some of my interventions have been, even to my eye, weak if not actually mean-spirited. There's something about this group that triggers comments from me that I'm not proud of. Because this forum is anonymous, I am willing to share them with you, hoping to better understand how this has emerged.

This weekly group of men and women has seats for ten members, which I know is large, but rarely have all ten members shown up at the same time. The age span is about 30 years, from 25 to 55, and the members range from halfway house patient, Marie, experiencing bipolar disorder to lawyer, Jim, experiencing job loss precipitated depression. So, the psychopathology ranges from severe to moderate, with essentially two subgroups of patients, namely, the more severely impaired who don't function well on a daily basis and the less impaired whose everyday lives are relatively successful. I should admit at this point that this is the case because, a year ago, I merged two of my groups when each dropped to three members.

From the start, I found it hard to deal with this mix of individuals, because some of what I thought were my better interventions—metaphors pitched at a reasonably high level—were met with confusion by some of the patients and disdain by others. Rarely did I feel I was speaking to the entire group, or more to the point, rarely did I feel the entire group was listening to me.

Then, Jim, the most intelligent member of the group—and a litigator—began to challenge my interventions on a weekly basis. He accused me of creating too large a group just for the money (which had a grain of truth to it) trying to be too clever by half leaving members like Marie puzzled and failing to improve his understanding of why he had been let go from his firm. This made me very angry, but I tried to hide my feelings with a professional demeanor and encouragement to Jim to keep sharing.

However, I didn't stop there. On one occasion, I found myself subtly inciting other group members to go after Jim. I made such comments as, "I wonder why the group allows Jim to take the floor all the time? Are people reluctant to tell me they agree with him, or to tell him that he's embarrassing himself with his aggression?" After making these comments, I winced internally, thinking, what am I doing? Unfortunately, the group rewarded me by taking Jim on, and challenging his attacks on me as wasting time and not giving them enough time to describe their own issues. Surprising to me, Marie often sided with Jim, even though I always felt warmly toward her and expressed it in the group. Momentarily, I would feel betrayed by Marie, and grateful to the other group members who defended me.

Within a few weeks, they were no longer defending me, but had joined Jim in the form of expressing dissatisfaction with their lack of progress. Jim's smug expression engendered fantasies in me of impaling him on my letter opener. I was then resorting to interventions such as, "The group is having a hard time letting my comments be useful to it." Several group members mentioned that they thought I sounded angry, but I typically interpreted these comments as projections of their own anger, perhaps at me, perhaps at other group members. Week after week I watched myself hoping that Jim would quit, because I viewed him as the ringleader. Week after week I entered the group with trepidation and left with anger and a sense of helplessness and failure. How did I get here? What can I do with my strong feelings, which are clearly being read by the group despite my attempts to hide them?

Dear Therapist:
All of us who conduct group therapy know firsthand the potential pitfalls as well as triumphs of this complicated endeavor. In fact, most good group therapists have had to learn to deal with mistakes in fruitful ways because we are sure to make them. We are two clinician–professor–researchers who have responded to your dilemma from a psychodynamic point of view.

Here are the main points: an adult outpatient group of women and men formed from two previous groups—one high functioning the other lower functioning—meeting weekly; an unusual feeling of incompetence for an experienced therapist as well as feelings of trepidation, anger, helplessness, and failure; member dissatisfaction; lack of progress; and an apparent mismatch between low and high functioning members.

Perhaps we should begin with the irrefutable proof that group therapy works. At least you aren't engaged in a futile endeavor! For almost 100 years group psychotherapy has been empirically examined from an array of angles: therapist–leader influence, group structure, member roles, member and leader nonspecific effects or common factors, and finally, leader and member specific effects (Barlow, Fuhriman, & Burlingame, 2000). From all of these angles, group process and outcome researchers have been able to examine the components of successful group psychotherapy; that is, groups wherein members get better by therapy's end and stay better (maintain their gains at 6-month follow-up). What might be the main culprits in your dilemma from the perspective of both research and psychodynamics?

Group structure
Composition and pre-group training are key issues in successful groups: how we prepare the members for their group experience; whom we refer to a group; what the likely combination of individuals will be; when, where, and for how long we are meeting; and the size of the group, expectations regarding adding new members, and the like. These structural elements are often overlooked because we aren't always in control of them. Outpatient psychotherapy groups appear to work best when members are carefully referred, the group consists of seven to nine members, the members meet approximately once a week for 1 to 2 hours, and have clear boundaries about inside versus outside group behavior—including consistent attendance and when to join or leave the group.

Perhaps your first mistake was combining the two former groups based on your convenience rather than the benefit for the members. Members at two different developmental levels will likely have different reactions to this disruption. Your interpretations (uncovering and observing character patterns) for the lower functioning members might be too destabilizing, just as your strong unacknowledged feelings can be. You must analyze reactions to these subgroups, as well as the reactions to each individual member and the group-as-a-whole.

It's not that groups haven't been combined before—it happens all the time in all kinds of agencies and private practices, but combined groups have a better chance to cohere when the therapist reinterviews all the members and tells them what they might expect from this reconstituted group. Had you actually begun a "new group"—where everyone went through the usual introductions and forming stages before moving on to deeper work —this would have set the stage for appropriate "storming" (dealing with conflicting needs) and "performing" (examining underlying motives). That is, dealing with conflict and hard work cannot follow if proper "forming" and "norming" haven't occurred (to use the group stage language of Tuckman, 1965).

Many of the difficulties you are now experiencing come from this problem with structure. Many group leaders groan at the extra time it will take to prepare members for a new group. But according to the research, even a 15 minute interview will do—asking what top three issues the client wants to work on; telling the client how this new group might be able to help with those goals; and inducting the client into a member role that includes awareness of people at different levels of functioning, and where he or she might expect to give or receive help. Even though reconstituted groups will still have their differences, the members feel more equipped to tackle them. The 2 or 3 hours this might take are well worth the investment.

Group dynamics

You are brave to be so honest. Consultation is essential for successful psychotherapy. The wonderful consequence of mistakes is that almost always they represent a patchwork of enactments. For instance, group members at different developmental levels vie to understand each other and compete for fulfillment of needs. Group leaders "do their best" under the circumstances, and instead of being appreciated, they are attacked: A group member ridicules you because the parent–leader is not meeting his needs. In this case, Jim may be accurately sensing your mistakes, but is still too raw from his recent firing; he may want you to be fired too! Of what is all this a repetition? What each of us brings to the interpersonal matrix creates the rich texture of group process, the very purpose for meeting. Perhaps in this group, the members were far too stirred up from what appears to be an ascendancy of your needs over their own that they could not observe their own and others' enactments, the analysis of which brings insight.

So, what might you consider now that you are already in the soup? Consider reinterviewing all the members, eliciting excitement for the new group. If this is not possible for some of the individuals, they could be placed on a waiting list and referred to individual therapy while another group is organized. If this doesn't seem feasible, initiate a discussion in the ongoing group about the current problem.

You must walk a fine line between being overly apologetic and inappropriately defensive. For instance, Jim is already having too much trouble with his aggressive affects and possibly feeling too powerful. If you take *too much* responsibility, Jim as well as the other members will not feel safe. If you take *too little* responsibility, the group will continue as it has been. The introduction might go something like this: "My role as leader and some of the choices I have made recently have had an impact on you. As you know, I put two groups together, which may have made group members feel like only numbers. Marie and Jim seem particularly displeased with me and I wonder if there are others."

Processing these comments could help group members separate out their own anger ("Why isn't this group working?"), envy ("Why do some people seem better than me?"), and enactments ("Why do I seem to get stuck in the same roles in here?") from other members' projections. Then, "Here's what I think you can do for each other even though you might be on different levels," delivers a message of hope regarding how the unique properties of group allow members to both give and receive help from each other, and to learn how other people think and feel even though they may be very different. "If you still believe we are too different, perhaps we should return to the two former groups? I will encourage my colleagues to refer more members so that you won't have to do all the work," which is often what happens in three-member groups—either that or individual therapy with an audience.

Jim appears to be right-on with his accusations. Maybe part of his character stance is "the voice of truth"—and it might be the unregulated use of this pounding veracity that gets him in trouble at work. What a great thing to work on! You will be far more able to do this once you have invited the group to re-examine the soup they're in and turn it into a more viable group. We all experience anger and countertransference—the key is to feel free enough from enactments or fast enough to recognize them when they do occur to engage members in fruitful examination.

Sally H. Barlow, PhD, CGP, ABPP, ABGP
Shawn M. Taylor, PhD

References

Barlow, S., Fuhriman, A., & Burlingame, G. (2000). The therapeutic application of groups: From Pratt's "thought control classes" to modern group psychotherapy. *Group Dynamics, 4*, 115–134.

Tuckman, B. (1965). Developmental sequence in small groups. *Psychological Bulletin, 63*, 384–399.

Dear Therapist:
As the army of the birds prepares to fight against the army of the beasts in Aesop's fable, "The Bat, the Birds, and the Beasts," members of each group passing by approach the bat and ask him to join them. The bat, however, hesitates and tells each group in turn, "I am a beast" to the birds, and "I am a bird" to the beasts.

Peace prevails and on this news the bat asks the birds if he can join them but they make him fly away. Then he goes to the beasts with a similar request but he has to retreat before being torn to pieces. "Ah," said the bat, "I see now that he that is neither one thing nor the other has no friends."

We could say to the bat, though, that they saw in him the absent friend. That neither of them knew about the other half of themselves as part beast or part bird, and could it be that the brief encounter of each army with the hesitant bat was the key to their making peace with each other? If so we could add that the bat is also repressed and that leads him to the false conclusion that he has no friends because he cannot come to terms with his true nature as bird *and* beast. Perhaps the therapist in this group is like the bat in the fable caught between the birds and the beasts. In this situation it is tempting but fatal to opt for the solution of being only a beast or only a bird.

In Freudian psychoanalysis as emphasized by Lacan, the analyst is seen by the patient as *the subject who is supposed to know*. The patient frequently expects the therapist to make him complete, a full ego, a full self. This is the *imaginary* realm of Lacan, but a full self in the Lacanian way of thinking is always a false self. It is not a good guide. It is the call of the Sirens. The place that Lacan assigns the therapist is the position of the *object of desire*. This object of desire, however, points to the human being's basic *lack of being*, part presence, part absence. Desire is fundamentally desire of the other's desire, desire to be desired. Lacan is talking here about unconscious desire, connected with a lack of the object, not with the actual object of object relations.

To assist us to sail between the Scylla and the Charybdis of the ego is the *symbolic*. It is in the word, the symbol, like in classical Freudian theory, where repression acts. The interpretation that frees the desire hidden in the unconscious is an intersubjective encounter of analyst and analysand: "It is only once it is formulated, named in the presence of the other, that desire, whatever it is, is recognized in the full sense of the term" (Lacan, 1988, p. 183).

From a Lacanian perspective, this dilemma brings out a most interesting paradox. On the one hand, something was missed in the formation of this group. Something was absent. On the other hand, the immediacy, the urgency of the feelings in the group as experienced by you, the therapist, points to an overwhelming presence. The feeling of trepidation that you face before each session, this bodily sensation, is an indication of what Lacan calls *the real*, that which has not yet been mentated, symbolized, and in this case, something that points to a traumatic experience in the group.

Let us look at the dilemma from this brief presentation of some of Lacan's ideas. To begin with, you say: "This is unusual for me" (the feeling of incompetence). So here some hope exists, that you usually feel like a good bird. But now in this group you feel like a beast. You are interested to find out how this whole thing has emerged. Again this is hopeful. And you are glad this forum is anonymous. Your wish for privacy may point to some basic threat to the safety of the self as the beast is mobilized in the group. This basic narcissism, of course, has to do with an early sense of one being the only object of mother's desire. There is nobody else but me.

You note that you have never felt that "the entire group was listening to me." But why should that be the case? After all, from your description I can identify at least three groups, if not four: the two original groups represented by three members left in each group; the third group is, of course, four new patients added to this group; and the fourth group would be the actual ten members as a group. This fourth group is rarely present in full attendance. Is it possible that the absences represent actual gaps in the composition of this group, and that not only are you looking for a group, but the members are looking for a therapist to give them a beginning sense of necessary (although false) sense of totalization, of oneness? In a sense each one of these groups has a different analyst, and of course, each different analyst has a different group.

To complicate things more, you feel that some of your "better interventions" have been met with confusion or disdain. So you are telling me how unwittingly you have contributed to trigger a competitive struggle between the members of these different groups. Of course, Jim, "the most intelligent member of the group" (may God help him!), has understood at some level the excitement and the danger of his position as the conveyor of your wisdom and feels entrapped by your seductions at the same time that he does not want to let go of them.

A fascinating byproduct of the special relation between you and Jim is the fact that Marie has found some liberation from her idealization of you and has sided with Jim. You feel the loss of the protection and affection of Marie. So you, Jim, and Marie are entangled in a powerful triangle as the members of the group struggle to find out how they are special (recognition, self) so they can move from being the chosen one to being a collaborator in the work of the therapy.

What is the trauma that you and these members are experiencing? It doesn't appear that you realize how difficult it was for these patients to move from their original groups to a new one, and for the four entirely new members it must be very confusing to enter a group so constituted. These may have become traumatic separations and premature births that have caught you by surprise and have sent everybody down to ground zero, to the original narcissism of false totalization, of idealization that, in this case, stimulates a high level of aggression to protect the group formation out of fight-flight and pairing dynamics (Bion, 1961) because the basic issues of dependency cannot be safely addressed yet.

You ask, "How did I get here? What can I do with my strong feelings, which are clearly being read by the group despite my attempts to hide them?" These are very good questions pointing to the possibility of learning for the whole group. Here the bat's hesitation in the fable may be helpful. This question, however, is of central importance, and theory and intervention will need to come together to be of service to the group. In spite of Lacan's mistrust of the ego, when we do psychotherapy instead of analysis we need to pay close attention to the self (ego) lest we cannot get to the soul; that is, to desire.

As useful and still valid for me as the concept of projective identification is, I am afraid that it can lead to premature and unhelpful interpretations by the therapist, especially in the heat of the conflict. Doing consulting and supervision has taught me useful lessons applicable to psychotherapy groups. A basic one is to try to maintain the conflict at the interpersonal level before rushing into the intrapsychic dimension. This can open up a number of possibilities, and one can even challenge the assumptions of the patients and act in a way that does not feel wimpy, yet never puts down the patient or the group, nor incites aggression to counteract the feeling of hurt the group members may feel. This creates an atmosphere of reciprocity, so it is easy to say, "I see what you mean," or even "I am baffled by that," or "But how does this match with what was said by some members in the previous session," or "Please let me know what is it that really bothered you so much," and so on.

In this group, you might ask what losses they felt when they moved from the previous groups. Do they see the present agitation as an attempt to come together? Perhaps you can say that you are puzzled by a number of things going on in the group and that you are developing a tolerance for this puzzlement, not without difficulty, and wonder if anybody else is puzzled. One therapist in a similar situation, when pushed more and more to answer back, said that he really didn't know at this time what was happening in the group and that he needed more time to say something that could be useful. He also invited the members of the group to give more thought to what was going on. This intervention opened up a different dialogue in the group. Your fantasy of impaling Jim on your letter opener may contain rich information on unconscious processes. Why a letter opener? Why not a knife, or a gun? Is Jim some kind of letter that contains crucial material for everybody in the group including Jim and you? What comes to mind with the word letter? Any memories about a murderous letter?

I am hopeful that you can preserve the hesitation of the bat in the fable. If you can pause and track down the absent element, whether it is bird or beast, some room for the unconscious may develop. The speech of your patients and that of your own fantasies may provide you with a letter that is alive and holds the power of the Symbolic to inform the group's dialogue. This would be more desirable than you finding yourself hostage to the traumatic Real represented by the letter opener that could impale you or your group or throw you into the arms of the ever present master, the death instinct, the death of the group.

Macario Giraldo, PhD

References

Bion, W. R. (1961). *Experiences in groups.* New York: Basic Books.

Lacan, J. (1988). *The seminar. Book I. Freud's papers on technique* (J. Forrester, Trans.). New York: Norton.

Fear and Loathing

Dear Consultant:

The most difficult feeling I deal with as a group therapist is fear about being attacked verbally. I'm now 6 months into an open-ended interpersonal group, and I have been experiencing this very intensely. As a 35-year-old woman leading this highly sophisticated group of young professionals, all of whom have lots of individual therapy experience, I'm sure you'll find my fear to be realistic, but I've crossed over into feeling real dread. I have actually looked at the calendar to see which Monday nights are holidays to see which nights I could cancel group.

Adding to this, when I am fearful, tears come to my eyes, and I am terrified the group will see this. Once, they have. On that occasion, one of the women, LuAnn, said something comforting—as though I am a group member—while another, Lisa, attacked my attacker. Two men, Bill and Jake, commented on their lack of progress, while Damon, who attacked me that evening for "uttering clichés," repeated his criticism, blaming me for the ills of the group. Three other group members, women, remained silent.

In a typical group, which I begin by remaining silent, Damon will say, "I'm telling you, this is the wrong way to start. She's got to direct us more. We don't know what we're supposed to do in here. Can't you see that?" LuAnn might then describe a work issue that has been troubling her, asking the group for counsel, which she gets. Even though I do not think that this path of advice-giving is a wise one, I am paralyzed and say nothing, knowing that to speak risks my bursting into tears. So, I'm collecting myself, hoping that the group will not pause and look to me. Usually, it continues its work, although Bill and Jake often look bored. Finally, when I am collected, I will make some comment, trying to avoid a cliché, but I am so anxious that I do utter them. If I am challenged about this, I will ask if the

177

group agrees with the challenger, and usually the group as a whole will reroute the conversation to something more mundane and safe. At times, I will then feel humiliated and enraged with my challenger, but have already retreated into my posture of silence. Thankfully, some of the group members are so adept at the therapeutic process, it's as though they can do their work without me, so the group goes on. I, however, do not feel helpful as I go through this cycle of dread and rage, punctuated by moments of intervention meant to keep the focus directed away from me.

At this stage, I feel trapped in this cycle. I may even have pressed the group to view me as the paid time-keeper while they try to figure out their own path. Were it not for Damon, Bill, and Jake complaining, and LuAnn taking the shallow path, I might even be able to persuade myself the group was functioning well.

I wonder whether my reactions are too powerful to lead a group. I feel so visible, so exposed, so at risk, that I long for the comfort of my individual therapy practice.

Dear Therapist:

The theoretical approach I choose to look at your challenging situation comes from an object relations perspective. This perspective concerns itself with the way an individual relates to the world as a result of a particular personality organization which has developed from fantasized and real early relationships with significant others. Therefore, object relations must be evaluated in terms of fantasy and not simply what is happening in the "real relationship" (Greenberg & Mitchell, 1983).

Bion's (1961) work on group development and regression gives us a frame to understand object relations theory as it applies to group psychotherapy. Bion believes that projective identification—defined as the projection of certain mental concepts from one person on and into another with a resulting alteration of behavior of the targeted person—is a crucial element in the functioning of groups. Projective identification is divided into two processes: the intrapsychic, or how it affects the person outside of the object; and the interpersonal, or how it affects the external object itself (Horwitz, 1983).

Initially, I looked at this dilemma from the latter point of view. This group has been meeting for only 6 months, which means that it is at a very early stage in its development given these primitive issues. Bion's (1961) basic assumptions of dependency, fight–flight, and pairing are relevant to this situation. A group can become stuck in trying to get its dependency needs met by the therapist. At the same time, the basic assumption of fight–

flight operates to protect the group against its demise and defends itself against primitive psychotic thinking. In your group, members express this fight–flight basic assumption through member fighting and the group rerouting the conversation to safer territory.

In this group, projective identification appears to be alive and well. The group has filled you with the fear, rage, and impotence it experiences as a result of the current developmental arrest. Perhaps you are so afraid of your own tears and rage that you have responded with silence, which parallels the group members' unexpressed nonverbal feelings. In a sense, you have become the willing scapegoat of the group. Both the group and you have unconsciously colluded in silencing these unacceptable feelings. The group has successfully avoided your interventions, and your continued silence may have conveyed to them your need for protection. This has recreated an atmosphere in which anger directed toward you and the other group members is taboo.

Now what to do: If you can understand how these dynamics are operating within this group, you may be able to free yourself from your silence. You pointedly refer to your ease in individual treatment so we can assume that you have some basic comfort level with therapy. It is essential that you comment to the group about unacceptable actions and likely unconscious consequences. For example, you might say, "The group wants me to start off by telling everyone what to say because you do not feel safe here nor able to take care of yourselves. If I take charge of the group, it will feel like I am effectively using our time and taking care of you." This comment may encourage members to talk about early needs and yearnings that have gone largely unmet. Early fighting between group members is often a substitute for anger toward the therapist for lack of protection and care. Encouraging individuals to express this anger directly at you would be very freeing to individual members, the group-as-a-whole, and you.

Usually members become the scapegoat rather than the therapist, so your dilemma suggests to me that you may be in a dual role in the group (i.e., both a member and the therapist). Your emotional constriction has been induced by the group, but your countertransference also is in play (Helfmann, 1976).

When Lisa attacked LuAnn for attacking the leader, you might have said, "Lisa, I wonder if it is safer for you to be angry at LuAnn rather than me." It is important for you to avoid participating in and colluding with this projective identification dynamic. You might say, "The group seems more comfortable when we retreat from strong feelings. In fact, sometimes I feel like that too. Maybe this is the way the group allows me to understand how uncomfortable and scary these feelings are." These interventions will give the group members opportunities to gain insight into their unconscious worlds. This supports the notion of the group as an in vivo laboratory that recapitulates there-and-then unresolved conflicts in the here-and-now.

Although my thinking has not dramatically changed over time relative to these theoretical underpinnings, my behavior as a leader has shifted. I am now more likely to reveal my reactions to the group. For example, in this case, I might disclose my feeling of inhibition and how it might relate to the group's reluctance to confront me. It is important to remember that one never knows the impact that your self-revelation will have on individual members or the group-as-a-whole, so you must be able to explore your impact and self-regulate when necessary.

Other ways exist to look at this dilemma as well. One approach is to focus on your experience and enactment of severe countertransference reactions. Your fear, anger, and lack of confidence may stem from unresolved internal conflicts. These feelings of exposure, humiliation, and paralysis are likely because of earlier unresolved psychic conflicts. I recommend you seek supervision where you can continue to look at how your issues dovetail with those in the group. Supervision can give you added support and perspective.

I do not know what has motivated you to start this group, how you selected the members, or your theoretical orientation. I do not know your level of experience, or whether you have training in group therapy. Finally, you mention the individual therapy experience of these group members. Are they all in combined individual and group? If so, who is–are the individual therapist(s)? These questions emphasize the preparation, training, motivation, and mental health of the therapist. Looking at it from this point of view puts the onus for healthy group functioning on the skill and training of the therapist.

You also need to consider ethical issues. You say you are so emotionally upset by leading this group that you wonder whether you should continue. Ethics require that we not practice outside our scope of expertise and competence. If you feel that you do not have the training or supervision to run this group ethically, then you are required to terminate the group and make sure all patients have been offered suitable therapeutic alternatives. You could find another therapist to replace you as an alternative.

Prior to such drastic action, however, I encourage you to get some help. An experienced group supervisor would enable you to understand how your own issues and group dynamics are operating. The supervisor might also provide sufficient support to allow you to break out of your trapped state. In addition, you might consider your own group therapy, which could prove invaluable. You often feel like a member in your current group, which may be the wish behind the fear. In your own group therapy you would experience the same feelings of group exposure that a member in your group experiences, which could be a growth-promoting opportunity.

I have not recommended a co-therapist here because I feel it avoids the issue. If you lean on someone else for help in this way you run the risk of creating a parallel process between your therapy group and the dynamics of the co-leadership.

Group is not for the faint of heart. Perhaps the main thing that has frightened therapists away from leading groups is the eight or nine against one phenomenon. Because of contagion, groups are better able to confront the therapist on his or her omissions, transgressions, and errors more easily than when members are involved with individual treatment. If you have trouble tolerating this type of exposure, group is not for you (Helfmann, 2001)!

Barry Helfmann, PsyD, CGP, ABPP

References

Bion, W. R. (1961). *Experiences in groups.* New York: Routledge.

Greenberg, S. A., & Mitchell, J. R. (1983). *Object relations in psychoanalytic theory.* Cambridge: Harvard University Press.

Helfmann, B. (1976). *Role differentiation in group development: The emergence of the scapegoat in a self-analytic group.* Unpublished dissertation. Dissertation Abstracts.

Helfmann, B. (2001). Developing a group psychotherapy practice. *New Jersey Psychologists, 51,* 16–18.

Horwitz, L. (1983). Projective identification in dyads and groups. *International Journal of Group Psychotherapy, 33,* 259–279.

Dear Therapist:

The theory that guides my clinical work is primarily psychodynamic, influenced by contributions from object relations, self psychology, and systems theories. From this point of view, countertransference can impede or promote treatment, depending on how it is used. To use countertransference effectively, one must first become aware of it, put it into words, and inhibit the tendency to enact it. One can then attempt to identify its source and the dynamic features in the group and in the therapist that are contributing to its emergence at this time in the treatment process. One can then consider whether, when, and how to use what one has learned.

Given this frame of reference, my first reaction to this clinical example is: Bravo! What courage it takes to bring these experiences to the table. Many clinicians would ignore, overlook, conceal, or deny such countertransference reactions. To acknowledge feeling fear, loathing, rage, and helplessness is, after all, fraught with shame. However, the biggest countertransference "mistake" that can be made in conducting group therapy is to not acknowledge these reactions or try to find ways to use them therapeutically. It is narcissistic folly to believe that one can conduct an enterprise as complex as a psychotherapy group without experiencing countertransference or making mistakes. After nearly 40 years of running groups, I have yet to run the perfect session, much less the perfect group. So, from a system's point of view, one might say you have spoken for all of us!

You appear to be caught up in the dynamics of what Bion would label the "fight–flight" basic assumption, or what others might call the storming–rebellion–antiauthority phase, when the group actively challenges the leader. Your silence at the beginning of sessions, and your fears of being verbally attacked or that you have nothing worthwhile to say may well be a manifestation of the members' deeper dependency needs. Damon, the self-appointed leader of the resistance, located a suitable enemy against whom he can mobilize the troops for battle. You, of course, are it. He verbalizes the group's dissatisfaction that you should "direct us more" and proceeds to attack your sense of authority and competence. This moment provides an excellent opportunity to examine how each of the group members align themselves and how subgroups (e.g., the attackers, the supporters–rescuers, the silent members, the men–women, and so on) form as the drama unfolds.

So far, so good. The group is, after all, 6 months old and is composed of "sophisticated" members with experience in individual psychotherapy. It seems perfectly reasonable that they should start challenging you, but you must be able to take the heat and find productive ways to channel and work with this energy. Alas, this is where things go awry. You feel overmatched and intimidated to the point where you are paralyzed. You worry that group members will lose control of their aggression, but I wonder if you worry, too, that you will lose control of your own aggression: that is, blame yourself for being defective, reveal your vulnerability, ineptitude, and help-lessness, abandon your role as therapist, and feel deeply humiliated and ashamed. Although you state, "I am sure you will find my fear to be realistic," you seem to take to heart the criticism from the group, and your fears–countertransference reactions appear to be significantly exaggerated.

Might there be a grain of truth in their criticism and your anticipation of attack? Yes, but you recognize that your responses might be "too powerful." It is the distorted and exaggerated nature of your fears and your ways of dealing with these—primarily through avoidance–denial–flight, helplessness, and extremely harsh self-criticism—that suggest the presence of countertransference. The problem here, from a group dynamics point of view, is that you, the identified enemy during this phase of the group's life, are in danger of becoming the group casualty. Not only is the group beating you up, but you are doing it to yourself as well. You no longer feel competent, knowledgeable, and concerned about your patients. Rather, you feel defective and deskilled and are concerned about your own survival and suitability for the job. You seem unable to think clearly about whether these feelings are coming from inside yourself (i.e., from unresolved aspects of your personal history), or are being induced in you via projective identification (i.e., are you the receptacle for the group members' disowned feelings?).

What, then, to do? If this were an ongoing supervision, I would: (a) empathize with how difficult it was for you to acknowledge and present these concerns, and underscore the trust and courage it took to do so; (b) normalize your countertransference experience; (c) assess your understanding of the group dynamics that might bear on your countertransference responses; (d) examine your fear of exposure, ridicule, attack, and humiliation in the group, and how realistic these are; (e) help you to explore and identify your expectations of yourself and your sense of shame, and how realistic these are; (f) examine how you are managing your own and others' aggression in the group; (g) shore up your resolve against entering into enactments; (h) explore the implications for the group of how you deal with your concerns; (i) encourage you to identify those factors in your personal history that might incline you to deal with things as you are; (j) examine your suitability for the role of casualty in the group; (k) consider some technical suggestions for how you might proceed with the group; and (l) address the importance of ongoing therapist self-care.

Because this is a one-time consultation, I will focus on the most salient features. Remember that no matter how much groups wish to overthrow or destroy us, they also need us and try to protect and preserve us. You are probably "holding" (via projective identification) a combination of your and the group's disowned helplessness, dependency, rage, and shame. You need to make it safe for the group to express these feelings so that they can be contained, detoxified, addressed, and worked through. I would encourage you to consider several possible empathic and interpretive interventions. For example, you could describe what you see happening in the group from a group dynamics perspective and empathically mirror and give voice to the group's frustration, disappointment, and impatience with you. This might make it possible to meaningfully examine their mounting unhappiness, dissatisfaction, and anger about what you are and are not doing for them. Their collective fears of losing control of their aggression might then be broached, as well as their concerns about their own underlying feelings of dependency and helplessness. You could explore how people aligned themselves when you were being verbally attacked and challenged. You could address how the roles they chose relate to their family histories, how these roles get played out in other areas of their lives, what impact this behavior has on others, and so on.

You might reveal to the group that you felt attacked and what that evoked in you. Such self-disclosure might provide an emotionally corrective experience for the group, demonstrate that one can talk about shameful feelings, and create a valuable opportunity for group members to address their aggression and vulnerability without the fear that they might be destroyed in the process. However, you must be clear about whether this self-disclosure is to help your patients or yourself; you cannot abandon the role of the therapist in order to become a patient in the group. Effective self-disclosure must be consistent with the overall therapeutic task and goals of your group. It requires that you be alert to the impact of such disclosures on the group.

Finally, the area of therapist self-care is often overlooked in our work. Two aspects of self-care that are worth considering are the professional and the personal. Professional self-care may include treatment, supervision, peer supervision, or participation in professional organizations, meetings, and seminars. On a personal level, we sometimes need to be reminded that we, too, need to get enough exercise, take vacations, eat healthy diets, make time for hobbies and pleasurable activities, and enjoy family and friends. If we maintain our own well-being, less temptation exists to try to gratify our own needs at the expense of our patients by becoming patients in the groups we lead.

Robert H. Klein, PhD, FAGPA

Tolerating the Intolerable

Dear Consultant:

I've been running a coed group of people ages 35 to 60 for the past 7 years. Two years ago I added a Jewish woman, Rebecca, to my group who complained of severe anxiety that was exacerbated by the plane crashes into the World Trade Center. Her parents were holocaust survivors and Rebecca had grown up in Brooklyn. She was in Brooklyn the day the planes hit and was devastated by what she saw. At first, she shared little of her history with the group. She might make a comment or two, but never said anything substantial. Once she shared a retaliatory fantasy against a person who had parked too close to her car. She said, "I wanted to blow torch his car so it melted like the Wicked Witch of the West." I was taken aback by this comment because her fantasy evoked images in me of the infernos of the Nazi death camps. My problem is that as Rebecca has opened up, her comments have become more bigoted. I consider myself a liberal, and feel that I tolerate a wide range of beliefs, but a recent event in my group has me questioning whether I can work with her.

My group has a number of patients from different nationalities in it. I love its diversity, and the chance I have to hear about and work with different cultures. I have a Chinese woman, Amy; an Indian man, Uppinder; three Americans (two Protestants and one Catholic), Jill, Jay, and Paula; and my Jewish patient, Rebecca. One day Uppinder, an engineer who has lived in the United States for 10 years, talked about his fear for his family's safety in India after there had been a scuffle between Pakistani and Indian troops on the border. This led to a discussion of the war in Iraq. Paula worried that there would be more terrorist attacks against Americans. I said, "It sounds like the group is wondering how safe it is in here." Rebecca ignored my comment and burst out that she was glad Bush had bombed Iraq and that she hoped he would ultimately destroy all Muslim countries. She said she found Muslims "dirty and despicable." She ended her tirade with the expressed belief that all non-Americans should be deported for the safety of Americans. Amy, who is very demure, said nothing, but Uppinder was furious and asked for an apology. Rebecca refused and said that her hatred of Arabs had nothing to do with how she felt about Uppinder, but yes, she still thought he should return to India. Since then Uppinder and Rebecca have not spoken to each other, and the group seems ready to burst at the seams with unspoken rage (including mine).

In my groups, I have found that patients are generally tolerant of each other's differences, and that they often tolerate behavior I wouldn't. This is the first time anyone has ever said anything so blatantly bigoted. I don't even know what to say, because I am so enraged by Rebecca's views and comments. I feel that she has insulted Amy and Uppinder, and that her views are damaging to the integrity of the group. I also feel tremendously ashamed that I did not say anything in response to her bigotry. I wanted to tell her that bigotry is not acceptable in my group, but I was paralyzed by my own anger. What should I say or do? How does a therapist tolerate the expression of beliefs so different from her own? How do I discuss prejudice in the group? I fear the group might disintegrate into name calling, or worse yet, the same kind of hatred that has fueled religious wars for centuries.

Dear Therapist:
The depictions of your therapy group, its members, and their interplay, contain the components of a potentially vibrant and textured setting for deep personal work. High and turbulent drama is present: intrigue, confrontation, hatred, hurt, shame, and perhaps even the seedlings for passionate attachment. These rich and exciting ingredients of human sentiments are cooking and churning in your group cauldron, and rather than despairing about the demise of your group, or being bogged down in your intolerable paralysis or wrath, you have the excellent opportunity to fashion an optimally functioning psychotherapy group whose objective is individual growth and change.

My own philosophical and clinical orientation to leading psychotherapy groups is psychodynamically informed (Rutan & Stone, 2001) with notable contributions from self psychology, object relations theories, and general systems thinking. Group members enter the group setting with their respective developmental wounds, hungering for the primary human need for connection to others, and predictably live out historically painful dramas in both obvious as well as coded ways. The group leader attempts to help create a sturdy group crucible where honest and courageous expression of deep affect as well as primitive subjective life can emerge and be understood, and thereby be available for the transformation of limiting and harmful life patterns. "In a psychodynamic group the counterintuitive and anxiety raising perspective of the disruptive and disorderly is nourished so individuals can maximize inner and outer freedom" (Elfant, 2003, p. 4).

Also, I believe that the group therapist's subjective experiences in the group process, once cleared of private debris, provide a bridge to helpful and insightful leadership. Countertransferential and projective identification processes, if reasonably differentiated from the therapist's own personal baggage, present multidimensional perspectives which can lead to creative interventions in the group's struggles. "The group leader's task involves containing and nourishing the intensity of passion and desire in the group as well as holding the urges to flee longing and desire" (Elfant, 2003, p. 5).

If I were leading this psychotherapy group, I would be uneasy about what comes across as 7 years of ossifying political correctness that must serve to obscure an avoidance of lively conflict and more genuine intimacy. Absent in your narrative are vigorous group member engagement, exchange, and inquiry. Why is this group so very frightened of pronounced divisiveness? What wishes and longings are being eschewed?

I would take the entry of the first Jewish member within the current group composition—together with her vociferous fears and defensive bigotry—as a wake-up call for a somnolent group and its leader seemingly basking in the warmth of congratulatory ethnic diversity. New members, especially those that revolt against the status quo, are gifts of a disturbing kind. Rebecca is definitely such a prize! She has declared the leader's nakedness, likely wishes to kill the Wicked Witch of the West by melting her with the requisite heat, and through her self-protective expressed prejudices has exposed the undifferentiated, vanilla underbelly of the group politic.

As the group leader, the impact of your impatience, intolerance, and paralyzing fury served to miss a much needed chance to connect to your group's primal struggles. The extent of your powerful responses shows evidence of personally incomplete issues regarding conflict, anger, dependence, shame, and, yes, differences. Your excessive need for surface cultural colorings in the group fabric and your incapacity to hold Rebecca's vitriolic utterings compromised your providing effective leadership. Professionally and ethically, a need exists for ongoing consultation, and likely some personal work as well.

Your group vignette focuses much on yourself, Rebecca, Uppinder, and Amy. Except for a terse mention of the terrified Paula, the remaining three members are relegated to name, being American, and religious affiliation.

So, I wonder about your own ethnic and religious origins and the possible existence of hurts from those beginnings. Also, the group dynamic of a provocative woman engaging and exciting a man, and from your vantage point hurting a meek woman too, all lead you to ally with the apparent victims as well as experience the urge to kill off the offender. I wonder what this triad and drama mean to you on deeper levels. Whatever might emanate from the questions I raise, I do think your silence was ultimately constructive, as you were not in an internal space to use your reactions to bridge to your group.

On a group level, the era of overt benign tolerance has ironically give way to scapegoating the bigoted newcomer. Bigotry has begotten shunning or worse, and the terrified have become the terrorists. Rebecca's initial silent and withholding period in the group was apparently never addressed, likely resulting in her own wounding. When she does speak, she talks of fiery violence when a stranger comes too close to her automobile. Her communicated fear of and likely wish for contact is unacknowledged, and although your associations to the Holocaust in Rebecca's fantasy may be quite perceptive, your own reaction served to actually alienate you from Rebecca. An opening was closed, having an impact on you, Rebecca, and the group.

Soon, the neglected Rebecca ups the ante, and spews forth racial hatreds, succeeding in pushing you and Uppinder into your own allied furies, while the group imitates its leader and seethes silently as well. Contrary to your notion that Rebecca ignored your comment about group danger, she poignantly confirmed what you said by indicating how much she needed a strong Presidential father to protect her from a rageful mother and mother's admiring entourage.

As a group leader, I see this commentary as offering a set of proposed possible meanings and associations to the group narrative. These hypotheses can lead group members to a fertile exploration of their group experience and how that experience pertains to their current lives and formative histories. When I was a younger clinician, if I were faced with the challenges current in this group, I might have gravitated toward more proactive and assertive confrontation around what I saw as the prominent terrifying group and group member themes. My clinical and personal journeys over more than 3 decades lead me now to value clear, persistent, gentle intervention on group, subgroup, and individual member levels. Such an approach gives greater potential to forward movement.

In terms of using your present reactions as a group leader for the good of your group, I believe you first need to work through your own undigested personal conflicts. Once that is in a manageable state, your impatience can be a conduit to connecting the group to its own unvoiced intolerances. Your anger can be helpful to sort out the group's struggle with speaking to hurt, rage, and deep intimacy. Your wish to evict the new group member can be a pathway to engage the group on its resistance to change and what may make for violent urges. Your feeling of paralysis can be a gateway to how scapegoating operates to defend against a host of anxiety-laden experiences, including helplessness. The long group history of exaggerated manifest politeness can be revisited as a way of fleeing conflict and sexuality. Being more in tune with yourself and the group could also lead the group to appreciate and learn from the many edges of genuinely experienced differences and similarities with others. Finally, depending on your own judgment within the unique context of given group moments, making effective use of your subjective reactions may or may not entail overt group therapist self disclosure in the here-and-now.

Allan B. Elfant, PhD, CGP, FAGPA, ABPP

References

Elfant, A. B. (2003, August). *Psychodynamic group psychotherapy and well-being: A passionate union.* Paper presented at the Annual Convention of the American Psychological Association, Toronto, Canada.

Rutan, J. S., & Stone, W. N. (2001). *Psychodynamic group psychotherapy* (3rd ed.). New York: Guilford Press.

Dear Therapist:

Your dilemma is an extremely rich one, and it captures a particular kind of real-life quandary that most therapists confront during their careers. Let me begin by describing the theoretical position which informs my clinical work, and therefore my responses to the dilemma as posed.

Psychodynamic perspectives, especially object relations theory and Yalom's interpersonal approach, inform my work. I believe people are primarily motivated by the wish to connect in gratifying ways with others; thus, I view treatment (particularly group treatment) as a forum in which to identify what prevents people from achieving this end. In terms of technique, I am an active participant in the treatment process and am someone who is willing to disclose aspects of my personal experience in a careful and judicious way.

I think differently about individual and group treatment. In individual treatment, the criterion for continuing versus terminating treatment with a person like Rebecca can be simply stated, though it is often difficult to figure out how it applies in a given situation. You should ask yourself, once she has revealed a side of herself that you find abhorrent, whether you can continue to be genuinely accepting of Rebecca. Your decision should be informed by whether you view this aspect of her persona as an overlay, underneath which she is a good and decent human being, or whether this aspect of her is so heinous that you can no longer maintain your empathy for her. What is most important is how you feel, not what you think.

I believe that most heinous feelings and behaviors are neurotic overlays, and that underneath we are all motivated by the wish and need to love and be loved. However, I cannot always maintain this view when I deal with other human beings, and if I cannot feel this fundamental acceptance of the person I'm working with, my feelings eventually will become discernible and will undermine the treatment experience. This is why an ethical imperative for therapists to be introspective exists.

It is not ethical to continue a treatment with someone for whom you have lost your ability to be genuinely empathic. If you permanently lose your empathy with an individual patient, you need to end the treatment. However, if the patient is in a group, you must ponder a second question before deciding whether you can continue: Did what the patient reveal irreparably damage the group climate? One factor is whether the person has so alienated others that most or all of the group members have lost their empathy for that person. Another aspect, which is relevant to the dilemma described, is whether others are feeling so put off that the group is no longer a place where they can do the work they came to do.

A pro-therapeutic group climate, which takes a great deal of time and effort to establish, can be destroyed quickly. I once had a patient whose angry outbursts were so scary to others in the group (who had been working together productively for over 3 years) that the therapeutic work shut down. The agenda that became most prominent was to be sure that no one said anything that would antagonize the angry new member. Once the patient left (at my behest), it took months to re-establish the sense of safety that is a sine qua non for doing effective work in a group. After that experience I stopped telling prospective patients that their role was to say anything and everything that they found themselves feeling during the course of each session. Instead, I now tell people that I generally want them to express what they feel, but that destructive, invalidating forms of expression have no place in a therapy group. Although constructive criticism has a place in my groups, there always needs to be an overarching commitment to try to be helpful to others in the group, and efforts to hurt others will not be tolerated.

In the present case, I would wonder whether the relationships between Rebecca and both Amy and Uppinder have been irrevocably ruined. Is it possible that, with time and candid discussion, some level of mutual understanding might emerge? If you do not think this is possible, you should remove Rebecca from the group. You could work with her individually (if she would) if you feel you can maintain an empathic stance with her, or you could refer her to another group, although you need to let the other therapist know what transpired to try to ensure that Rebecca does not again have the experience of being extruded from a group.

Do you think it would be beneficial to Rebecca to get feedback about how her views impact those around her (not only the foreign-born members)? Sometimes feedback can be transforming for a patient, but in other instances it falls on deaf ears and is without value. A corollary question is whether any value exists for Amy, Uppinder, and others to articulate to her their feelings about what Rebecca expressed. Because minorities in this country (and others I am sure) inevitably experience bigotry at various times in their lives, they undoubtedly have accumulated feelings about being seen the way Rebecca indicated she sees them. In a well-functioning group climate, this can be valuable work. But if the climate is irretrievably poisoned, this work cannot occur.

If you decide that you are going to work with the situation as it has developed, then you should process your personal experience of Rebecca. As indicated above, the first step is introspection about whether you can continue to maintain a positive valence toward her. If you can, then think about whether some sort of feedback from you might be constructive, both for Rebecca and for the rest of the group. First consider what others in the group have been able to express, and what you believe they will be able to express as time goes on. Can Amy, Uppinder, and others in the group find words to express what was evoked in them, and can they do so constructively? If not, you need to give expression to your own reactions.

In my experience, often other members cannot express the depth of feeling that has been evoked in them. The avoidance of what people are feeling, Rebecca included, becomes like the proverbial elephant in the room. When this persists, it is up to you to break the ice. You should only attempt this with people with whom you have a positive therapeutic alliance. This consists of two parts: do you still genuinely like and care about this person, and does he or she believe that you are genuinely committed to being helpful?

If your alliance is strong enough to make this effort, try to find language that captures what you feel but that is focused on feedback for the patient rather than your own self-expression. You can express your positive regard while not being mealy-mouthed. You might say to Rebecca, "There is a lot I like and admire about you"—and be as specific as you can be about this— "but at the same time I find myself feeling angry about and rejecting of your sentiments about foreigners in the United States. Although I don't want you or others to feel they need to be politically correct, your sentiments seem to me to be both bigoted and prejudiced, and such sentiments are antithetical to values that I hold dear."

You could then ask whether she had thought about what her sentiments might have evoked in others, whether she had experience with expressing such sentiments in other settings, and so on. In this way, you would: (a) get the group to talk about the elephant in the room rather than collude in the avoidance; (b) focus on her in a caring way rather than elaborate on what led you to develop the feelings that she had evoked in you; and (c) model for group members how difficult feedback can be delivered in a constructive manner.

I cannot emphasize the third point too strongly. Group therapy is not only a setting in which people can learn basic social skills; it is also a place where people can develop very advanced social skills, one of which is offering difficult, but constructive, feedback.

Two additional points must be made about giving such feedback. The first is that you must be extraordinarily sensitive to the cues you receive from the patient. Specifically, if you begin to offer Rebecca the sort of feedback I'm suggesting, you need to note the nonverbal cues she emits about how she is receiving what you are saying. If you sense that she is very hurt or otherwise unable to take in and make use of what you are saying, you should stop. Sometimes therapists have the need to finish what they have started, even when it is evidently not going well, which is a mistake.

Second, be wary of the potential for scapegoating. Although others might build on your feedback, you should be quick to intervene in a protective way if scapegoating begins to emerge. It can be destructive for not only the recipient, but for the group-as-a-whole.

Patients like Rebecca pose an enormous challenge for the group therapist and for the group-as-a-whole. As with many other phenomena that might emerge in a group, great potential exists for everyone to learn and grow from confronting what has been said and the feelings it has evoked in each member. However, this ideal often is not realistic, and it is incumbent on you to be realistic in determining whether to continue a treatment in which the group climate is so threatened or damaged. As we develop experience, it is hoped that we become better and better able to discern the difference between an unachievable ideal and a realistically achievable goal.

Harold Bernard, PhD, CGP, FAGPA, ABPP

Section VI
Self-Disclosure

Overview

In the HBO series *The Sopranos,* the analytically oriented therapist, Dr. Melfi, discloses to her Mafia patient, Tony, that she has been afraid of him, and that her interventions have been affected by this fear. Nowhere in her classical training, we expect, was there a model for such self-disclosure, or perhaps even permission for it, but the therapeutic times have changed, and self-disclosure is now more generally accepted. What remains murky, however, is how much to disclose, when, and to whom? These questions are compounded for the group therapist who, in a group session, is disclosing to *all,* whereas in individual sessions may have only disclosed to some. Let alone what is disclosed inadvertently.

In his chapter, *How Far Should I Go?,* Joel Frost explores the history of therapist self-disclosure and changes in our views about it, as well as addressing some of the complex questions highlighted above. Then, in *Breaking Up the Family or the Fantasy?* consultants Sara Emerson and Gil Spielberg address the dilemma of the divorcing therapist whose work performance is suffering as a result, but who is unclear whether to disclose anything about his personal state to his group. Emerson empathizes with the therapist's wish to protect the patients and himself but suggests that disclosure can "expand and deepen the therapeutic space." Spielberg emphasizes the therapist's need first to examine his countertransference reactions and then to have the courage to confront the "terrors" he shares in parallel with the group.

Next, in *If I Did It, Why Can't You?*, we meet the personally shy, physically abused, and formerly quick-tempered therapist who has overcome these issues and wonders whether telling the group about his success might help them. Marti Kranzberg and Meg Sharpe respond and independently agree that disclosure in these areas is unwise. Kranzberg invites the therapist to consider whether envy about the desire to be a group *member* is a motivating force here. Sharpe wonders whether the therapist's wish to be idealized or to avoid anxiety or the group's aggression may be fueling the desire to disclose.

Finally, a female therapist, in *Sharing at the Exit*, is terminating her women's group after several years and is being asked personal questions by some members, whereas others expressly don't want to know. Bernard Frankel, who explored "shared existential meanings of our common mortality" with his patients after 9/11, highlights the need to process underlying feelings about the death of the group, rather than worry too much about personal disclosure. Brenda Smith advises against biographical disclosure for this therapist who has been opaque to the group prior to the termination, but recommends disclosure of feelings about what is happening in the group.

How Far Should I Go?

JOEL C. FROST, EDD, FAGPA, ABPP

The subject of self-disclosure has received increased attention in the clinical literature. Whether presented as a concept or a technique, self-disclosure rarely has a clear and unitary meaning. In this chapter, I suggest that self-disclosure is best understood as existing along a continuum with three distinct perspectives or levels. An examination of the differences in these perspectives, as well as attention to the overlap among them, will help the reader make sense of the sometimes confusing usage of the concept in the extant literature.

Self-disclosure as technical modification

Therapists are continually faced with opportunities for self-disclosure. The therapist who routinely strives for anonymity may at times elect to self-disclose toward a particular therapeutic goal. Telling a group, for example, where you are going for vacation or that you missed a session because you were ill may serve, for example, to humanize the therapist when the group is feeling a sense of anxiety or abandonment. Other therapeutic goals might include the solidification of the therapeutic alliance at the beginning of therapy, the gradual diminution of the transference toward the end of the work, or the reduction of the negative transference during heated periods of treatment. At this level of technique, self-disclosure represents one addition to a therapist's repertoire of interventions, to be used for a specific purpose, at a particular time, with a particular patient. Such instances of self-disclosure need to be understood by the therapist with respect to goal, meaning to the patient, and impact.

Self-disclosure as structural shift

In some treatments, the therapist may move further along the self-disclosure continuum to include more frequent and extensive self-disclosure. For example, the therapist might routinely answer direct questions in contrast to solely exploring the meaning behind them. With the goal of becoming more "accessible" to the patient, self-disclosing therapists may more extensively or consistently share countertransference feelings, broadly defined to include all personal reactions such as fleeting personal associations, musings, reveries, tentative hypotheses, passing affective states, and the like. This level is characterized by a broad opening up of oneself *in response to the patient's request* for sharing, which, in the literature, is frequently referred to as the "therapist's use-of-self" (Epstein, 1990; Wright, 2000). Rather than offer an occasional self-disclosure, from this perspective the therapist alters the very structure and frame of the therapeutic relationship. A group therapist may more frequently acknowledge that he or she is confused, angry, hurt, or detached when asked about his or her subjective state in the group. Most authors who endorse the use of self-disclosure work at this level.

Self-disclosure as philosophical underpinning

Some therapists move another step along the continuum. For them, the therapeutic project is to develop a genuine relationship between active co-participants who commonly and openly share many of their thoughts, feelings, and life experiences. At this level, therapists may initiate self-disclosure *in response to the patient's material* even without being asked. Here a group therapist might actively introduce his or her confusion into the group process, present a dream or personal fantasy, or ask members to offer feedback on the therapist's behavior or countertransference that is not evident to the therapist. Such a therapeutic stance constitutes an evolutionary shift in the general philosophy of the therapeutic relationship, and moves considerably beyond the occasional revealing of oneself to the patient or group. An extreme example of this position was described by Ferenczi (1932), who entered into a mutual analysis with a patient. Although proponents of this level of intervention are currently rare, an increasing number of authors and clinicians are grappling with how far toward this position they are willing to move.

The subject of self-disclosure covers a lot of ground, and various authors limit their examination to one or another of these perspectives, often without recognizing the continuum described above. To summarize, for some therapists, self-disclosure is an *intervention*, a giving of something personal to a patient; for others, it reflects a *shift in structure* toward becoming an active coparticipant; and for the rest, it represents a radical change in the *philosophy* of psychotherapy.

The theory of self-disclosure is evolving, and has been more focused on providing rationales for its use than presenting clear practical guidelines. Thus far, the literature has paid insufficient attention to what, when, and how much to disclose in the service of enhancing the treatment outcome.

Within the psychoanalytic community, discussions of self-disclosure were originally focused on the one-to-one setting of analysis. Since that time, there has been continued discourse regarding its acceptability. Greenberg (1995) framed it well:

> Thus contemporary psychoanalysts are faced with what is, to say the least, a vexing problem of adjudication. On the one hand we have the testimony of the founder himself that self-disclosure demonstrably undermines our attempts to conduct an analysis. On the other hand we have the testimony of the man who was widely acknowledged to be the foremost clinician of his day that refusing to reveal ourselves demonstrably undermines our attempts to conduct an analysis. The same arguments that Freud and Ferenczi made, putatively based upon the same empirical observations, are regularly repeated in contemporary discussions of the issue. The clinician, faced many times each day with the need to act one way or another, is buffeted by strongly held, anecdotally supported, diametrically opposed injunctions. (p. 195)

Freud and Ferenczi disagreed on many aspects of theory and clinical practice, and self-disclosure was no exception. Both based their positions on clinical experience as well as on theory but came to different conclusions, as have clinicians who have followed after them. Consider, for example, Greenberg's comment, "Self-disclosure is necessary because it works" (1995, p. 195) and its opposite, made by West and Livesley (1986):

> Those who advocate self-disclosure may propose that this tactic is beneficial because it imparts the notion of the therapist's humaneness and thus removes an artificial barrier existent between therapist and member. A consequence of these modifications of the therapeutic boundary is that the therapeutic frame, and hence the basis of therapy is compromised. (pp. 11–12)

Levenson, in more even-handed fashion, reveals, "I am much more wary about self-disclosure. I have had some striking successes, but also some disasters" (1996, p. 247).

Freud himself used self-disclosure, but subsequently took a position against it for four reasons: resistance becomes more difficult; transference resolution is more difficult as well; the patient becomes insatiable for more information; and the patient realizes that the analyst is more interesting than him- or herself. However, most authors arguing against the use of self-disclosure cite Freud, but generally focus their position on his views on therapist anonymity—that is, the need to remain a "blank screen." Those writing in favor of self-disclosure generally include in their argument the works of Ferenczi, who proposed a very different type of therapy frame with a more egalitarian and horizontally based relationship (Ferenczi, 1932).

Ferenczi (1928, 1932) introduced the use of analyst self-disclosure in the 1920s. He had begun to accept as reality the analysand's experience, rather than assigning it solely to neurosis. He responded to this by a willingness to disclose his subjective experiences in the analysis. He took the position that extensive self-disclosure would act to counter the dishonest, silent, troubled communications many patients had had with their parents.

Rachman (1990, 1999), having studied the works of Ferenczi for 20 years, highlights the historical development of self-disclosure as an integral aspect of the development of psychoanalytic theory from a one-person, to two-person, to an intersubjective psychology. He asserts that this shift is a natural outgrowth of the concept of empathy, is inherent to the interpersonal process, and is required of an authentic relationship. Thus, although Rachman is a strong supporter of the use of self-disclosure, he seems unwilling to go as far as Ferenczi. He struggles with the line between *when a therapist self-discloses in response to a patient's initiation* (judicious self-disclosure), and *when a therapist self-discloses on his or her own initiative* (conspicuous self-disclosure), but cannot actively practice at the third level of self-disclosure.

Renik, a proponent of the third level, although writing that we need to review what we mean by self-disclosure, leapfrogs the issue entirely to argue that therapist anonymity is a myth. He begins with the position that we are *always* self-disclosing, and must therefore look at "how to manage the unavoidable condition of constant disclosure" (Renik, 1995, p. 468). He refers here to the types of self-disclosures elsewhere referred to as "inadvertent self-disclosures" (Pizer, 1997).

Inadvertent or inevitable self-disclosures

Inadvertent self-disclosure concerns what we selectively reveal to patients in our everyday interactions in the office. Such disclosures include information we reveal by where we practice, how we dress, how we decorate our space, and religious holidays we observe. What fees do we charge, how do we manage the bills, what importance do we give to money? What do clients pick up about our values, opinions, beliefs, and attitudes by observing magazines we have in our waiting room, the car we drive, the jewelry we wear? What can they access about us on the Internet? Because patients have access to this kind of inadvertently disclosed information, and already have thoughts and feelings as a result, to take a strict stance of anonymity can be seen as counter-therapeutic. In this way, self-disclosure that acknowledges what patients already know supports their reality testing, affirms the therapeutic alliance, facilitates mutual empathy, and makes the treatment feel more authentic.

Hoffman (1983), Aron (1991), Greenberg (1995), Rachman (1990, 1999), Basescu (1990), Levenson (1996), Ehrenberg (1996), and Renik (1995, 1999), all agree that the blank-screen position is a myth, that such a screen is impossible to maintain, and that attempts to hold too strongly to it can cause iatrogenic trauma for the patient. As Levenson writes, "If self-revelation can be defined as what the patient may see, through a veil darkly, regardless of the therapist's efforts at inscrutability (not neutrality, which I don't believe possible or desirable), then the only issue is whether the therapist confirms or, at least, acknowledges what the patient sees" (1996, p. 239). In asserting that self-revelation is inevitable, Levenson distinguishes between inadvertent self-revelation and deliberate self-disclosure. Again, the reader can see the shift in terminology as reflective of the continuing confusion regarding self-disclosure.

With regard to countertransference disclosure (defined here as the sharing of any of our responses to our patients, including our feelings and reactions in our groups, and even our dreams about members or the group), Ehrenberg writes about an "emotional joining" through the "constructive use of countertransference disclosure," (1996, p. 277) which furthers and deepens the work. She sees this "spontaneous, authentic reaction" (1996, p. 278) on the part of the therapist as not only a leveling of the playing field, but a diminishing of the patronizing, authoritarian approach on the part of the more emotionally removed (non self-disclosing) therapist. The fact that a therapist does not practice self-disclosure does not in itself suggest emotional unavailability or distance, but the inference in the literature is just that. Proponents of self-disclosure make frequent reference to their work being authentic, honest, inviting, respectful, more horizontal than vertical, and genuine.

Complete agreement exists that the therapist should acknowledge, admit, explore, or even invite the patient's material regarding self-revelation or inadvertent self-disclosure. General agreement also exists that the therapist should perceive the patient as a coparticipant in the therapy, construing the patient's contributions as valuable as those of the therapist. Agreement exists that, at some times and with some patients, countertransference self-disclosure benefits the therapy. However, therapists disagree whether creating an atmosphere of "playing one's cards face up in analysis is a useful overall policy" (Renik, 1999).

Ferenczi proposed creating such an atmosphere and policy of open and intentional self-disclosure in analysis (1928, 1932). Renik (1995, 1996, 1998, 1999) is the modern-day proponent of Ferenczi's stance. Both are the central proponents of the third level, that self-disclosure become central to the very philosophy of treatment, thereby recasting the entire structure of the therapeutic relationship.

Against self-disclosure

Although a compelling case has been made for therapist self-disclosure, a number of cogent arguments against its use exist. The first is the value of preserving therapist anonymity, of remaining the "blank screen" on which the patient can project. Anonymity helps the therapist to be objective, non-judgmental, and to not intrude into the intrapsychic space of the patient's internal world. Another major argument against self-disclosure centers on countertransference and the concern that a therapist "acts in" via self-disclosure, which may presage a slide down the slippery slope toward acting out with a patient. A third argument concerns the nature of the analytic relationship itself, that it is to be primarily intellectual, objective, and removed for the analyst, and emotional for the patient (West & Livesley, 1986).

West and Livesley take the strongest position against therapist self-disclosure in a group psychotherapy setting. They see it as a frame violation, preferring the value of anonymity, total confidentiality, and neutrality. They write that "the frame refers to the nature of the relationship between therapist and patient in which both relinquish a desire for a real relationship in favor of an 'as-if' quality that then permits the relationship itself to be a focus of examination" (1986, p. 6). They view the therapeutic relationship as an intellectual process for the therapist and an emotional process for the patients. Thus, any motivation for the therapist to self-disclose (break the frame) would be seen as an expression of therapist "object hunger" because of an inability to tolerate mutual deprivation. They argue that a therapist's move toward establishing a real relationship can only arise from the therapist's narcissistic and exhibitionistic tendencies. Although advocating against self-disclosure, they also advocate against the therapist striving too completely to be a blank screen because that might create a "nonhuman atmosphere" (1986, p. 17).

Indeed, proponents of self-disclosure seize on this very argument. They see it as essential to shift away from the "as-if" relationship to one of greater equality and authenticity. This enhances the benefits of therapy: "Intimate self-disclosure begets intimate self-disclosure" (Jourard, 1971, p. 17).

Group therapy

These above arguments concern therapist self-disclosure in the analytic or individual psychotherapy setting. Theorizing about the use of self-disclosure in group psychotherapy often follows the same thinking that applies to the individual relationship. Yalom (1995) writes that self-disclosure facilitates reality testing on the part of group members, and should be used increasingly as the therapy progresses:

> Therapists help patients to confirm or disconfirm their impressions of the therapist by gradually revealing more of themselves. The patient is pressed to deal with the therapist as a real person in the here and-now. Thus you respond to the patient, you share your feelings, you acknowledge or refute motives attributed to you, you look at your own blind spots, you demonstrate respect for the feedback the members offer you. In the face of this mounting real life data, patients are propelled to examine the nature and basis of their fictitious beliefs about the therapist (p. 202).

Thus, as Yalom's groups mature, he uses increasing self-disclosure to actively reduce transference distortions.

Group clinicians, writing in support of therapist self-disclosure, present case examples that describe how to use self-disclosure, often in the form of modeling for the group members. For example, Sternbach (2003) models how difficult it is to reveal oneself in a men's group, thus increasing empathy for men's difficulties with normal socialization. He decides how much and when to self-disclose through titration—that is, "the smallest amount of an agent that will produce the desired reaction in the substance being acted upon" (p. 69). Cohen and Schermer (2001) model intimate communication within the group, with their self-disclosure also serving as an "intersubjective bridge" to allow group members access to the therapist's subjective world. They cite an example in which a group therapist discloses that he felt "vulnerable, hurt, and attacked" (p. 48) after providing what he had viewed as helpful interpretations. They further cite three selfobject transference configurations through which to understand this self-disclosure.

In 1990, an entire section of *Group* was devoted to the use of self in group psychotherapy. In the lead article, Rachman (1990) presents his personal reactions after being attacked by a group member. He describes numerous self-disclosures as he works through the group's insistent request that he validate a member's experience of feeling ridiculed by Rachman's smile. Rachman openly discloses feeling attacked and misunderstood by the group, and characterizes his smile as one of anxiety rather than hostility. He owns his contribution, but he also validates the group member's experience of the current reality as a re-enactment of earlier family-based trauma. This process of self-disclosure broke the impasse in group and accelerated the development of trust.

Also in this issue of *Group*, Epstein (1990) cites examples of encouraging the group to offer their reactions to his actions (such as his turning away from a male patient toward a female patient, or favoring the women over the men). He also describes his willingness to validate their perceptions while openly discussing his confusion as to the countertransference meaning of his actions. For Epstein, self-disclosure is an important element in working through his empathic failures.

Practical questions and guidelines

Although theoretical notions about the use of self-disclosure in group therapy can readily be found, practical guidelines are almost nonexistent. For example, should one disclose less in a new group than an ongoing group, or more in a support group than a psychoanalytic group? Many clinicians seem implicitly to decide which of the three levels they are comfortable with, and then practice from that level. Even Yalom (1995), who comes closest to offering guidelines, attends little to variations in self-disclosure such as when a new member enters a group, thereby changing the group. Moreover, little attention is paid to a self-disclosure which can be advantageous for some members in a group and simultaneously problematic for others within the same group.

Similarly, it can be difficult to balance the types and extent of self-disclosure in individual psychotherapy with a patient also treated in a group setting. What does the patient in group feel free to reveal when it was material disclosed in the individual therapy? How is a patient's reaction to a therapist's disclosure different within the context of the group? Is the therapist as comfortable self-disclosing when eight people are watching and reacting? Can the therapist tolerate having inadvertent self-disclosures "distorted" by a group member's transference, even after such a distortion was "corrected" through self-disclosure? Do therapists practice the same level of self-disclosure in each of multiple groups? Are we as willing to validate accurate negative perceptions of inadvertent self-disclosures as we are of the more positive?

Cohen and Schermer (2001) present a solid case for preparing group members for self-disclosure so that members are not "shocked" when it occurs. They also describe the increased *symmetry* and *parity* that occurs when they disclose. Although they focus on the rationale for and benefits of self-disclosure, they too offer little practical advice. Wright (2000) also embracing a philosophy of self-disclosure, cites a willingness to engage in mutual communication, to more openly use countertransference reactions, to talk about one's responses (for example, when a therapist tears up in a group), to use playfulness, humor, teasing, and spontaneity—even sharing "unprepared thoughts or ideas in the making" (p. 190). He notes the value of creating a norm of self-disclosure in his groups, but, as is common, offers little in the way of specifics.

In an attempt to establish some guidelines regarding the use of self-disclosure for group therapists, agreement exists on several points. First, inadvertent self-disclosures occur naturally, constantly, and often without our intention or awareness. Therapists cannot control their occurrence; however, we can choose whether to validate them and open them for discussion in the service of group progress. To deny the truth of a patient's perception of us can be counter-therapeutic. Yet this is complicated because in a group, multiple "truths" always exist.

Second, when we decide to actively self-disclose in our groups, we are altering the frame and changing the way group members are able to interact with us. Such alteration should be done thoughtfully and consistently, and its effects should be thoroughly analyzed. Once we have started down this road of self-disclosure, a later decision to discontinue it can be felt by the group to be unfair.

Third, allowing the group to have greater access to the therapist as a person will vary according to personal style, comfort with such exposure, and confidence that we have sufficient self-awareness. Thus, it is reasonable that there be wide variation in the type of self-disclosures in which one may engage, ranging from sharing fleeting thoughts, musings, tentative clinical hypotheses, countertransference reactions, or even one's own pain. Whatever is disclosed should always be offered for the benefit of the patient or group, and not in the service of the therapist's personal needs.

As the literature suggests, clinicians routinely struggle with when, what, and how much to disclose. We are always operating within a complex intersubjective environment in which we are characteristically more subjective and have revealed more than we may have thought. With an increased focus in the field on empathy and the need for genuine interactions, we more often feel the pull to self-disclose, either when reacting to a patient's request, or initiating in response to a patient's material. For many generations of therapists, firm and clear boundaries about therapist anonymity served to protect the therapist from such struggles. Recently, the tide has shifted toward a view of self-disclosure as not only acceptable but, in many instances, as desirable. Even as our theoretical and philosophical ideas undergo transformation, however, practical guidelines remain evanescent. Clearly, we are witness to a concept in evolution.

References

Aron, L. (1991). The patient's experience of the analyst's subjectivity. *Psychoanalytic Dialogues, 1*, 29–51.

Basecu, S. (1990). Tools of the trade: The use of the self in psychotherapy. *Group, 14*, 157–165.

Cohen, B. D., & Schermer, V. L. (2001). Therapist self-disclosure in group psychotherapy from an intersubjective and self psychological standpoint. *Group, 25*, 41–57.

Ehrenberg, D. B. (1996). On the analyst's emotional availability and vulnerability. *Contemporary Psychoanalysis, 32*, 275–286.

Epstein, L. (1990). Some reflections on the therapeutic use of the self. *Group, 14*, 151–156.

Ferenczi, S. (1928). The elasticity of psychoanalytic technique. In M. Balint (Ed.), *Final contributions to the problem of psychoanalysis* (Vol. 3, pp. 87–102). New York: Basic Books. (Original work published 1955)

Ferenczi, S. (1932). *Ferenczi's clinical diary*. (J. Dupont, Ed.). Cambridge, MA: Harvard University Press. (Original work published 1989)

Greenberg, J. (l995). Self-disclosure: Is it psychoanalytic? *Contemporary Psychoanalysis, 31*, 193–205.

Hoffman, I. Z. (1983). The patient as interpreter of the analyst's experience. *Contemporary Psychoanalysis, 19*, 389–422.

Jourard, J. M. (1971). *An experimental analysis of the transparent self*. New York: Wiley-Interscience.

Levenson, E. A. (1996). Aspects of self-revelation and self-disclosure. *Contemporary Psychoanalysis, 32*, 237–248.

Pizer, B. (1997). When the analyst is ill: Dimensions of self-disclosure. *Psychoanalytic Quarterly, 66*, 450–469.

Rachman, A. W. (1990). Judicious self-disclosure in group analysis. *Group, 14*, 132–144.

Rachman, A. W. (1999). Sandor Ferenczi's ideas and methods and their relevance to group psychotherapy. *Group, 23*, 121–144.

Renik, O. (1995). The ideal of the anonymous analyst and the problem of self-disclosure. *Psychoanalytic Quarterly, 64*, 466–495.

Renik, O. (l996). The perils of neutrality. *Psychoanalytic Quarterly, 65*, 495–516.

Renik, O. (1998). Getting real in analysis. *Psychoanalytic Quarterly, 67*, 566–593.

Renik, O. (1999). Playing one's cards face up in analysis: An approach to the problem of self-disclosure. *Psychoanalytic Quarterly, 68*, 521–539.

Sternbach, J. (2003). Self-disclosure with all-male groups. *International Journal of Group Psychotherapy, 53*, 61–81.

West, M., & Livesley, W. J. (1986). Therapist transparency and the frame for group psychotherapy. *International Journal of Group Psychotherapy, 36*, 5–19.

Wright, F. (2000). The use of the self in group leadership: A relational perspective. *International Journal of Group Psychotherapy, 50*, 181–198.

Yalom, I. (1995). *The theory and practice of group psychotherapy*. New York: Basic Books.

Breaking Up the Family or the Fantasy?

Dear Consultant:

I have an office outside my home where I run my practice. I prefer the privacy that an outside office provides me. Recently, however, there have been a number of changes in my personal life that are going to affect where and when I practice. I'd like to know how to handle these changes.

My wife and I are going through an extremely conflictual divorce. We have two children, ages five and eight. One result of our divorce is that each of us will have less money on which to live; another is that I will share custody of the kids so that I will be responsible for them 2 days during the week and all weekend every other week. I now practice Monday through Thursday and all day on Saturday. Because of custody arrangements, I will have to change my Saturday schedule, which includes moving a group to another day and time after it has been meeting on Saturdays for 5 years. In addition, I will need to move my office to one that is less expensive.

The members of my group include four women and three men. One woman, Jane, was diagnosed with breast cancer a month ago, and is recovering from a mastectomy. Paul, an aggressive businessman, just broke up with a girlfriend of 10 years. Another patient, George, lost his mother last week to multiple sclerosis after many years of watching her deteriorate. Although this group is pretty high functioning, I'm anxious about telling them about the changes in time and location of the group. I know my patients will ask why I am moving my office and the time of the group, and I don't really want to tell them. I feel they are dealing with a lot themselves right now, and that I should be strong for them. I also feel raw and quite ashamed about my divorce. I'm afraid that if I tell the group about what is happening I might start to cry. On the other hand, I don't want to lie to them.

Historically, I have not told my patients much about myself. When I was in training, I was taught to ask for fantasies, thoughts, and associations to their questions, but not to reveal the answer for fear of interfering with the transference. This has served me well because I tend to be a private person. My patients do not even know where I live or whether I have children! Yet, now I wonder what they know about what is going on for me. I am sometimes distracted and more distant than I usually am. Last week I was late to group—a first for me—and now that I have custody of my two children, I sometimes get paged in the middle of a session when they are sick at school. Should I tell my patients about what is going on? How much do I say? How do I handle the transition to the new office and time of group? How do I make sure they know I am taking care of myself and they do not need to take care of me?

Dear Therapist:

Your current situation, as painful as it is for you, provides a wonderful arena in which theory, practice, and real life collide. It points out the paradox of our work: the need to hold to theory and our theoretical guidelines as a compass, while at the same time managing and incorporating the way in which real life impinges on us and thus on our patients. Psychotherapy and psychotherapeutic practice, despite our best efforts to protect the relationships and the boundaries, is subject to the vicissitudes of life—ours and theirs. Under the "best of circumstances" our anonymity is highly questionable. To my mind the question is as much what to disclose as it is how to manage the continual and inevitable self-disclosures which continually occur. How you manage this very painful and absorbing life crisis with which you are confronted and understandably absorbed, given the way you have practiced, raises important and complex clinical questions.

I will attempt to answer the questions you pose directly as well as speak to some of the underlying issues you raise in the description of your current situation. As I understand your dilemma, initially you want suggestions as to what and how much to tell your patients. This simple question raises a number of complex issues: self-disclosure and anonymity–privacy, what is therapeutic, and the impact and influence of our world (internal and external) on our patient's lives. You say that you don't want to "lie" to your group, yet you don't want to tell them the truth. However, the events of your life will have a significant impact on their treatment, if only because of the change of time and office space. Second, you wonder about how to protect your group members and "be strong for them," and have a wish to reassure them that "they do not need to take care of" you. Finally, you feel shame about the separation and divorce and fear exposure, especially that you might cry, which is out of character for you.

You are aware on many levels how the divorce has had an impact on you; you were late, you were beeped, and the most glaring and concrete: the need to change your office space and the time of this particular group. Obviously the concrete has to be addressed: Why are you moving and changing the group time? Even if this were staying the same, the group members would be attuned to the fact that things have changed with you. You are preoccupied, grieving, and trying to manage a new life situation. It is an extremely tough and demanding situation.

Your current state of being, with all of its fluctuations, will clearly have an impact on your group patients. When our world and our own psychic reality intersect with our patients' treatments, we have a responsibility to honor and help speak what may feel to be the unspeakable. Of course you have the right to your privacy, and our patients have a right to a confirmation of what is real and truthful. You need to make decisions about how to maintain your privacy, and the amount of information needed to help the group and the individual patients feel safe and contained. It is important not to unnecessarily increase the group's anxiety by a lack of information, thus leaving them alone to their fantasies or projections, or to deny their own perceptions, as it is important not to flood them with your own affect.

In this case, you are right to wonder who you are protecting: yourself or your patients? Here is where theory, practice, and life collide. Is telling the group members about your current situation therapeutically sound or self-serving? You are absolutely correct in wondering what your patients may be picking up from you.

Your current situation raises a broader question of the image we have of ourselves, of our personal and professional selves, and how we wish our patients to perceive us. As "professional helpers" we strive to have our best selves present with our patients. So what happens to us when, in fact, our best self is intruded on, shaken, disrupted? We are then confronted with an internal dissonance and a real dilemma or problem of how to manage that interface between our world and our patients. Groups may be a complex arena in which to hide as we are continually scrutinized by a number of people and subjected to the vast amount of affect that is generated in a group.

At the very least, the group is entitled to a statement from you that you are undergoing changes in your personal life. The events in your life are not life threatening, but will require that you make some changes that will have an impact on them—specifically, a change in the office space and meeting time of the group. Feinsilver (1998) notes that "the therapeutic importance of a disclosure is not just that it reveals something previously not known or hidden, but whether or not it begins deliberately to bring ego resources to an issue that is potentially threatening" (p. 1143) because it is unspoken or unacknowledged by the therapist. Disclosure, to my mind, can expand and deepen the therapeutic space rather than collapse it. The process of disclosing provides the group and the therapist with a multitude of therapeutic challenges and opportunities. What you will be sharing with your patients has to do with your own humanity, it "involves basic human concerns: life and death, change, loss and grief [which are] at the center of human experience and growth" (Pizer, 1997, p. 456).

With respect to your wish to be strong for your group members and assure them that you are taking care of yourself, I have a number of thoughts. You have no more power to protect the members of your group from the real losses and tragedies that they are confronting in their lives than you have to protect yourself and them from this crisis in your life. You do, however, have the capacity and the skill to provide a contained, safe environment in which they can explore and verbalize their feelings. In this setting, they can express and metabolize their own feelings about you and your life situation, and reflect on their lives and life events. Our "power" is in our capacity to invite and contain affect, speak the unspeakable, and thus, integrate and accept the members' feelings.

Let me briefly address your very understandable feelings of shame. As your separation (divorce) may represent a failure, it also disrupts the "fantasy" you hoped your group members (and patients) held and the image you held of yourself. This kind of "failure" is indeed experienced as shameful. Shame is one of the more difficult affects to address in ourselves and with our groups. To cry may be more of a gift than a mistake. It reveals our humanity; we too exist in the real world. Such an experience provides our patients the chance to express compassion and caring for us—a rare opportunity.

You will best be able to assure your patients that they don't need to take care of you by in fact making sure that you are taking care of yourself as best you can. Clearly, your community and support system, professionally and personally, are crucial right now.

Finally, as a model of communication, therapist self-disclosure "can also encourage members, who may fear letting others into their own private domains, the implicit assurance that it is possible to do so and yet survive as a psychologically intact and responsive participant in the group's work" (Cohen & Schermer, 2001, p. 51).

Indeed you are in the midst of major personal and professional decisions. My heart goes out to you, having been in a similar situation many years ago.

Sara J. Emerson, LICSW, CGP, FAGPA

References

Cohen, B. D., & Schermer, V. L. (2001). Therapist self-disclosure in group psychotherapy from an intersubjective and self psychological standpoint. *Group, 25,* 41–57.

Feinsilver, D. B. (1998). The therapist as a person facing death: The hardest of external realities and therapeutic action. *International Journal of Psycho-Analysis, 79,* 1131–1150.

Pizer, B. (1997). When the analyst is ill: Dimensions of self-disclosure. *Psychoanalytic Quarterly, 66,* 450–469.

Dear Therapist:

Times appear in one's life and the life of a group when everyone hopes to hold on and survive. If the group and the therapist can learn along the way, so much the better. This is clearly one of those times. The fact that this dilemma appears in a section on self-disclosure provides an obvious focus for the nature of the problem that is confronting you and your group. A rich and complex literature exists on this topic, filled with historical notions of what is proper therapeutic technique and what has actually been done. Although self-disclosure is a clinical decision influenced by one's particular theoretical model, here the underlying issue is the global dilemma of therapist countertransference.

You are indeed struggling to make decisions as to how much you want to reveal about yourself and how much might be revealed whether you intend it or not. This is an interesting problem in itself. Given any amount of unconscious attunement between you and the group, plus some natural curiosity, we can assume that emotionally a great deal will be communicated with or without your verbal expression or conscious attempt to do so. You seem clearly to understand this aspect of this dilemma when you pose the question in the final sentence that, roughly paraphrased, might read as follows: "Who gets taken care of in this situation—the group or the therapist —and what emotional cost will be paid?" Again, at bottom this is a countertransference issue.

The title of this dilemma is also revealing. From the background given, you are deliberately ambiguous about which family is being broken up. Several exist to choose from here. Is it the group itself, the real families of some of the members, the virtual group family, or your own family? With each loss, real or imagined, the accompanying loss of both the cherished object and the underlying fantasies begin to explicate the meaning of the loss. This might include themes regarding one's place in the interpersonal world, how one controls the world, and cherished aspects of the self. Phrased in this manner, the lurking dangers here are not only of the disruptive isolation, despair, and grief but also of the internal experience of potentially traumatic disillusionment for the group members and you alike. In many ways, uncomfortably so, you and the members are confronted with parallel terrors. Who teaches whom and who leads whom might be the most relevant questions.

Definitions of countertransference cover a broad spectrum from the most inclusive to the most narrow. The more narrow definitions include only those idiosyncratic responses of the therapist to the patient's transference. The broader definitions cover all therapist responses to the entire clinical situation. Although the size of the universe of responses to this definitional problem is debatable, the more relevant consideration is the capacity of the therapist to develop an exquisite awareness of his personal responses, attitudes, and behaviors. Gradually, over decades of clinical practice and evolution of clinical theory, it has become clear to me that any deeply meaningful therapeutic encounter demands the emotional involvement of both the patient and the therapist.

The therapist is asked to attune himself to the emotional realities, or, better put, the emotional experience of the patient. Clinical theory has migrated from privileging the interpretation as the central element of therapeutic efficacy to conceptualizing empathy in that role—both as a data-gathering tool and a clinical intervention. Consequently, the centrality of the empathic perspective requires the therapist to place himself closer to the experiential world of the patient. To do this, the therapist is asked both to immerse himself in the patient's world while simultaneously maintaining a clinical–observational perspective. Stepping into the patient's world through partial identifications and the use of the countertransference is both a source of vital creative transformative energy and the slippery slope of dangerous countertransference enactments.

Theory, consultation, self-knowledge, and experience all contribute to the therapist's capacity to have the ego resources to both emotionally immerse oneself in the patient's or group's experience and maintain sufficient emotional distance to provide the functions necessary for psychotherapy to progress. When overwhelming life events occur, especially within areas of vulnerability for the therapist, this capacity shrinks. This describes the current group dilemma.

You are overwhelmed with your own sense of loss and shame. You are struggling to keep yourself from being flooded by these feelings while attempting to provide an emotional space within the group for the members to explore and contain their own overwhelming feelings, and you predict that group members will likely inquire as to the reasons for the changes in group time and venue.

My experiences have born this out. When I once switched the time and day of an ongoing group, I was met with a brief silence and then several questions about the change. Patients had some interest in knowing about the realities surrounding this change of the situation. However, on further exploration it became apparent that the questions were prompted mostly by unnamed or unexpressed anxieties. As these anxieties within the group were explored and understood, a reduction in the interest around the specifics of my circumstances occurred. I had minimal concern about sharing my situation; the topic had little personal vulnerability for me.

Looking back, this emotional position allowed me, most importantly, to not need any particular confirming or empathic response from the group. I had the luxury of not feeling afraid of my feelings or theirs. I was free to direct my attention to exploring the meaning of the associations from the group and the personal meanings that were being shared. I could even venture to inquire about what was too dangerous to speak about.

However, in this emotionally overwrought situation you describe, I would strongly recommend you to make creative use of your professional resources. This is the right time to be either in personal therapy, professional consultation, or both. This is a time of potential personal and professional transition, and the more support to develop new coping skills the better. In addition, a therapist whose personal needs are being addressed constructively is less likely to act on those needs within his professional life.

Within the group context, I would begin by suggesting that you do what you are accustomed to doing. Obviously, this is what has worked thus far with this group and for you. It has been my experience that keeping in mind my baseline way of functioning within the group, and noting if I begin to deviate from this, provides me with a reference point for my countertransference reactions. I would advise you to maintain as much awareness as possible of your own feelings during and after the group. Although this might be painful, it actually immerses you in the same task as the group is being asked to accomplish. As you pay exquisite attention to your emotional experience, fantasies, memories, thoughts, and feelings, this will provide a deeper level of resonance to the experience of the patients, as well as assist you to not defend yourself from your experience, but rather to learn from it.

I would also advise you to keep the initial announcement about the upcoming changes brief and fact-oriented. As the group reacts to the announcement of the changes, it is useful to study their associations and begin to assist the group to develop the meanings both for the group and the individual patients in terms of the struggles and changes in their lives. If personal questions do arise, I would recommend you check with the group as to how to understand the emotional message involved in the question.

Because each self-disclosure involves the entire group, it is helpful to monitor the participation of all group members during this discussion. Beware of a uniformity of views. Transference needs are often conflicted and group conformity is usually a signal of defensive operations rather than a free flow of experience. Direct requests for emotional contact, especially if they signal something new that is a shift in the transference relationship paradigm, are best met with direct answers. These interchanges tend to be progressive toward emotional growth. If the questions seem too exposing or uncomfortable in some way, a direct communication to the group about your unwillingness to answer that question, with a short explanation, is useful. Omissions and prevarications are never useful in building the trust and cohesion essential for the group to function in such times of distress.

Gil Spielberg, PhD, CGP, FAGPA

If I Did It, Why Can't You?

Dear Consultant:

For years, I have been trying to figure out if self-disclosure has a place in my groups. I've been practicing for about 10 years and I am comfortable sharing aspects of my personal life with my individual patients, but I'm more reluctant in my groups. This has to do with my training and with my not being clear of the effects on group members because they can react from such different places. I have three typical examples of personal areas I would love to disclose but do not.

First, in groups I have run with individuals who have experienced earlier deprivation and neglect, if not frank physical or sexual abuse, I often want to tell them that I was physically abused by my father, cursed at by my mother, neglected in general, and here I am anyway. My hope would be to serve as a model of identification for group members, but I have been hesitant to mention anything because I just don't know whether this is wise or right.

Second, although I lead groups, I am shy in social gatherings, and prefer to avoid them, although I go to many of them as a matter of course, and manage to interact with general success. This is not at all how my group members typically view me. Instead, they often have an idealizing view of me as popular, poised, and socially at ease, because in the group I am rarely flustered and can display a decent sense of humor. When group members speak of hating themselves because of their self-described childish, embarrassing, or shameful social interactions, I have urges to blurt that it's common to be shy and not a terrible thing, especially if they can find a good friend or two, which is what I have done. I'm afraid though that this might diminish their idealization of me, which I enjoy, or that they would

213

pay less attention to my interventions about ways to manage their social anxieties.

Third, I used to have a fairly quick temper, but have worked hard to suppress that in my daily interactions with good success. The group never sees me flare up, or at least I don't think they do because I come from the school of "the fewer interventions, the better," so I listen a lot. Some group members are working on controlling their anger, yet feel hopeless about it, arguing that "as the twig is bent, so is the tree inclined." Again, if I tell them, "Wait, I've overcome my anger—for the most part anyway—so there's hope for you," would that be productive?

So, I guess I'm asking whether a group therapist's earlier history, personal anxieties, or problematic impulses or feelings should ever be disclosed and if so, are there rules of thumb to help one know when optimally to share?

Dear Therapist:

Therapist self-disclosure is a thorny therapeutic issue, particularly so in group therapy where divulging personal information may result in a profusion of unwitting effects that the clinician can hardly imagine, much less control. Although this is true for any therapeutic intervention, therapist self-disclosure is *personal* in a way that other types of interventions are not. Further, reasons for disclosure are also more personal, creating an added dimension to clinical decisions that do not somehow encroach on the therapist's personal life. In looking at the dilemma presented for this chapter, I think you did an excellent job of highlighting potential pitfalls of revealing personal information and addressing the complexity of decisions to self-disclose. These include therapist motives for sharing personal information, attention to dual roles, recognizing the limits of control over how clients experience the therapist, dangers of wanting to help, and the ever-present necessity for therapist self-care.

My lens for examining self-disclosure is Redecision therapy, an existential, humanistic theory that is action-oriented in its emphasis on identifying and changing maladaptive behaviors and transferring this learning into the client's life outside of the therapy office. The group structure involves individual work in which the therapist and group members play crucial roles as they witness, support, confront, and validate. Although group-as-a-whole interventions are not part of Redecision group process, I am attentive to effects of interventions on individuals and the group itself and may comment on commonalities, differences, themes, and other aspects of the process of group.

Using this context, I turn to the issues you raise. I would likely not disclose information about abuse by my parents unless the issue arose in the context of a specific therapeutic situation. I do not usually reveal personal information about a specific issue because to do so seems more connected to something I am wanting for myself than to what is happening in the group. I am persistently curious about my motives for self-disclosure anytime I consider revealing personal information. When my desire to disclose is not contingent on a particular situation in the group, I am skeptical, and, if I am aware of strong affect, as reflected in your comment that you would "love" to reveal abuse by your family, I am downright suspicious. The central issue is whether the self-disclosure is in the interest of the client or the therapist.

At times, therapists can experience a desire to become members of their own group. This *group envy* can be powerful, and clinicians may unwittingly use self-disclosure as a way to "join" the group and abdicate the therapist role. I experienced this when I moved to a new city with few friends and little emotional support. As therapist for a cohesive group of women who were working through deeply-felt abuse issues, I noticed that I was envious of their intimacy and my desire to use the group to assuage my loneliness. With this awareness, I was able to acknowledge my vulnerability, attend to getting an appropriate support network, and keep group boundaries intact.

Another issue raised in your dilemma is your desire to serve as a "model of identification" for group members with similar personal histories. Although wanting to serve as a role model may be admirable, it is not therapy and results in a dual role. These overlapping relationships cannot always be avoided, as therapists in small towns, for example, can attest. These roles are also not necessarily harmful to the client. The clinician, however, needs to be thoughtful and clear about how she or he bends boundaries in order to protect the primacy of the therapeutic relationship. In an experience of overlapping roles with clients in a professional organization, I began to notice that I wanted to be liked in a way that was not a concern when my only role was therapist. The danger became that I might abdicate my role as therapist because I was reluctant to make interventions that would result in the clients' potential to become angry or dislike me.

I would also be unlikely to reveal personal information about my social skills (or lack of them) unless the disclosure would be useful for a particular client in a specific situation. In this connection, you identify a desire to maintain your clients' assumed idealization of you. Idealization is a part of the therapeutic process and can be a heady experience for a therapist. It is, however, irrational to believe that we can control how clients see us, and perhaps a relief to give up trying.

In addition, we have little control over whether clients "pay less attention" to our interventions, another aspect of your dilemma. Although we might like for all of our interventions to be welcomed as brilliant (or at least useful), we have little control over that, as well. Our task is to offer what we can, and let clients take what is useful to them. Carl Whitaker, in his wisdom, says we should honor our impotence as our most valuable asset.

The issue of motives for self-disclosure is again raised when you note "urges to blurt" information about yourself. It is important to be suspicious of these urges and make decisions about disclosure on the basis of the needs of clients.

I would be unlikely to disclose information about my former "fairly quick temper," unless there were some compelling reason to do so in a specific situation. It may be surprising for you to learn, however, that group members already know about your temper. Indeed, we are likely to be more transparent to our clients than we know or care to know. The bad news is that we can't hide some aspects of ourselves that we might want to hide, and the good news is that we don't have to expend energy trying.

Finally, in this particular vignette, you express your hope that self-disclosure might prevent clients from feeling hopeless. Most of us enter the profession because we want to help people in pain. It is hoped that we lose our naiveté and get on with the business of being therapists. If we address our own hopelessness and tolerate being in the presence of human suffering, we can sit with clients without having to change their hopelessness to please us.

I did not always take the positions I describe above. My views of self-disclosure have changed as a result of my work as a therapist and from the many simple and profound lessons I have learned from my clients. Perhaps equally significant for me have been ongoing professional development, unrelenting consultation, and my personal therapy. I am now less likely to identify with clients who have similar issues. I can maintain both compassion for their pain and distance from it that allows me to think more clearly about how to work with them. I feel less attached to whether I self-disclose and let the situation be the guide. I have fewer delusions that I can help clients. As a result, I am willing to do what is possible and let the clients do what they will. These have helped me to change and grow as a therapist and to observe, time after time, that no *right* way to do therapy exists.

This triad of self-care has also served as a means to avert ethical breaches that often result from a failure of self-care. Therapy helps me to avoid inflicting my unresolved issues on my clients. Ongoing consultation in a group format has provided me a place to discuss clients, my reactions to them, and strategies for clinical work. Finally, professional development throughout my career keeps me fresh in the work and open to new ideas.

Together these provide a forum for addressing the impact of self-disclosure and other ethical issues, as well as support for me as a clinician and a measure of protection for the client.

Marti B. Kranzberg, PhD, CGP, FAGPA

Dear Therapist:

My initial response to this three part dilemma is a negative one on all counts. My underlying reasons derive from my therapeutic standpoint about self-disclosure, which has not changed over the years.

Group psychotherapy is a widely accepted discipline and many different theoretical models and trainings exist. My own orientation is psychoanalytic and I work both as a group analyst and an individual analyst (Jungian). After many years I am firmly rooted in this discipline and my clinical work is informed and guided by this.

Briefly, group analysis was developed by S. H. Foulkes and its roots are in sociology and psychology. It is treatment of the individual in the group, of the group, and by the group, including the therapist. The role of the group analyst is that of a "participant observer" rather than an active leader (Foulkes, 1964). Like group analysts, Jungian analysts maintain a fairly low profile by trying to be appropriately self-contained, neither a blank screen nor overly active.

In your presentation of the dilemma, you appear comfortable sharing personal aspects with individuals and are reluctant to do so in groups. I find this to be a deeply ambivalent position. I work mainly in analytic groups with transference and countertransference and resist the temptation to give personal information to patients that might not contribute to and might divert or impede the development of the group or individuals within it.

The dominant thought in my mind is "Will this help the patient?" In my experience the answer is usually no. Nevertheless, patients may ask personal questions, and in this event I try to answer simply, without elaboration, preferring first to explore fantasy: "I may be happy to give you the information but could you explore first why you need it?" In most cases, this leads the questioner in another direction. At other times a fragile patient may need to know where I am going on vacation, not out of curiosity alone, but to feel safer knowing where I might be physically located in the world.

Self-disclosure also has an ethical facet. It may lead patients to question their own ability to contain *their* self-disclosure. Total trustworthiness is the essence of ethical behavior. Responding with personal information could be interpreted as acting out. It may occur when the analyst feels defeated or a failure. Staying with one's own helplessness instead of volunteering how one has overcome a similar trauma can be more therapeutic. In other words, remember and think before speaking and acting. "Let no day pass without humbly remembering that everything still has to be learned" (Jung, 1970, p. 255).

I believe it is important for a therapist to develop a capacity to sustain a high level of anxiety that can arise in both the therapist and the group. How much is this group (individual) pushing this therapist's boundaries so that he or she feels a self-revelatory response is needed or may be helpful? Foulkes (1964) wrote about achieving the right equilibrium between human involvement and a desirable detachment. Group therapy is a search for understanding; finding the location of anxiety gets near to this understanding.

I recommend my students to read Patrick Casement's *On Learning From the Patient* (1985). He illustrates vividly how he has learned to monitor the implications of his own contributions by metaphorically lying alongside the patient on the couch. We as group therapists can all benefit from his experiences.

In dealing with the dilemma over anger, you should not be under any illusion that the group does not recognize the signs, particularly if it is a well established group. Therapists sometimes do become angry and show it. In doing so, we may illustrate we can cope with anger and even apologize when it might be a faulty response. No, it would not be productive to say, "I overcame my anger." So what? If the therapist needs to discuss personal problems and achievements, join a group, have supervision, but do not use the patient group for therapy or self-congratulatory purposes.

When dealing with major traumas that affect organizations, communities, or cities, the group will well know if you are involved and are suffering too. It is still extremely difficult to try to contain one's own grief and deal with the group's as well. If you find you cannot, then abstain from leading the group until you feel able to deal with extreme stress and anxiety. The group has first claim on the therapist's professional skills; however much they may be depleted by private trauma, it is not the group's role to help with the therapist's problems.

Remember that you—indeed, all therapists—are not invisible. We reveal ourselves from the very first encounter: how we look, dress, speak, have facial expressions, and decorate the office. Just as we learn over time to read our group's expressions and moods fairly accurately, so does the group learn to read the therapist and will surely pick up a clue if something is wrong or the therapist appears distracted or subdued. A colleague once reported hearing about a close friend's death in a car accident just before her group. She got through the group but could recall little of what went on. In the next session, a patient said, "We knew something was wrong with you so we just carried on as usual."

Some therapists leave informative messages for the group if they are unable to attend: "have the flu," "delayed in heavy traffic," "work crises," and so on. These kinds of messages are most likely to avoid or block any kind of aggression that might be felt by the group in response. A simple message such as "please meet without me" leaves it open for patients' reactions without blocking them with reality.

Let us assume it is a basic instinct to want to make ourselves look good as therapists. However, when it comes to idealization, the sooner this is diminished, the better. In writing about transference and countertransference, Menninger and Holtzman (1973) discuss the therapist's inability to understand certain kinds of material that touch on one's own personal problems, and they discuss narcissistic devices such as trying to impress the patient in various ways. "One must be constantly alert to the existence of countertransference . . . recognizing both its pitfalls and its uses" (Menninger & Holtzman, 1973, p. 93).

Patients are basically—and rightly—really only interested in their own progress. Therapists are not indispensable. Groups survive even if the therapist does not—a sobering thought (Sharpe, 1991). In any event, patients assume the therapist has had a good enough analysis and is a step ahead of them. To reveal one's own personal struggle may make the therapist feel better: "I am like you only I'm okay now." The patient may be encouraged that change is possible or the patient may feel he can never achieve that and thus become more depressed and despondent.

Enid Balint (1993), writing about the mirror in "The Mirror and Receiver," discussed the distance of the analyst from the patient: "A patient may feel more alone, more isolated, more distant from the analyst when the analyst is friendly or sympathetic and deviating from the mirror model . . . . Although the healthier part of the patient may feel some satisfaction or even gratification from the sympathetic analyst, the ill part of him which is seeking help may feel out of contact and not reached or even ignored" (p. 59). The mirror model enables "the analyst to be neither distant nor close, but just there." Finally Jean Cocteau's advice "Know how far to go not to go too far" illustrates the delicate balance the therapist must hold and attain all the time while working through transference and countertransference, which are the center of therapeutic work.

Meg Sharpe, BA (Hons), MInst GA, CGP

References

Balint, E. (1993). *Before I was I*. London: Free Association Books.

Casement, P. (1985). *On learning from the patient*. London: Social Science Paperbacks, Tavistock Publications.

Foulkes, S. H. (1964). *Therapeutic group analysis*. London: Routledge.

Jung, C. G. (1970). *Collected works: The practice of psychotherapy* (Vol. 16). London: Routledge.

Menninger, K., & Holtzman, P. (1973). *Theory of analytic technique*. New York: Basic Books,

Sharpe, M. (1991). Death and the practice. In J. Roberts & M. Pines (Eds.), *The practice of group analysis*. London: Routledge, Keegan, Paul.

Sharing at the Exit

Dear Consultant:

In an unusual coincidence of timing, my coed psychodynamic group is ending after 3 years. All the patients are in their mid-thirties and five of the six members are moving to other states because they have just graduated or are getting married to someone who has taken a job elsewhere. During my work with them, I have revealed few details of my personal life. Because my office is located outside my home, my patients do not know where I live, what church I attend, or whether I have children. The issue of whether I have children has become particularly salient because one of the group members just had a baby. In the past, I have asked for fantasies from the group members, which have ranged from yes, I have one special needs child to I'm infertile to I hate children and lead a romantic and adventurous life with a handsome husband. As our termination ends, the group members have become more curious about my life. When they ask questions, we have long discussions about what it would mean to them to know.

Recently, one member, June, left the group when she graduated from law school. Before she left, she asked me again if I have children. As I always do, I asked the group for their fantasies, but this time June said she really wanted to know before she left, rather than just having me explore the fantasies. Because other members, especially Martha, said they didn't want to know, I decided not to tell June the answer and she became very angry. Ultimately, we were unable to resolve the issue before she left. I felt horrible because I really liked her and we had done some good work together. I also know it may have been easier for her to leave in anger.

My question is whether one should answer questions more openly if a group is going to end. I often answer questions as I near the end of individual therapy with patients, but not so many as to interfere with the transference if they should return at a later date. In group, it seems much more complicated. Some patients want to know pieces of information about me and others don't. How do you decide to whom to tell what, because they are all present at the same time? In addition, Paul, the lone group patient who showed up last week, told me he had looked me up on the Internet. He read every reference to me and my family. He found out I am president of my church, that I am on the Board of the Arts Counsel, and that I was involved in a law suit regarding a land dispute with a neighbor. When Paul revealed to me that he had done so, he said he felt closer to me now that he knew more about me, even though he also felt somewhat embarrassed. Initially I felt his action was intrusive, but then I saw his remorse as containing boundaries. However, I don't know how to handle it in group. Is this an out-of-group contact? Does it need to be told to the entire group? What if I do raise it in the group and all the patients look me up on the Internet? I think I will feel that my privacy has been invaded. How is his disclosure related to my ambivalence about answering the group's questions about my personal life?

Dear Therapist:

My own theoretical position about self-disclosure is that it depends on the context and the values of the therapist. By context, I mean the immediate situation that the group, including the therapist, is consciously and unconsciously experiencing. By values, I mean the criteria the therapist uses in defining the relationship between himself or herself and the group that maximizes purpose and meaning to the group experience.

A therapist's pursuit or belief in his or her objectivity or neutrality as a means for conducting psychodynamic group psychotherapy is bound to fail, as you are discovering. Two dramatic examples from my practice illustrate the folly of neutrality to which you are trying rigidly to adhere. One is the New York City blackout of 1981 when I had a penthouse office on the 26th floor. The other is 9/11. In each instance, the context is a crisis that severely disrupts the sense of order and safety in an expected dependable world.

During the blackout, patients and I trudged up 26 floors to hold our sessions. Scheduled appointments could not be maintained, people came when they could, and I arranged spontaneous groupings of three or four patients, depending on arrival time. One group that evening had ten patients, at least five of whom were not group members. The ordinary boundaries of time allotments for patients were suspended. Hierarchical positions of leader and patient, object and subject, were transcended by the common humanity of us all, mortal, vulnerable, anxious, and dependent. We were like the pioneers that went west in covered wagons, braving dangers together.

Although 9/11 was more intense in the arousal of fear and horror, it was also a wake-up call in my practice as to shared existential meanings of our common mortality and the desire to expose our authentic selves. I acknowledged openly my fear and anger about the terrorist attack. I noted the limitations of protecting ourselves and assuring safety. I cried with others about the loss of life and the devastation to families. I recognized that, although the group is at times a safe harbor from the outside world, I must still remember that we also all live outside the group in a different reality that may be suspended momentarily, but cannot be denied by a group cocoon. I also expressed my awareness that I live in a larger world and have a responsibility to be more aware of the limitations of my control over events and of my own vulnerability. My comments that day and subsequently were in the context of a deeply shared consciousness among group members and a recognition of a previously unstated intimacy.

The dilemma you are facing is not about maintaining your theoretical frame in the midst of the invasive attempts of patients. It is about the crisis of the impending death of a living entity. To provide meaning to this death, literal and symbolic mourning requires a shared experience for all members, including yourself. As I see it, the question is not whether openly answering questions and concerns will affect your neutrality or dilute the transference. It is whether you and the group can process the finality of ending as a subjective experience of mutual sadness, remembering shared and treasured moments and accepting the limitations of knowing. Like the affects associated with death and dying, attention needs to be paid to anger, relief, grief, bargaining for more time, and acceptance. You need to lead by personally venturing into your own affects and then making them acceptable to the group. You must announce a definitive date for ending the group that will serve as an organizing and structural boundary.

Once a concentration on mutually shared feelings appears, you may find it more natural to disclose yourself. You certainly can state what the group has meant to you personally. I find it useful at these times to compare the group to a mutually tended baby that all have contributed to "raising," including moments of endangered survival. Now this older child is leaving the nest and entering the world. I might also review moments in the group's history when there was a threat to its existence, and such a crisis impinged on me and promoted growth. I might reveal what I have learned from the members individually and collectively as a way of personally being involved.

I would not worry about compromising the transference. I would make distinctions between transferential curiosity and normative curiosity. Transferential curiosity is when a patient asks you for personal information with an underlying motive of enlarging or diminishing an existing fantasy about you. Paul's extensive search for Internet information, then, is more in the transferential category. However, he may be acting for other members who are disturbed by your placing a higher priority on the "work" while Rome is burning. His intrusive behavior may reflect a group wish to take you with them as the group ends, or it may be to concretize a memory of you, like a keepsake.

Although Paul told you what he did while alone with you, you need to treat this as group material, to be brought up in the group. You can acknowledge your initial anger and shame but this might be seen as turning the tables. I would advise a response that embraces resistance through a joining approach that recognizes the context: "Paul, you are to be complimented for taking such a huge risk and treading on eviction. You seem to want to lead the group to see the necessity of changing our boundaries as the group is ending." You might admit how hard it is for everyone to end the group with so much that is unfinished and so little time left. Everybody needs their version of a favorite doll—for example, personal information: "I have my own hardship about ending the group. My continued emphasis on eliciting fantasies is my own resistance to the inevitable ending."

In individual analysis, frustration of oral cravings is intended to promote regression and deepen transference by a neutral stance. This is not comparable to group therapy. From the onset of group, members are in constant view of each other. Words, inflections, expressions, posture, tone, and a host of other personal signals are self-disclosing all the time.

Because the topic of children seems often to be raised in this group and has been subject to considerable conflict, I want to discuss this in greater depth. Questions about whether you have children are laden with meaning about hope and the future because children carry the previous generation. For many, this is the promise of immortality, of not simply disappearing. This group may be communicating their fear of dying and not being remembered, or this focus on children might indicate hidden wishes to be the only child, the favored child, the rejected child, and so on.

It is impossible to feel the same way about each patient. Each patient has a different valence for us that is not simply countertransference. You might review and disclose the valence each patient and the group has for you before the group ends. You may even disclose how your views have changed from the beginning of the group to the present. Each patient deserves to know something about what meaning they have for you. A device I have used is to have each person, including you, compose a short poem spontaneously about each other. If I were to compose a short poem about you, the therapist, it would go as follows:

> Science is but a tool for human use
> There is always an infinity of knowledge
> Keep low to the ground
> Observe with your ears
> Seeing is not believing

No psychodynamic group is meaningful if it does not enhance the quality of life for its members. This is my value. Spending my time with a group is equivalent to spending my life. Time and life are inseparable.

Bernard Frankel, PhD, CGP, FAGPA, BCD

Dear Therapist:

My first thought in responding to you is that I probably have more questions than answers for you. I would love to sit and talk with you so that I could listen, watch, feel, respond to you, and ask many questions. Because I cannot sit with you, I will imagine you and the consultation in my mind's eye. In our consultation session I would inquire about your theoretical base and your style. You did not make a clear statement about this. However, within the range of choices you had about the dimensions of your role, you appear to have chosen to be more passive than active, perhaps more frustrating to the group than gratifying, rather more opaque than transparent, and to place a focus on transference and fantasy. Therefore, I "hear" in your choices that you are somewhat of a traditionalist, and I will base my comments on that assumption.

Your description of the early stages of the group's development seems to indicate that you felt the group was working well. You mentioned that there was earlier testing, perhaps in the power and control stage, and that it came in the form of a challenge to you to self-disclose whether you had children. You comfortably decided to deal with this by exploring group members' fantasies and what meaning this would have for them. If my assumption about you being a traditionalist is correct, your decision not to disclose seems in keeping with your theoretical base. However, you are less clear about this decision when June, who is about to terminate, repeats her question about whether you have children. You have selected an opaque position during earlier stages of the group, so why waver now? If you thought that using self-disclosure could be a productive intervention, then I wonder why you didn't choose to use it more throughout the life of the group. Perhaps you have not had the opportunity to think through your position about using self-disclosure in a group or perhaps if self-disclosure would be a departure from your style, your ambivalence means that something else is going on for you.

Some psychodynamic group therapists are comfortable with including self-disclosure in their role, whereas others would not self-disclose and would advise you to remain opaque. Although at one point in my development as a group therapist I would not have self-disclosed, I now have come to use it in a limited way, and I feel transparency can be a helpful option in a therapist's repertoire. It is critical that self-disclosure be used only in the service of the group's work. Members are expected to self-disclose, but therapists should self-disclose only if its clear intent is to help the group or an individual.

I have thought about your comment that as the group nears termination the members are more curious about your life. I think group members are always curious about us. They watch, listen, and interpret everything they can about us throughout the life of the group. They want to use us as role models and teachers, as well as therapists. If we can use self-disclosure in an appropriate and comfortable way, then something can be gained. You wrote that you often answer direct questions as you near the end of therapy with individual patients. I am not sure why you choose to do this with individuals, but you should understand the meaning of this heightened curiosity and the push for you to disclose personal information. You are right to understand that using self-disclosure with an individual patient is different from using it in group. We do not decide to whom to tell what; we decide if we are going to disclose to the group-as-a-whole. I think you are also correct that the members are picking up on your ambivalence. Perhaps Martha and June are representing both sides of your ambivalence, one wanting you to disclose and one not. Your question about whether Paul's disclosure is related to your ambivalence is best answered by exploring this in the group. Paul has already brought up his out-of-group actions in a group session and it is important to continue to process this with the entire group. Another possibility is that you are all focusing on whether you will share to avoid the more important question about whether the group and you will process this termination.

Although your focus in this dilemma is on self-disclosure, equally important is the unexpected termination of the group. Your attention is on your sense of being invaded and the loss of your neutrality, but if I focus solely on this issue, perhaps I would be colluding with you and the group in avoiding the real issues. I wonder if this parallels what is going on in the group—that is, the group and you are colluding to not deal with termination by focusing instead on what you will, or will not, disclose.

Let us look at the fact that you were quite distressed with the process of June's termination. She was a member who did good work, but at the end the sadness, anger, pride, and joy of her "graduation" seem not to have been processed. The focus stayed on whether you would disclose personal facts about your life. The group is coming to an end. What are your feelings? What are the members feeling about terminating after 3 years of very personal interaction? What are the feelings of the member who is not moving and is losing the group? I think the question of "to share or not to share" is not about you sharing your personal information, but about whether you and the group will share in the personal experience of terminating your relationships. Will these feelings be avoided while you and the group focus on whether you share factual information, and in doing so, replay June's termination— that is, does the style with which June, the group, and you handled June's termination become a group norm? In this light, a member pursued through cyberspace personal information about you and brought it into the group. This is now a group issue and exploring this along with other issues of termination is the work.

I have found that sharing my feelings about what is happening in the group has been consistently more productive and valuable as an intervention than sharing biographical details. My wish is that you and the group can find a way to appreciate what you have accomplished together and what the group has meant to each of you before you end. I wish you a rich and productive termination.

Brenda L. Smith, MSW, LICSW, CGP

Section VII
Time-Limited Groups

Overview

For many of us, the passage of time serves as the quiet backdrop to our lives. Events occur, however, which force time into the spotlight. For the astronauts on Apollo 13, time was the enemy as their oxygen, water, and electricity diminished, jeopardizing their successful return to Earth. Facing death, their rescue efforts quickened as the clock ticked. Less dramatically, but no less compellingly, for those who experience psychological distress, time can be the enemy as well. On one hand, suffering can feel endless, whereas on the other, the time available for treatment can be short. As it happens, we have developed treatments that take time into account.

In his chapter *Working with the Clock Ticking*, Ted Powers explores the recent surge in time-limited group treatments, the structure of such treatments, and the powerful—at times paradoxical—benefits that derive from limited time.

In the first dilemma of this section, *Stand By Your Stance*, the finitude of time takes on deep meaning for the therapist and his cancer support group, as several of them press for the time-limited group to continue beyond its endpoint and are upset with the therapist for holding firm. Both Ramon Ganzarain and William Piper respond by supporting the therapist's decision and emphasize the centrality of loss as a theme for these patients—of the group and possibly of their lives. Ganzarain is clear that such patients "need to learn very difficult lessons about how to end and how to die." Piper agrees, and also reflects on the time-limited clinician's common counter-transferential resistance to saying goodbye, which can lead the therapist "to collude with patients' irrational wishes" to continue indefinitely.

In *Manage My Stress*, the therapist expresses confusion and dissatisfaction that his stress management group never achieved traction or intensity and ended with nary a whimper. Consultant Pamela Enders offers suggestions about structuring a group differently the next time, highlighting the therapist's failure to address significant issues in creating this group. Arthur Horne also emphasizes pre-group planning as "the key to solving many possible problems."

In contrast to the tepid nature of the stress management group noted above, the trauma survivors group described in *Containing Contagion* experiences too much intensity. Consultant Helen Riess notes the inevitability of this group's regression given its failure to end when initially planned and the lack of a clear contract or boundaries in its second phase. Mark Sorensen focuses not only on technical strategies to avoid regression in such groups but also on the need for the supervisor and the therapist to recognize and own their powerful countertransferential reactions.

Working with the Clock Ticking

THEODORE A. POWERS, PHD

"The time has arrived for brief group treatment," Poey declared in 1985 (p. 331), but what is "brief group treatment," and has its time really arrived? To be sure, the past 30 years have seen a tremendous surge in the use of time-limited groups and time-limited therapies in general. Although many approaches to group treatment are well researched and produce empirically established results, there are still a number of factors that continue to inhibit the wide appeal and comprehensive use of time-limited groups. This chapter will examine time-limited group psychotherapy, its theory and practice, as well as its utility and future.

Introduction

Traditionally, effective group therapy was thought of as necessarily long-term treatment. Economic realities and theoretical shifts, however, converged to produce substantial changes in the health care delivery system leading to the development of more efficient and cost-effective treatment modalities. Group treatment was not to be left out of these tectonic shifts in the practice of psychotherapy. The *International Journal of Group Psychotherapy* produced a special issue in 1985 devoted to the practice of brief or short-term group therapy. Several of the now seminal articles chronicling the origins of short-term groups were published in this special issue (Dies, 1985; Klein, 1985; Poey, 1985). These writings provide some of the early guidelines and principles for the practice of brief group therapy.

The majority of early short-term therapy groups were reality based, focused on problem solving, and delivered in an inpatient setting (Klein, 1977), crisis group (Donovan, Bennett, & McElroy, 1979), marathon group

(Mintz, 1971), or psychoeducational group format (Drum & Knott, 1977). Developments in theory and technique led to the emergence of outpatient time-limited psychotherapy groups of a psychodynamic and interpersonal nature (Budman & Gurman, 1988; MacKenzie, 1990; Piper, McCallum, & Azim, 1992). Both Klein (1985) and Poey (1985) discuss the theoretical considerations and technical aspects of brief therapy groups. Klein (1985) summarizes the shared technical characteristics of short-term groups such as group composition, patient selection, preparation, and contracting. With Dies (1985), he emphasizes the role and therapeutic stance of the leader.

Klein (1985) also raises the supportive–interpretive question, which has been consistently debated throughout the brief therapy literature. He argues that the short-term therapist must be active, but that the therapeutic stance, whether supportive or interpretive, needs to be fashioned in response to the level of pathology and ego adaptive capacity of the group members, the therapist's level of competence and experience, the goals of the group, and the constraints on the treatment, such as the amount of time. Although maintaining that carefully selected, healthier, and well-prepared patients may benefit from an essentially interpretive stance, he suggests that in the short-term group it may only be possible to identify core internal or interpersonal conflicts and examine their interpersonal effects, but not to work these through or achieve lasting structural change. In sum, he states that the therapist's role in short-term group therapy should tend toward the supportive and include several essential elements, such as: quickly engaging the patient and promoting positive transference; maintaining an active goal-directed approach; maintaining a primarily ahistorical, conscious, and preconscious focus on ego functioning; strengthening healthier defenses; and even incorporating cognitive and didactic elements into the group process.

The important distinction between short-term psychotherapy and time-limited psychotherapy was drawn by Budman and Gurman (1988) who correctly point out that the question of how short is short is not particularly meaningful. Instead, we need to be asking how much time, or for that matter how much therapy, is required to accomplish a particular goal with a particular individual at a particular point in time. The duration of therapy, therefore, becomes a function of the specific focus and purpose of a particular group. Budman and Gurman maintain that the duration ought to be the shortest amount of time necessary to achieve the goals of the group. As such, the duration of a circumscribed crisis-oriented group may be eight sessions, whereas a developmental life transition group may last 15 sessions, and a group focused on chronic dysfunctional interpersonal patterns may last 60 to 70 sessions. The emphasis is, therefore, on time-consciousness and time-effectiveness rather than merely on brevity.

MacKenzie (1990, 1994, 1997), a major contributor to the theory and practice of time-limited group psychotherapy, notes that the time-limited group spends most of its time saying hello and saying goodbye, and he provides a theory of the development of time-limited groups applying the basic principles of traditional interpersonal group work. He lays out the basic principles for conducting time-limited psychotherapy, such as the establishment of the time limit; the need for careful assessment and selection; the explicit establishment of circumscribed goals and group foci; and the use and mobilization of resources within and without the therapy. Like Budman and Gurman (1988), he focuses on the stages of group development and the therapeutic tasks for the members and the role of the leader during each of these stages.

Variations on a theme

As MacKenzie (1994) correctly observed, the term *group psychotherapy* is not very meaningful or informative. Rather, group *psychotherapies* refer to a range of therapeutic formats delivering treatment from a variety of theoretical perspectives within a group setting. Certainly the same applies to time-limited group therapy as a subset. Time-limited groups are used for a wide array of problems with a variety of patients across the diagnostic spectrum. These groups have been vehicles for psychoeducation and skills training, altering interpersonal patterns, and uncovering intrapsychic dynamics. Some groups are based on specific diagnostic criteria (e.g., bulimia, panic disorder, depression, medical illness), others are formed around specific situational or developmental issues (e.g., bereavement, divorce, middle age), and some are organized around more general interpersonal concerns.

There are a number of ways to consider the variations in time-limited group psychotherapies. These distinctions are discussed elsewhere (Levenson, Butler, Powers, & Beitman, 2002) and are summarized here. In broad terms, time-limited group therapy modalities vary along a number of conceptually imprecise but potentially useful continua. These continua are derived to some extent from theoretical distinctions, but they are firmly rooted in consideration of the basic purposes and goals of the particular groups. For example, time-limited group therapies can be said to vary in the extent to which they are structured or unstructured, supportive or expressive–interpretive, and focused on changing specific behaviors, interpersonal patterns, or intrapsychic dynamics. Debate continues in the literature over the centrality of these and other dimensions, and like many sets of distinctions they inevitably fade in the reality of therapeutic practice (Scheidlinger, 1997). Space does not permit a comprehensive discussion of all the various treatment modalities applied to the time-limited group psychotherapy enterprise. Instead, the basic and fundamental characteristics shared by most are presented here in an effort to convey the essence of time-limited group therapy as a vehicle for change.

Technical considerations

Time-limited psychotherapy in general and time-limited group therapy more specifically differs from longer-term or open-ended therapy in a number of important respects. A case can be made, however, that time-limited work differs most decidedly from open-ended therapy in saying hello and saying goodbye. Because the time-limited group spends most of its time beginning and ending, the therapist needs to be keenly aware of and sensitive to the particular dynamics of joining and leaving, and must be equipped with the necessary knowledge and tools to manage these fundamental passages for the therapeutic work to have any hope of success.

The differences between time-limited and open-ended or long-term therapy have been reviewed throughout the literature (Budman & Gurman, 1988; Levenson, Butler, Powers, & Beitman, 2002; MacKenzie, 1990). Although there is a fair degree of variability among time-limited therapies, the essential differences appear to lie in the following areas: (a) selection and preparation for treatment; (b) group focus; (c) active therapist stance; and (d) the paradox of time-limits.

Selection and preparation for treatment   Although careful screening and preparation are important for any group therapy, they are essential for time-limited groups. When the clock is ticking, the group needs to be able to "hit the ground running." Time-limited groups cannot withstand substantial dropouts or gradual evolution of the group that longer-term groups can. Selection criteria for time-limited groups obviously follow from the theoretical orientation of the group as well as the group's purpose and focus. Selection for more expressive–interpretive and therefore more potentially anxiety-provoking groups tend to be more stringent than for supportive or cognitive–behaviorally oriented groups. General exclusion criteria for any time-limited groups include: active psychosis; paranoid, schizoid, and sociopathic character pathology; active suicidal or homicidal ideation; rigid externalizing and somatizing; excessive disorganization, withdrawal, or rage; monopolizing behavior; and active substance abuse, unless the abuse is the focus of the group. Inclusion criteria include a minimum ability to relate, to articulate a focus, and to possess a substantial degree of motivation. Klein (1985) nicely summarizes the selection process by emphasizing the most important factor—congruence between the identified goals and tasks of the group and the ego capacity and motivation of the member to accomplish them.

The processes of screening and preparation are to some degree intertwined. Assessing whether a patient will be an appropriate group member involves a collaborative effort of framing the patient's presenting concerns in direct relation to the focus and objectives of the current group, which is also part of preparing a patient for group. One question in this regard is whether screening and preparation should be conducted individually or in a group. Budman and Gurman (1988) recommend a combination of both. They suggest at least some brief individual contact with the group leader as well as a group screening and preparation workshop. The individual interview is intended to provide information to the patient about groups in general and about the particular group, and to initiate a bond between the therapist and potential group member. This interview also provides an opportunity to frame the patient's concerns in a form that is conducive to making optimal use of the group experience. The therapist helps the patient to articulate an individual focus, to tie that focus to the focus of the group, and to articulate circumscribed, achievable goals. The pre-group workshop, used to assess and prepare potential members for the group experience, also can provide the best sample of in-group behavior for the therapist and the best example of what the group experience may be like for the patient. There is evidence that the use of a pre-group workshop can reduce the likelihood of premature dropouts, which are considerably disruptive to a time-limited group (Piper, Debbane, Garant, et al., 1979).

With respect to group membership, there is debate about whether groups should be open to including new members after the start of the group (MacKenzie, 1993). In an inpatient setting or crisis group format, membership into the group is necessarily open, because of practical constraints. However, for time-limited groups, particularly of brief duration of 15 sessions or less, closed membership provides some decided advantages. Designing the groups to have all members begin and end at the same time can maximize the development of the group process, enhance the all-important development of group cohesion, and minimize disruptions to the group such as premature dropouts. Longer-term time-limited groups can, and sometimes are forced to, manage the inclusion of new members, and this may require the use of renewable group commitments (Budman, Cooley, et al., 1996).

Group focus The concept of focus is central to any form of time-limited therapy. It is the job of the group therapist to clearly define and articulate the workspace for the group. This process involves clarifying and accepting that some things fall within the circumscribed area of the group's work, whereas other things do not. This process of focusing is difficult in any therapy but can be particularly challenging to achieve in a group with different people and multiple agendas. Foci will vary as a function of the particular theoretical perspective of a given group. Therefore, one finds foci that are interpersonal in nature, intrapsychic, behavioral, cognitive, and so forth. Groups can be symptom focused, focused on interaction patterns, or corrective emotional experience. When developing a focus, the group therapist must strike a balance between foci that are too narrowly defined and therefore pertain too specifically to any particular individual, and foci that are too general and thereby apply so loosely to everyone that they lack vitality or meaning. Budman and Gurman (1988) distinguish between a working focus that is established a priori by the therapist and the emergent focus, which is unique to each group and stems from the particular issues and dynamics present in that particular group. In the preparation for group, potential members need to be helped to construe their presenting issues through the lens of the group focus.

Establishing the focus of the group begins to define the identity of the group and fosters group cohesion and homogeneity of group membership. Homogeneity is to some degree a function of the selection process, but this process follows from the purpose and focus of the group. Homogeneity can be sought along concrete dimensions like age or more abstract dimensions like dysfunctional interpersonal patterns. Two particularly important dimensions are homogeneity of coping capacity (ego strength) and homogeneity of purpose. Homogeneity of purpose can begin to develop through the definition and acceptance of the focus. Unlike open-ended groups, which can tolerate or even embrace a greater degree of heterogeneity, time-limited group therapy generally requires a more homogeneous mix in order to promote the necessary rapid coalescence of the group.

The focus of the group also instructs other important decisions, such as group composition, size, and duration. Once the focus has been established, it is the role of the group leader to maintain that focus. The leader maintains the focus by consistently rearticulating it for the group and empathically but firmly and consistently bringing members back to that focus. It is not at all unusual for a time-limited group therapist to express directly to a member or subgroup that the group simply cannot accomplish its goals if the group attempts to cover all territories rather than the agreed upon landscape.

Active therapist stance   There is uniform agreement in the literature on time-limited therapy that the therapist must adopt an active therapeutic stance (Budman & Gurman, 1988; Klein 1985; Poey, 1985). The exact nature of this activity varies with the theoretical model, but all agree there is no time to wait for the unfolding emergence of group process in a time-limited group. Rather, the therapist facilitates, evokes, and even provokes the processes of the group work.

This active stance is assumed from the very beginning of the group and, with some variations appropriate to the developmental stage of the group, is maintained for the duration. The activity of the therapist includes instigating the group to get started when necessary, drawing in group members, setting limits on behaviors that may be potentially harmful to the group, and tying themes back to the central focus of the group (Budman, Cooley, et al., 1996). This active stance is not intended to be manipulative or coercive, but rather facilitative of the group interaction and the power of the group members to help one another (Budman & Gurman, 1988; Dies, 1985). Such activity can have implications for the group process, in particular for the development of transferences. An active, and therefore less abstinent, stance may constrain the transferences that develop; however, this potentially limiting effect is offset by the rapid cohesion and accelerated movement facilitated by this activity.

The paradox of time limits Setting a time limit or a number of sessions for the group clearly distinguishes the time-limited from the open-ended therapeutic approach. The limit itself establishes the beginning, middle, and end of the therapy experience. The compression of time defined by the limit can serve to instigate the process and motivate the group members. Existential finiteness can serve to concentrate the mind and the will.

Although the time limit highlights the limited resources within the group, it simultaneously focuses attention on, encourages, and even forces the mobilization of the resources outside and beyond the group. So the focus on limit is paradoxically paired with the notion of limitlessness. The time-limited group therapist encourages work outside of the group as well as the use of external resources, emphasizing that growth continues long after the group stops meeting. The time-limited therapist also overtly recognizes the current group experience as a part of a much larger constellation of therapeutic experiences that a person may have throughout the lifespan.

Stages of group development
An understanding of group dynamics is essential to all group psychotherapy, and time-limited group therapy is no exception. To understand group dynamics in general, it is useful to understand the stages of group development. Although this awareness is important for all group therapies, it is

particularly important in time-limited groups, precisely because there is a greater need to maximize every moment and every interaction, with less opportunity for error or miscalculation. The therapist needs a comprehensive knowledge of the specific group tasks and the requisite technical considerations involved in each of the group stages.

Different time-limited group theorists propose slightly different stages of group development (Budman & Gurman, 1988; MacKenzie, 1990). However, as discussed previously, there is clear agreement about the critical nature of the beginning and ending stages of the group. The beginning stage is marked by the process of engagement, and the basic concerns are safety and acceptance, boundaries and rules, and roles that will be assumed by the leader and the group members. The major task of the group during this phase is cohesion, and the leader's role is to facilitate this cohesion and the development of universality and acceptance by pointing out similarities among the group members, making joining statements, focusing on emergent themes, and tying those themes to the group focus. Although the issue of time is often a remote concern during this stage, the leader must maintain the awareness of the time limit by consistently reminding the group each session of the number of sessions remaining.

The termination stage is also an extremely important one for the success of the group. Emotions can run high, as the group faces the existential finiteness of time, the limits of accomplishment, and the reality of loss. The reactions to termination are mixed and varied, including "forgetting" that the end has arrived, and asking to extend the life of the group. The leader must remain aware of his or her feelings, countertransferential and otherwise, and manage temptations to keep the group going. The leader needs to remain positively focused on consolidating the gains of the group and must steadfastly adhere to the task of facing the end together. The group members need to be supported and encouraged to grieve the loss of the group along with the personal losses evoked by this process in order to find a new and better way to say goodbye.

Why time-limited groups?

The potential benefits of time-limited group psychotherapy have been extensively discussed throughout the literature (Budman & Gurman, 1988; Levenson, 2002; MacKenzie, 1997, 2000) and are briefly summarized here. There exists a substantial body of evidence that time-limited group therapy is effective (Piper & Joyce, 1996). Likewise, time-limited groups can surely be a cost-effective treatment modality. However, in addition to possible cost-savings, there are several potential therapeutic advantages of the use of time limits in group therapy.

Potential patients often perceive time-limited groups as more manage-able, and therefore they may be more likely to commit to the group for the circumscribed period of time. In addition, time limits can decrease the development of prolonged dependency on therapy and can reduce the like-lihood of harmful regression (Budman et al. 1996). As discussed previously, the time limit itself can produce an intensely evocative experience by high-lighting the existential issues of time and meaning (Mann, 1973). The per-sistent recognition and acknowledgement of the finiteness of time can activate and inspire the group process. The imposition of a time limit may also be useful in helping patients move beyond the stance of victim by pro-moting a greater sense of personal agency.

Conclusion

The effectiveness and efficiency of time-limited group psychotherapy cer-tainly make it an attractive treatment alternative, especially in the world of cost-conscious managed care and resource limitations. But, has the arrived for time-limited group psychotherapy? Although the potential advantages of a comprehensive group program appear obvious, there have been a number of obstacles to the implementation of these programs, resulting in their underutilization (MacKenzie, 2000; Piper & Joyce, 1996; Rosenberg & Zimet, 1995; Steenbarger & Budman, 1996). Attitudinal biases against group therapy and time-limited therapy persist among both patients and therapists who view these therapies as "second best." Other possible limit-ing factors include the potential for side effects like increased anxiety with time-limited groups, or structural–institutional factors such as the difficult logistics of establishing time-limited groups and the degree of insurance coverage for group therapy.

An additional factor limiting the expansion of group therapy use is the training of therapists. Few therapists have been adequately trained in group therapy and even fewer in the various time-effective treatment modalities. MacKenzie (2001) envisions the day when most group therapists will feel comfortable running a cognitive-behavioral group in the morning and a psychodynamic group in the afternoon, but that day has not yet come. These limitations, among others, have led some to conclude that the rou-tine use of group therapy as a primary therapeutic modality may still be in the distance (Piper & Joyce, 1996).

MacKenzie (1997, 2000) argues that a comprehensive group therapy program should be part of any mental health delivery system of the future, and that time-limited group therapy should play a significant role within that program. He suggests that a comprehensive group program would provide a range of groups designed to address the different levels of clinical need. This program would include time-limited groups designed for crisis intervention and situational disturbances such as bereavement; diagnosis-specific groups for people experiencing, for example, anxiety or bulimia; psychoeducation and skills building groups; and general interpersonal groups. He also recommends longer-term groups for those patients requiring ongoing care.

Powers and Alonso (2004) and others argue that time-limited therapy was never intended to be all things to all people. Just as the open-ended treatment of all comers constituted a clinical and economic Procrustean bed, so does the ill-considered attempt to fit all comers into the modern Procrustean bed of time-limited therapy. Time-limited therapy is good at what it does for the appropriate patients and appropriate needs, but as Piper and Joyce (1996) indicate, it is by no means a panacea. Time-limited group psychotherapy, then, is best thought of as part of a larger, more comprehensive constellation of therapeutic offerings.

Reflecting on the state of time-limited group therapy, there are those that predict increasing health and prosperity (MacKenzie, 2001; Scheidlinger, 2000). Others recognize that certain conditions need to be met for that prosperity to be realized (Steenbarger & Budman 1996). These conditions include a better informed consumer, better trained clinicians, and a health care system that has been educated about the clear benefits of group therapy. We may be well on the road to those conditions, but we are not there yet.

References

Budman S. H., Cooley, S., Demby A., Koppenaal, G., Koslof, J. & Powers, T. A. (1996). A model of time-effective group psychotherapy for patients with personality disorders: The clinical model. *International Journal of Group Psychotherapy, 46,* 329–355.

Budman S. H., & Gurman A. S. (1988). *Theory and practice of brief therapy.* New York: Guilford Press.

Dies, R. (1985). Leadership in short-term group therapy: Manipulation or facilitation? *International Journal of Group Psychotherapy, 35,* 435–455.

Donovan, J. M., Bennett, M. M., & McElroy, C. M. (1979). The crisis group: An outcome study. *American Journal of Psychiatry, 136,* 906–910.

Drum, D. J., & Knott, J. E. (1977). *Structured groups for facilitating development.* New York: Human Sciences Press.

Klein, R. H. (1977). Inpatient group psychotherapy: Practical considerations and special problems. *International Journal of Group Psychotherapy, 27,* 210–214.

Klein, R. H. (1985). Some principles of short-term group therapy. *International Journal of Group Psychotherapy, 35,* 309–329.

Levenson, H., Butler, S. F., Powers, T. A. & Beitman, B. D. (2002). *Concise guide to brief dynamic and interpersonal therapy* (2nd ed.). Washington, DC: American Psychiatric Press.

MacKenzie, K. R. (1990). *Introduction to time-limited group psychotherapy.* Washington, DC: American Psychiatric Press.

MacKenzie, K. R. (1993). Time-limited group theory and technique. In A. Alonso & H. I. Swiller (Eds.), *Group therapy in clinical practice* (pp. 423–447). Washington, DC: American Psychiatric Press.

MacKenzie K. R. (1994). Where is here and when is now? The adaptational challenge of mental health reform for group psychotherapy. *International Journal of Group Psychotherapy, 44,* 407–428.

MacKenzie, K. R. (1997). *Time-managed group psychotherapy: Effective clinical applications.* Washington, DC: American Psychiatric Press.

MacKenzie, K. R. (2000). Group psychotherapies and managed care. In A. J. Kent & M. Hersen (Eds.), *A psychologist's proactive guide to managed mental health care.* Mahwah, NJ: Erlbaum.

MacKenzie, K. R. (2001). An expectation of radical changes in the future of group psychotherapy. *International Journal of Group Psychotherapy, 51,* 175–180.

Mann, J. (1973). *Time-limited psychotherapy.* Cambridge, MA: Harvard University Press.

Mintz, E. E. (1971). *Marathon groups: Reality and symbol.* New York: Appleton-Century-Crofts.

Piper, W. E., & Joyce, A. S. (1996). A consideration of factors influencing the utilization of time-limited short-term group psychotherapy. *International Journal of Group Psychotherapy, 46,* 311–328.

Piper, W. E., Debbane, E. G., Garant, J., et al. (1979). Pretraining for group psychotherapy: A cognitive-experiential approach. *Archives of General Psychiatry, 36,* 1250–1256.

Piper, W. E., McCallum, M., & Azim, H. F. A. (1992). *Adaptation to loss through short-term group psychotherapy.* New York: Guilford Press.

Poey, K. (1985). Guidelines for the practice of brief, dynamic group therapy. *International Journal of Group Psychotherapy, 35,* 331–354.

Powers, T. A., & Alonso, A. (2004). Dynamic psychotherapy and the problem of time. *Journal of Contemporary Psychotherapy, 34,* 125–139.

Rosenberg, S. A., & Zimet, C. N. (1995). Brief group treatment and managed mental health care. *International Journal of Group Psychotherapy, 45,* 367–379.

Scheidlinger, S. (1997). Group dynamics and group psychotherapy revisited: Four decades later. *International Journal of Group Psychotherapy, 47,* 141–159.

Steenbarger, B. N., & Budman, S. H. (1996). Group psychotherapy and managed behavioral health care: Current trends and future challenges. *International Journal of Group Psychotherapy, 46,* 297–309.

Stand by Your Stance

Dear Consultant:

I have recently begun leading support groups for individuals with cancer and two problems have arisen. The groups, located in a general hospital, are structured to run for a 12-week cycle with the same members, except that new members can join during the first 3 weeks of the cycle. Each group lasts for 2 hours, and the typical membership is 12 to 14 people, both men and women, although generally there are more women than men. The format of the groups is to have some educational portion at the beginning of each session, followed by an open discussion that ranges from expected discussion about cancer in general to very deeply personal, and painful, sharing of current experiences. Very often, the group feels very much like a psychotherapy group and indeed two members in particular have been asking to eliminate the educational portion entirely, wanting to have more time for personal sharing.

For 2 weeks, it was looking like five other members were beginning to be persuaded that this was a good idea, but I did not permit a vote, and fortunately, two of the more powerful group members argued for continuing the structure as is. Consequently, I did not accept the proposed shift in structure because I see a central element of my task as providing useful educational material especially for those members who have a hard time accessing or speaking directly with their doctors, or who can share more easily around more clinical discussion. Because I'll be leading more groups of this sort in the future, my first question is: What should I do if the majority of group members desire a shift in the structure and push for it, for example, to do away with the educational piece? Should I adopt a more democratic, perhaps humane, approach to differences with my structure, especially given that the group members have so little control over the cancers that they are battling?

243

Second, about ten of the group members want to continue meeting beyond the 12-week cycle, asking me to be the leader of a less structured group for them, although they haven't defined whether they would want a supportive group or an exploratory psychotherapy group. They just don't want to stop meeting. My training has been to stick with the structure—that is, to end the groups as planned, and to encourage members to seek other group venues to continue their work if they choose. This has occasioned unhappiness in many of the members, and anger toward me from some of them, and it has been hard for me to stand up for my position because I'm not really sure it's the best or correct decision. Can you help me think about this more clearly?

Dear Therapist:

I agree with stopping your group within the time limits of the initial contract and also with helping those who wish to continue in a more exploratory psychotherapy to form another group. They may be a core of "old timers" who, after sharing a previous educational therapy, may join in a new group of other "old timers" with similar experiences.

I'll try now to understand better what had been happening with your technical approach as well as the rationale in planning a second "more psychotherapeutic" phase to help your clients. When you wonder if you should adopt a more humane approach to differences with the structure, your countertransference is inviting you to reflect about the meaning of "termination" for these patients with a likely "terminal" disease. You correctly link your clients' democratic voting to continue beyond 12 weeks and to shift the structure with their having "so little control over the cancers that they are battling." Indeed, voting may give them a sense of power to influence their future instead of painfully realizing their helplessness. If we compare such illusory exercise of power with the unconscious meaning of terminating after 12 weeks, we realize how termination evokes their concerns about the threat of ending their lives, dying of cancer.

Your educational approach seems to offer—on the one hand—some hope that by learning about cancer they might gain control of their future by applying their newly acquired knowledge, thus reinforcing the defensive omnipotent denial of their difficulties. Such an approach may be especially welcome when starting a new group of cancer patients. However, as they spontaneously engage in more "exploratory" exchanges, they develop a group cohesiveness and a transference to you, to their group mates, and to their group, finding support and understanding from each other, thus feeling less anxiously lonely facing their possible death from cancer. Because they wish to continue living, they do not want to "terminate" and would like to be able to take control of their future and of their group.

Furthermore, your technical approach was not always 100% educational. Instead your sessions became increasingly supportive and sometimes even exploratory of "very deeply personal and painful" current events. Such exchanges were possible because your clients had by then developed a transference neurosis to the therapist, to the other members, and to their group.

As you know, the arrival of a relatively established transference neurosis to the psychotherapy process can be recognized by the fact that the patients talk more and more about their current experiences, particularly those in the "here-and-now," instead of focusing on their pasts. Analyzing the unconscious meaning of the group's "termination" should be included there as a paramount agenda item. Naturally it will increase the intensity of their feelings, particularly their anger at their "bad luck" and their frustration with not being able to control their future. Hence they are prone to "act out" (Ganzarain & Buchele, 1987) their resentment rooted in their helplessness on facing their illness. Their transferred anger at you may then distort the planned termination as a stubborn exercise on your part to impose your "malignant" power over them, metaphorically comparable to their threatening fate. Their acting out may succeed in making you feel guilty and mean, in spite of the fact that they initially agreed with the 12-week contract.

Your flexible technical approach may allow you to help them explore more their anxiety and anger about dying, without sticking rigidly to your educational approach while enforcing the agreed time-limited contract. Their exploratory work may help them to learn how to say good-bye, how to graciously end their group and their lives. They need to learn very difficult lessons about how to end and how to die. Such learning may be slowly acquired through their exploratory "working through" (Ganzarain, 1983) in a new group formed by those motivated to continue, emigrating together to another psychotherapeutic group.

Ramon Ganzarain, MD, FAGPA

References

Ganzarain, R. (1983). Working through in analytic group psychotherapy. *International Journal of Group Psychotherapy, 33,* 281–296.

Ganzarain, R., & Buchele, B. (1987). Acting out during group psychotherapy for incest. *International Journal of Group Psychotherapy, 37,* 185–200.

Dear Therapist:

As you have indicated, two problems are apparent. First, some of the patients want to change the structure of the group from one that provides the combination of psychoeducation and open discussion to one that provides only open discussion. Others do not want this change. Second, most members want to continue the group with you as therapist beyond the 12-week time limit. Some do not. The basic conflict that characterizes both problems is whether to change the nature of your group after the group has begun.

My own theoretical orientation is psychodynamic and interpersonal, which is well represented in texts by Rutan and Stone (2001) and by Yalom (1995). I also strongly believe in the usefulness of interventions addressed to the group-as-a-whole, particularly in short-term groups with homogeneous compositions such as your therapy group with cancer patients. From the information that you have conveyed about the group and its patients, I believe that primary consideration must be given to the initial agreement or contract that was formulated between each patient and you before the group began. I am presuming that there was an agreement and that it included a description of what the general structure and process of the group would probably be like. Unless the group has been ineffective or harmful, which is not apparent from what you have described, I believe that, as therapist, you have the responsibility to honor the initial agreement and preserve the structure and process of the group for all members. This is true even if most members favor the change and the remaining members do not, or do not express their opinions. The silent minority may feel coerced by the more dominant members, and may be reluctant to voice their preference to maintain the present structure that was agreed on initially.

The initial stage of most, if not all, therapy groups is characterized by apprehension and anxiety about what will ensue—in particular, how one will be treated by the other patients and therapist. Building trust, a sense of safety, a therapeutic alliance with the therapist, and cohesion among members are the main objectives of the therapist at this stage as the tasks of the group begin to be addressed. In the case of a short-term group such as yours, these achievements must occur rapidly. Once established, these early achievements should not be undermined by the therapist changing basic structural characteristics of the group. A new stage of trust reformation would be required, which would take away valuable time from the working stages of the short-term group. It also may precipitate dropouts among the patients who do not wish to change the group structure to which they agreed.

There is a second important reason for preserving the structure of the group. Similar to the patients, you should not be coerced. You have stated that you believe that providing psychoeducational material is useful for the patients, in part because they often do not have the opportunity to obtain such information from their physicians, and in part because it helps more inhibited patients participate in the discussion. These are worthy objectives. In addition, you may not feel comfortable conducting a different kind of group with this patient population. You may lack training and experience in conducting what would amount to expressive group therapy with cancer patients, or you may believe that 12 sessions of expressive group therapy with as many as 12 to 14 cancer patients is simply not sufficient. As the patients' therapist, you have the ethical responsibility of providing what you believe to be the most useful treatment and for refraining from treatment for which you lack skills or you believe is not sufficient.

Conducting expressive, short-term group therapy is a demanding task for both the therapist and the patients. As a therapist, you must be well primed conceptually, because interventions must be made without the benefit of an accumulation of considerable clinical material. As you have observed, despite the short-term nature of the group, patients often share "very deeply personal and painful" experiences. They need time to open up, reflect on their experiences, and attempt to understand them in light of the current difficulties that they are facing. They also need some time to close up and engage in the ending processes of their therapy group.

Given the demands of the therapy group and the limited time, it is quite common for patients of time-limited groups to want to extend their length and for some patients to voice this wish to the therapist in the group. In addition to representing a realistic concern—that is, whether there will be enough time to achieve benefit—this wish may represent an attempt to avoid experiencing the endings of relationships. Because cancer often leads to death and the ending of relationships, experiencing endings in the group can be a painful precursor to what may follow in their lives outside the group. As you have also surmised, the expressed wish may represent an attempt to assume greater control of the group and greater control of you as its leader. As you have noted, loss of control is a central issue for cancer patients. If one is conducting an expressive therapy group, the wish to extend the group can be interpreted along these lines and members can use the eventual ending of the group to productively examine and understand the associated conflicts. If one is conducting a supportive group, the members can less ambitiously, but also usefully, benefit by simply learning to say good-bye to people to whom they have become attached.

We should remember that therapists are also vulnerable to the wish to not terminate gratifying working relationships with patients. Conducting short-term therapy groups on a regular basis confronts therapists with the reality of having to terminate relationships with a large number of patients.

This requires repeatedly investing considerable energy in recruiting, selecting, preparing, and treating patients who will soon depart when therapy is completed. Countertransferential resistance to doing so can sometimes cause therapists to collude with patients' irrational wishes. In the situation that you describe in your group, the patients can be reassured that after this group ends, their needs and wishes regarding future treatment alternatives will be considered. Of course, this will not prevent the therapist from being the target of criticism and transferential patient reactions during the current group. These can be interpreted or simply managed depending on the nature of the group.

Depending on a number of factors, different types of agreements or contracts can be made for future groups that you plan to conduct with cancer patients. If you possess the skills to conduct expressive, short-term group therapy and the patients are functioning well enough physically and psychologically to endure the associated demands, you may decide to conduct such groups. For 12-week expressive therapy groups, a somewhat smaller number of patients (e.g., eight to ten) would be recommended. Again, depending on your capabilities and those of the patients, it may even be possible to envision conducting a group where the patients assumed some of the responsibility in determining the structure of sessions as the group progressed. This, of course, would be clearly understood by the patients before the group began and would be subject to your judgment regarding the usefulness of their suggestions.

William E. Piper, PhD, CGP

References

Rutan, J. S., & Stone, W. N. (2001). *Psychodynamic group psychotherapy* (3rd ed.). New York: Guilford Press.

Yalom, I. D. (1995). *The theory and practice of group psychotherapy* (4th ed.). New York: Basic Books.

Manage My Stress

Dear Consultant:

I don't know if I'm looking for forgiveness or scolding, but I'm sure that I'm looking for advice. Years ago, I led my first and only short-term group, and only a relative would tell you it was a success. From beginning to end, I made mistakes that I came to appreciate as such only after the fact. I'm at a clinic where I've been given the task of setting up a 4-month anger management group and I want this group to succeed, so I want to do a postmortem on my last group.

That group was a 3-month outpatient stress management group run in a psychiatric hospital setting as part of my job as a social worker in the hospital. The plan was for it to have up to ten members and to run from September through November, ending just before Thanksgiving. Referrals were made to me by staff psychiatrists, psychologists, and social workers who treated the outpatients referred. Even though I had announced my group in June, 3 months prior to the start date, by the end of August I had only four members. Given the outpatient department's pressure to get the group going, I decided to begin in September as planned, but to allow new members to join within the first 2 weeks of the group's start. Because I got only one new member during that 2-week period, and there were three ready to go in week four, I stretched to allow entries into that fourth week.

Now I had a group of eight members, but they had begun at three different time periods, which presented immediate complications. Twice, I had to repeat the introduction to the group I had presented in week one, and some of the early exercises I had taught in the first 3 weeks I felt necessary to repeat, albeit cursorily, for the three newest members who came late. The first four members expressed acceptance of this plan, but I did pick up nonverbal signs of impatience such as yawning, examining books on the shelves, and even one member who left for a long bathroom break. I joked with the original members about the structure offering good practice for managing stress, and I thought they chuckled.

Then, in week five, a friend of mine persuaded me to include her patient who was experiencing acute stress having just caught her husband in an affair. In screening this patient for the group, I did tell her that I wasn't going to start from the beginning, because I had sequential work sheets from which I was working, and she agreed to start where the group was. Within 2 weeks, though, she left the group stating that she had transportation issues, which I did not believe. Also, another member from the original batch never returned after this, without explanation.

These comings and goings threw me even though I had permitted them, and I always had in my mind the differential entries of the members, especially because the four originals and then the three who came as a group later seemed to develop greater interest in their own cohort, and rarely asked questions of the other cohort.

In addition, given the way the group developed, I offered in mid-October to extend the group through the middle of December, to which all but one person responded tepidly. That one person, one of the newer additions, was fervent about continuing, and the more fervent, the more tepid the others became. So, ultimately, I abandoned the idea, without really addressing it.

We ended as originally planned just before Thanksgiving, with the group exchanging pleasantries and some warmth during the good-bye, but it felt more like individuals parting after a long train ride together, rather than an intensely connected group. I can stand frankness, so please help me plan this next group so that it is more apt to succeed.

Dear Therapist:
You have asked me to help you plan your next group and to evaluate what went awry with your last group. You seem to have an inkling why your previous group failed, but you didn't specify how you might rectify the problems you encountered. Rather than conduct an extensive postmortem on your stress management group, let me suggest how to avoid recreating those problems in your future anger management group.

Because my clinical training has been in both behavioral and psychodynamic approaches, my orientation can be described as pragmatic-psychodynamic. I value clarity and structure, especially in time-limited groups, and I attend to and use the process of the individual and group dynamics in order to facilitate change.

With that in mind, let's create a practical framework with which to design and implement your next group. Consider several pertinent questions: What kind of group will you be offering? Who are the members? What is the purpose of the group and how will you achieve your purpose? Why offer group and not dyadic therapy? Each of these questions relate to one another; thus, the answers are interdependent.

Too often, clinicians agree to run groups in a hospital or clinic without considering exactly what they are getting themselves into. Vagueness is the clinician's enemy. So, let's first consider the importance of clarity. The clearer you can be concerning your vision of the group, the better it will be. For example, imagine sitting with the group. What are the members like? What is the conversation like? Do you feel comfortable sitting with this imagined group?

You have been asked to set up a 4-month anger management group within a clinic setting. What exactly will you be offering and to whom? You can't really answer the "what" until you consider the "who." Will your prospective group members be convicted felons mandated by the court to manage their aggression? Will they be people who have engaged in domestic violence? Will they be individuals who get a bit riled up now and then and who could benefit from learning a few coping skills? Will you limit it to men? Women? Both? Will they be adults? Adolescents? You will see, I hope, that you can't offer the same kind of group to this diverse collection of people. Their needs are vastly different. You must be clear what your criteria for membership are before you start advertising your group.

The "what" of the group refers to the overarching purpose of the group. Is the purpose of the group to provide information, skills training, and support? Is it to promote intrapsychic and interpersonal change? Keep in mind your population—the "who." Convicted felons mandated by the court to attend a group may not be the best candidates for insight-oriented work. Don't allow your lofty ambitions to blind you to the reality of your potential group population. Once you have answered the "what" you can consider the "how"—that is, how you will structure the group in order to achieve your purpose. Again, you can't really answer one (the what) without considering the other (the how).

The what and the how constitute the fundamental building blocks of any therapeutic encounter, not just group. Your role (i.e., what you do and what you represent) is dependent on the way you answer the what and the how. For example, if you see that the purpose of your group is to provide information and teach skills, you will be seen as the expert guide who provides the needed information. You will be more active and directive in this kind of group. If the purpose of your group is to provide a safe, secure place in which to promote intrapsychic and interpersonal change, you will probably be less active, less directive, and your interventions will be geared to highlighting the underlying process of the group dynamics and to the transferences that occur.

I might add that no matter what kind of group you lead, you will need to attend to the task (e.g., teaching a relaxation strategy), the process (e.g., how the group responds to the task—with eager compliance or bored withdrawal), and the maintenance functions of the group (e.g., managing the time frame).

The final question is: Why group therapy? Why not offer your treatment in a dyadic context? Aside from the fact that group is more cost-effective for the clinician and the patients, how would you answer this?

To put it simply, things happen in a group that cannot happen in individual therapy: From the very first meeting, a person can recognize that she or he is not alone; he or she finds that others experience similar feelings of anxiety, despair, or loneliness. This sense of universality combats feelings of isolation and strangeness. To be accepted in the group despite past experiences or current symptoms or behaviors serves as an antidote to demoralization. The patient's own words can help others, and this sense of altruism enhances self-esteem. The combination of these factors helps to develop a sense of greater mastery over self and problems, diminishing the feelings of helplessness that existed before. Finally, the alliance that is formed with other group members can be stronger than the dependency that could get established with the therapist. The patient sees the value of peer relationships and notices the possibility of being one's own authority.

If you really appreciate the power of group therapy, you will be able to capitalize on this in the group you will be leading. For example, instead of focusing so much on what you want to teach, you will encourage interaction among group members, highlighting similarities and making connections. Learn to use the process of the group to support your psychoeducational aims. You bemoaned the lack of "an intensely connected group" in your last experience. Indeed, you had more of a chaotic class than a therapy group. This is because you failed to promote and secure group cohesion (a sense of "groupness") by the revolving door policy you haphazardly established and because you seemed preoccupied with what you had to teach and did not attend to the process. A structured support group requires attention to process even when the orientation is behavioral. A general rule of thumb is that if the task is being thwarted, attend to the process.

I do think that your future group can be a success if you carefully answer the questions I have presented here for you. Other critically important steps to take are to develop a group contract that includes the basic "rules" of the group, and screen all group members in person using this time to begin preparing the individual for the group. At the end of this meeting, the patient should know where, when, and for how long the group will meet; what the overall purpose of the group is; what her or his own goal is; what the group fee is; and what the group contract is. Finally, send out a reminder letter prior to the first group meeting. Good luck!

Pamela L. Enders, PhD, CGP

Dear Therapist:

Thank you for the invitation to provide some feedback and recommendations regarding your group work. I have been working with groups for 30 years now and have great feeling for the concerns you have shared regarding your initial group. My theoretical orientation is quite general in that I see advantages to all models, but as my following responses will likely indicate, I have approached your dilemma mostly from a social learning perspective.

From your description of your earlier group, you seem to have high expectations, positive intentions, and considerable enthusiasm for your work. By all means maintain that approach, for I believe that a group leader's optimism accounts for much of the positive impact group therapy has on its members. However, the leader's optimism is necessary, but not sufficient. In addition, there are basic principles of group work that must be addressed, including what I call Setting Up for Success. Your original group was not set up for success so let's discuss what some of those characteristics are and how you may include them in your next group.

Preparing for the group

Pre-group planning is the key to solving many possible problems. The planning includes what Smead (1995) has defined as organizing the group experience. This involves: (a) conducting a needs assessment (Who needs the group and why?); (b) preparing a written plan or proposal that will serve as a treatment plan and a roadmap for where you are headed; (c) announcing the group and recruiting members; (d) conducting pre-group interviews; (e) selecting members; (f) administering a pre-group evaluation; (g) conducting sessions; (h) evaluating the group effectiveness; and (i) providing follow through with members and referring staff.

It seems you may have had difficulty setting up for success from the beginning because I'm not sure there was a needs assessment done; that is, it isn't clear that there was a need for your group. It took a long time to recruit a minimal number of members, which represents neither a large need in the community nor support from the referring staff, who would have provided patients if this were seen as a necessary service. As part of defining the need, it is essential to determine for your next group what type of anger control group will be offered; that is, whether a support, psychoeducational, counseling, or therapy group will be given, for each has a different focus and goal (Fleckenstein & Horne, 2003).

From the description of your stress management group, it appears that a psychoeducational model was appropriate, but may not have been fully developed. Although I'm certain you reviewed what would go into the group, it doesn't seem that a treatment plan for the stress management group was developed, at least not one thoroughly set up that could be shared with the group members in advance in order to prepare them. An effective group leader will engage in skill building activities with the group, but will be effectively processing the dynamics of the group as well—that is, they will cover the content of the group, but also observe interactions among and between the group members, and will use the power of the group interactions to bring the content home to each member. What makes the group so powerful is the ability to experience growth from interactions with the leader and all the members of the group.

Part of the treatment plan is determining whether the group will be open or closed. In order to establish a cohesive group addressing a specific problem in a limited time, a closed group is generally more appropriate (Gazda, Ginter & Horne, 2001). For your stress management group, the 5-week period of time for accepting members into the group was such that the early group members had to be exposed to the same material several times as new members joined, and new members received a less thorough introduction to the materials as a result of your attempts to move through the material quickly so as to not be too repetitious for early members. The result was dissatisfaction for both the early and the late members. The diversity of entry into the program worked against developing positive group cohesiveness.

Group cohesiveness is a major concern for all groups, for it is understood that the leader has a goal of promoting group cohesiveness, fulfilling the expectation that goals will be met, tasks will be completed, and the group will function effectively (MacNair-Semands, 2000). Group cohesiveness is easier to establish if all members begin together, have a common introduction to the process, and engage in early group rule development and guidelines. Posthuma (2002) encourages thinking of the group process in developmental terms, meaning that the group moves through a series of stages. However, the meaning individual members make of their experience will depend also on their own developmental level in the group, their initial experiences in the group, and the extent of connection they have with the other members.

Your group appears to have had members at many different levels of development, thus with many differing views of the group, and therefore lacking cohesion. Members seemed to have aligned with their starting cohort rather than the group at large, which can lead to dissatisfaction and early drop-out. Several studies have demonstrated that those who drop out of groups report fewer positive feelings than those who remain (McCallum, Piper, Ogrodniczuk, & Joyce, 2002).

Another aspect of group cohesiveness is similarity and differences of group members. It was unclear from your earlier group whether members were experiencing acute or crisis level problems and it wasn't clear whether you knew which it was for each group member. A screening intake interview may serve you well in the future, for it will allow you to understand the compatibility of members, the appropriateness of the group to the needs of each member, and your ability to create a cohesive group. One aspect of member selection and screening is examining diversity of membership and compatibility of members on the basis of many factors, including severity of the problem for the individuals involved, age, ethnicity, economics, and other aspects of diversity that can—and do—influence the outcome of a group. Further, the screening provides you an opportunity of setting up for success by reviewing group goals, defining expectations of members, setting limits of confidentiality and respect, and assisting the member in preparing to enter the group ready to work. A clear presentation of what is expected and planned at the beginning may cut down on anxiety and discomfort for everyone involved.

Ethical considerations

One aspect of effective group work is to be certain that professional and ethical standards are followed. To ensure this, you might get appropriate supervision for your work. Because a standard of practice is to be trained in the skills you are teaching, it is essential that you, as the leader, possess the knowledge and skills to be covered by the focus of the group—in this case, anger management. In addition, the availability of supervision even during the group—with an experienced co-leader, for instance—provides the opportunity of staying on track and correcting problems in the moment, rather than as a reflective exercise later. It also provides protective shared coverage of responsibility if the group does not have satisfactory outcomes.

A supervision process might have facilitated the management of several of the problems you encountered but were unable to manage well, including the issue of the member who joined late and then dropped out. Although this member could not be forced to remain, discussing the situation candidly with remaining group members can be essential for maintaining trust and respect with these members.

The supervision process would also have facilitated a more effective closing for the group. Termination issues must be addressed therapeutically and having a group just fade away gives members the impression that the group was not important and reduces the likelihood of generalization of skills and experiences to outside the group.

Arthur Horne, PhD

References

Fleckenstein, L., & Horne, A. (2003). Anger management groups. In J. DeLucia-Waack, D. Gerrity, C. Kolodner, & M. Riva (Eds.), *Handbook of group counseling and psychotherapy.* Thousand Oaks, CA: Sage Publishing Company.

Gazda, G., Ginter, E., & Horne, A. (2001). *Group counseling and group psychotherapy.* Boston: Allyn & Bacon.

McCallum, M., Piper, W., Ogrodniczuk, J., & Joyce, (2002). Early process and dropping out from short-term therapy for complicated grief. *Group Dynamics, 6,* 243–254.

MacNair-Semands, R. (2000). Examining the beneficial components of groups: Commentary on Estabrooks and Carron (2000) and Terry et al. (2000). *Group Dynamics, 4,* 254–258.

Posthuma, B. W. (2002). *Small groups in counseling and therapy: Process and leadership.* Boston, MA: Allyn & Bacon.

Smead, R. (1995). *Skills and techniques for group work with children and adolescents.* Champaign, IL: Research Press.

Containing Contagion

Dear Consultant:

I was trained in psychodynamic group psychotherapy and have no experience running short-term groups. In a recent job change, one of my tasks is to supervise nurses who run short-term wellness, obesity, cancer support, trauma, and medical illness groups. Many of the groups are started with patients who come into specific clinics. They sign up for the groups and there is virtually no screening of patients before they begin. This leads to a lot of early drop out and sometimes has led to chaos.

Although I have done some reading about short-term groups, I feel lost supervising because I don't know what to tell my supervisees about the screening of patients, how structured the groups should be, and how and whether to address group dynamics that emerge. In addition, in my ongoing groups my group agreements discourage outside social contact, but many of the patients in these short-term groups routinely give each other their phone numbers and meet frequently outside meetings.

Recently, a supervisee of mine ran a structured 12-week group for childhood sexual abuse survivors that went well. Each week one of the eight members told her story, with no interruption from the group members. At the end of each meeting, the group was allotted 15 minutes to support the person who shared her story. The last 4 weeks of the group, the supervisee presented information about symptom management and creating emotional safety for oneself. After the 12 weeks, a follow-up 12-week group was offered to the women, with this group to be less-structured. All eight decided to sign up, and there was no additional screening. The group goal was to help the women cope with the symptoms of posttraumatic stress that they experienced. The first half of each group was psychoeducational and the second half included the sharing of experiences.

According to the leader, the first 2 weeks went well, but in the third week one member, Sue, complained that she couldn't understand how another member, Amy, permitted her cousin to continually have sex with her as a child when she knew it was wrong. This created a deep tension in the group, with the group fracturing into two camps, one that was compassionate toward Sue and the other toward Amy. After this conflict, Sue and another member, Benji, began to meet for coffee outside the group where they talked about the other members. When the members found out, two women precipitously dropped out. After that, Sue's symptoms worsened, including an incident where she superficially cut her wrists. Her disclosure of this self-cutting led to several other members reporting a lack of safety and increased anxiety.

In the sixth week, several other women reported that they too had recently been cutting. As a psychodynamic therapist, I know that contagion occurs in groups, but I was unsure how to address the issue in a short-term group where the process is noted but not necessarily talked about. How do I help my supervisee make the group safer? Should there have been a different screening process for the second group? How does contagion get contained in a short-term group? Does one ever ask a group member to leave a short-term group? Should I have had my supervisee require that all the group members have individual therapists? Like my supervisee, I am feeling overwhelmed and wonder whether I should have my supervisee end the group before its natural time.

Dear Therapist:

Frequently, time-limited groups are begun in an effort to offer timely, affordable treatments not requiring the longer lead-time needed to begin open-ended psychodynamic groups. Difficulties arise when group therapists, in the interest of time, omit general principles of group therapy and do not recognize that time-limited groups can be organized around psychodynamic tenets. Given the place of boundary violations in this group's member histories, if ever a group needed screening, structure, and boundaries, this was the one!

I will approach this vignette with an emphasis on boundary violations, pre-group agreements, the addition of an unplanned second group, and management of the resulting dilemmas. Despite these problems, I think this group can work.

The most predictable cause of failure of any group is a lack of clear agreements and goals to which each member consents. "If anything, careful patient selection and preparation is even more meaningful in time limited groups" (Rutan & Stone, 2001, p. 322). These survivors come to group therapy with histories fraught with trust and boundary violations and need screening for two reasons. First, members need to know the goals and what they are agreeing to. Second, group leaders need to know whom they are inviting into the group and whether enough homogeneity exists for time-limited therapy.

Pre-group screening meetings give prospective members information about agreements regarding time, fees, confidentiality, outside contact, and group structure. Informed consent will be a critical factor determining whether an individual will want to join the group. A commitment to 12 weeks of structured group therapy is very different than to a longer, less structured group. Pre-group agreements provide a safe envelope for the member and represent a reference that leaders can refer to when boundary violations occur.

You should remind the leader that group homogeneity is among the strongest predictors for group cohesion in time-limited groups (Brotman, Alonso, & Herzog, 1986). If members are too far apart developmentally, they will tend to focus on differences rather than similarities. Pre-group screenings allow leaders to learn of histories of suicide attempts, hospitalizations, affective disorders, substance abuse, or mutilation. In a 12-week group one would not combine members with these behaviors with members who had no such symptoms. Factions and group splitting are more likely to occur.

Lack of screening was not an important factor in the first group. It was structured in a highly protected manner: uninterrupted self-disclosure (like "no cross-talk" in an Alcoholics Anonymous model), followed by 15 minutes of "support" (no confrontations), didactic information, and symptom management.

Then, something very interesting happened. The group did not end! This is when trouble began to roil. This group originally agreed to meet for 12 weeks. A wish to continue time-limited groups is almost ubiquitous when the group has been supportive and helpful. The fear of aloneness and abandonment can be a powerful obstacle to ending a group. With a temptation to turn into a less structured group, the leader thought she was doing what was best for the group, and soon realized that extending the group was not part of the original agreement, was actually a boundary violation, and may have been unethical. Peer pressure is a powerful phenomenon. The group may be swept up by a strong wish to continue, but those who don't want to may be afraid to speak up. This may be where the real "contagion" got started. It was clear to everyone after 12 weeks that the work was not complete. Rather than deal with ending and the disappointment that more was not accomplished, they started another group with less protection. What ensued demonstrated some members wanted an exit, but didn't know how to leave.

The group therapist must be sensitive to what members' choices are saying about their readiness to do exploratory work. Often populations desiring time-limited treatments want the safety and certainty of an easy entry and exit to treatment. Expanding the depth of psychiatric work before members are ready can lead to regression, acting out, and ultimately destruction of a group before it overwhelms an individual.

The first group needed to end, as planned. If a second group is to be formed, a separate set of agreements needs to be clearly stated, with an exit for members who want to leave and openings for new members.

In the second group, Sue may have followed the unspoken rules of the new group. Although vague, there was some type of consent that the second group would have deeper and more honest discussion. Sensing this, she tested the waters asking Amy why she continued to have sex with her cousin when she knew it was wrong. This question is really central for many sexual abuse victims: "Why did I allow it to continue?" She pushed the group to move deeper in terms of sharing real and embarrassing feelings, but because her question was confrontational rather than supportive, the group became threatened and split. Not everyone was ready for things to go deeper!

Sensing increased tension in the room, the leader must acknowledge that something new has happened, and give permission to the group to talk about this by modeling. She could ask, "Amy, what do you experience when Sue offers you the gift of her authentic, if difficult, feelings?" She could say to Sue, "It takes an expert to pose a question like that; you must have asked yourself that question many times." She could ask the group their reaction to Sue's question. Group safety is increased when the leader acknowledges that they are navigating in new waters. She could have turned this into a group-as-a-whole issue, rather than allowing it to divide the group.

Because the group contract was so vague and the leader didn't make this confrontation discussible, more boundary violations occurred. Sue and Benji met for coffee and talked about the other members. When the other members found out, two women dropped out, Sue cut her wrists, and others followed.

Rather than "group contagion," this looks more like a cry for help. As supervisor, you noted your own confusion when you said you don't know how to address the issue in a short-term group where process is noted but not necessarily talked about. You seem confused about the fact that a time-limited group *can be* psychodynamic, not realizing that the group will self-regulate, knowing how much time they have to delve into material

(Mann, 1973). You contemplate yet another boundary violation: ending this group now.

If you apply your knowledge of psychodynamics, you might interpret the cutting as a distress signal regarding the lack of group safety. The implied message that the group would deepen was never made explicit, thus the group became confused about what could or could not be talked about. At this point, your supervisee needed to acknowledge the boundary violation unwittingly made by extending the group without a clear contract. She wanted to help them continue the work without recognizing that not everyone was ready. The issue is not about asking a member to leave the group or sending members to individual therapy, but whether an honest discussion of what happened can re-establish safety in the group: "I need to take responsibility for what happened here. By not maintaining the boundary of the first 12-week group, I recapitulated a boundary violation. We have an opportunity here to mend the boundary. Sue took the implied invitation to go deeper, but we didn't all agree to do this. The cutting that is going on in the group is showing me that you are all hurting. From here we can decide whether the group can come together around a set of agreements that will create safer boundaries. Each member can decide if she can agree to protective group agreements and then make her own decision."

A solid group contract will provide safe boundaries to talk about the difficult feelings that inevitably arise in a group of frightened but courageous women seeking a healing experience. With these boundaries in place there is hope that, through your supervision, your supervisee can facilitate recovery.

Helen Riess, MD

References

Brotman, A. W., Alonso, A., & Herzog, D. B. (1986). Group therapy for bulimia: Clinical experience and practical recommendations. *Group, 9,* 15–23.

Mann, J. (1973). *Time-limited psychotherapy.* Cambridge, MA: Harvard University Press.

Rutan, J. S., & Stone, W. N. (2001). *Psychodynamic group psychotherapy* (3rd ed.). New York: Guilford Press.

Dear Therapist:

It is significant that "emotional contagion" is occurring in a group of trauma survivors. This population often struggles with deficits in their capacity to modulate their affect and one can anticipate their difficulty insulating themselves from the emotional displays of others in a group setting. One critical aspect in leading short-term groups is to construct the group in a way that addresses the population-specific needs of the patients. It is the mismatch between the structure of this time-limited trauma group and the developmental lag in the acquisition of affect management skills typically found in incest survivors that needs to be addressed. My comments reflect an integrative theoretical perspective incorporating object relations theory, Silvan Tomkins' affect theory and script theory (Tomkins, 1979, 1982), general systems theory, and cognitive-behavioral theory.

The first intervention that I would recommend is preemptive and involves careful assessment, composition, and preparation prior to group formation (Klein, 1993). When forming short-term groups, screening for homogeneous group composition allows for the rapid cohesion and universality required to get the work done in a brief period of time. This trauma group is heterogeneous along the dimension of when the sexual trauma ended. Someone who is still enmeshed in an incestuous relationship should not be in a group with others for whom the exploitation was over years ago. Although other group members may struggle as Amy must have with complicated feelings toward their abuser, such an issue emerging in a short-term group is bound to trigger affect that can easily distract the group from their task of coping with the sequelae of trauma.

One central aspect of childhood trauma is that boundaries were exploited in unexpected ways by a person in a position of relative power over a child, leading to feelings of powerlessness, confusion, and fear about what to expect in relationships. Therefore, this population needs clarity of boundaries more than most in order to keep affect in the manageable range. The group described was apparently not presented with a group contract prior to the group. If the group members had known what to expect and in that context agreed to the contract, this itself might have helped to "inoculate" the group from emotional contagion.

Although it is often the case that a group decides to continue past its termination date, that decision should not be made until the group is over so that the group can benefit from facing the task of termination while remaining focused on accomplishing their goals in the time allotted. When the group shifted from a support-focused group to a more psychoeducational group, it would have been advisable to have membership become open at that time. Members of the old group could be assessed at that point to see if the new group format is one that suits them. Perhaps Amy might then have articulated feeling out of place in the group or Sue might have expressed her discomfort with Amy's ongoing abuse in ways that would have allowed for a reconsideration of the fit between them and the group.

A useful group contract will state expectations regarding confidentiality, attendance, putting thoughts and feelings into words, staying for the duration of the group, and socializing outside of group (Rutan & Stone, 2001).

In an open-ended group, acting out is something that can be explored over time whereas in a time-limited group acting out needs to be dealt with more actively. The ground rules will provide the leader with the leverage to move the focus from what has triggered the acting out behaviors (which are usually accompanied by intense affect) to a more cognitive appreciation of the connection between triggers and behaviors. This will typically mute the intensity of the affect and limit the acting out.

There are differing opinions about the wisdom of extra-group socializing for trauma groups. Some view it as an important source of support, whereas others regard it as complicating the work. My personal experience with these groups, which includes having had contracts that allowed socializing as well as those that precluded it, leads me to endorse the latter view. The likelihood of expressing feelings generated in group through self-sabotaging actions that take place outside of group is much greater in a group of traumatized adults for whom impairment in social relationships is common.

Even if careful screening and preparation had been done, you and your supervisee might still have found yourselves having to address the problem of contagion in the group. The group task of developing coping skills is meant to be accomplished through psychoeducation, support, and problem-solving rather than an examination of group process. As Goodman and Nowak-Scibelli (1985) point out in their experience with time-limited groups for adults with histories of incest, the chronic feelings of helplessness need to be balanced by a group focus that minimizes regression and reinforces strengths. With this focus there is going to be an emphasis on mastery through the process of thinking and behaving differently in response to their feelings. This is the development of "realistic thinking," which can be conceived of both as a goal of cognitive-behavioral techniques as well as a process central to the "working through" of transference-based distortions of relationships.

When Sue has her reaction to Amy's ongoing relationship to an abuser, it would be important for the therapist to intervene to highlight the relevant affect that is driving Amy's behavior and to which Sue is reacting. For example, the therapist could point out that one of the ubiquitous effects of trauma is intense shame that arises from powerlessness, and that Sue is expressing the kind of outrage at the abuser that serves to protect oneself from such feelings. At the same time, Amy is also expressing self-destructive feelings that are an attempt to manage the shame and to which everyone in the group resonates. The task for the time-limited group focused on developing coping skills is to be aware of the costs of their attempts to manage their shame and to begin to develop an attitude of acceptance of oneself as the only nondefensive antidote to the toxic effects of humiliation (Nathanson,

1992). By stressing that beneath the conflict the members are expressing solutions to the same problem, the leader creates a bridge rather than a breach.

The last aspect I would like to address is countertransference in response to group contagion. I suspect both you and your supervisee have found yourselves in a situation where you feel inadequate in terms of experience and also "de-skilled" by the presence of negative affect run amok. I think it likely that you are also experiencing the contagion of the feelings of shame felt by the group. Rather than handling these difficult emotions by asking members to leave or by terminating the group prematurely, the therapist, with your help, might own the mistakes made in managing the group boundaries, disclose her feelings of shame about this with the group, and draw the parallel between what she is feeling and what the group members are feeling. She can then renegotiate aspects of the contract (e.g., no socializing outside of group, putting thoughts and feelings into words, staying for the duration of the group). This instance of therapist self-disclosure will provide a model for handling shame through increased awareness, acceptance, and electing a nonreactive response. Such honest and empathic behavior by a leader offers a reparative solution that was usually missing in the families of group members during and after their trauma.

Mark Sorensen, PhD, CGP, FAGPA

References

Goodman, B., & Nowak-Scibelli, D. (1985). Group treatment for women incestuously abused as children. *International Journal of Group Psychotherapy, 35*, 531–544.

Klein, R. H. (1983). Short-term group psychotherapy. In H. I. Kaplan & B. J. Sadock (Eds.), *Comprehensive Group Psychotherapy* (3rd ed., pp. 256–270). Baltimore: Williams and Wilkins.

Nathanson, D. L. (1992). *Shame and pride: Affect, sex and the birth of the self.* New York: Norton.

Rutan, J. S., & Stone, W. N. (2001). *Psychodynamic group psychotherapy* (3rd ed.). New York: Guilford Press.

Tomkins, S. S. (1979). Script theory: Differential magnification of affects. In H. E. Howe & R. A. Dienstbier (Eds.), *Nebraska symposium on motivation, 26*, 201–236.

Tomkins, S. S. (1982). Affect theory. In P. Ekman (Ed.), *Emotion in the human face* (2nd ed., pp. 353–395). New York: Cambridge University Press.

The Challenge of the Group Psychotherapist
The Confidence to Be Humble

JOSEPH SHAY, PHD, CGP AND LISE MOTHERWELL, PSYD, CGP

There is a wonderfully humorous group therapy scene in *The Sopranos* in which young mobster Christopher is confronted by his mobster "family" and his actual family in an attempt at an "intervention" for his substance abuse. The group leader—immediately recognized by Christopher as the thief who "stole all those pork loins"—initiates the intervention calmly, but, within minutes, the group deteriorates into name-calling, chaotic communication, and ultimately physical violence. Not exactly a testament to the efficacy of group therapy!

Many group therapists are familiar with such a runaway process, and many individual therapists who contemplate becoming group therapists fear it, to the point of avoiding group therapy entirely. Perhaps LeBon spoke to them when he wrote,

> By the mere fact that he forms part of an organized group, man de-
> scends several rungs in the ladder of civilization. Isolated he may be a
> cultivated individual; in a crowd he is a barbarian—that is, a creature
> acting by instinct. (1895/1920, p. 36)

We created this book to help both beginning and experienced group therapists—as well as "Are you kidding? Me, run a group?" therapists—feel less anxious and more skilled in leading groups, recognizing that complex and challenging situations are a given in group therapy.

265

Consider this comment, applicable to clinicians at all levels of experience:

> Beginning group therapists are confronted with an extraordinary challenge when they approach their first group experience. They must lead their initial treatment group without knowing where they are going or how to get there! . . . There is no shortage of theoretical prescriptions for how to conduct group therapy, but it is difficult for the novice and *even the seasoned practitioner* to sort through the various models to establish a coherent framework for therapeutic change. Differences exist in the recommended target of interventions, the appropriate leadership style or focus, the nature if therapist verbalizations, structured activities, and the therapeutic factors promoting clinical improvement. (italics added; Dies, 1994, p. 60)

Not only is knowledge of individual dynamics an obvious prerequisite for the therapist, but so is at least passing familiarity with group dynamics (Cartwright & Zander, 1998; Forsyth, 1998; Stacey, 2003), systems theory (Agazarian, 1997; Durkin, 1981; von Bertalanffy, 1968), and models of change in group therapy (cf., Dies, 1992; Fuhriman & Burlingame, 1994; Kaplan & Sadock, 1993; Klein, Bernard, & Singer, 1992; Lieberman, Yalom, & Miles, 1973; Rutan & Stone, 2001; Yalom, 1995).

Is this not a recipe for deep anxiety in the therapist? In this context, our hope is for this book to serve as a partial antidote to anxiety by describing and illustrating common challenges for group therapists, and presenting thoughtful answers to these challenges. Underpinning our attempt to elucidate these typical dilemmas and their resolutions is a profound belief in the unique value of group therapy that makes tolerating one's anxiety worthwhile.

Much has been written about the distinctive contribution of group therapy for troubled souls (see, among others, Alonso & Swiller, 1993; Bion, 1959; DeChant, 1996; Ettin, 1992; Kutash & Wolf, 1990; MacKenzie, 1997; Marziali & Monroe-Blum, 1994; Roth, Stone, & Kibel, 1990; Rutan & Stone, 2001; White & Freeman, 2000; Yalom, 1995). Group therapy offers an inimitable context for the *in vivo* exposure and resolution of myriad psychological and interpersonal issues. Immense benefit accrues from experiencing a sense of belonging, divulging shameful secrets, viewing one's problems as universal, developing self-awareness in real interpersonal situations, improving social skills, and so on—all unique advantages inherent to group therapy.

Fortunately, our clinical experience of benefit is supported by the research literature demonstrating the efficacy of group therapy, and occasionally even its superiority (Leszcz & Goodwin, 1998; MacKenzie, 1996; McRoberts, Burlingame, & Hoag, 1998; Piper, 1993; Smith, Glass, & Miller, 1980; Toseland & Siporin, 1988). Much comfort, at least at the cognitive level, is afforded by this evidence.

Such substantive theoretical or research benefits offer little comfort, however, to the group therapist who is challenged by members who want to flee the group, openly fight the payment plan, or resent the addition of a privileged new member (Section I, *Boundary Issues*); faces supremely angry, narcissistic, or sexualizing members (Section II, *Difficult Patients*); manages attacking, passive, or murderous patients (Section III, *Complex Defenses*); is tested by a dying group, a resistant clinic setting, or a suicidal depressed patient (Section IV, *Destructive Forces*); must tolerate personal feelings of sadism, humiliation, or disgust (Section V, *Powerful Therapist Reactions*); struggles with revealing personal failings, triumphs, or biographical information (Section VI, *Self-Disclosure*); or, with the clock ticking, deals with loss, too little progress, or too much intensity (Section VII, *Time-Limited Groups*).

So, we are back to anxiety in the group therapist (Alonso & Rutan, 1996; Billow, 2001; Brightman, 1984; Gans & Alonso, 1998; Horwitz, 2000; Markus & Abernathy, 2001; Nitsun, 1996; Roller, 1984; Rosenberg, 1993). Not only are there multiple perspectives to choose from as suggested above, but also—in contrast to individual therapy—more mouths are in the room wanting to suck at or bite or fondle the breast, a dearth of skilled supervisors to consult with, virtually no peer support groups, and fewer extant journals offering help.

Leading a group can feel like walking a tightrope without a net.

As we hope the reader of this volume has experienced, however, frameworks of understanding and meaning-making exist that can contain this anxiety and uncertainty, and return the therapist to a fundamental belief in the unique power of group therapy. Although the dilemmas in this volume amply illustrate the complexities and challenges of group therapy, the authors of the chapters and responses suggest underlying pathways to resolution. Similar to the wisdom held by senior clinicians specializing in individual psychotherapy (Shay & Wheelis, 2000), what virtually all of our authors share is a belief in a consistent model of treatment (which can vary from therapist to therapist); the willingness to tolerate anxiety and uncertainty; the courage to acknowledge one's own expectably intense personal reactions; the versatility to be flexible and creative in the face of rapidly shifting group processes; a readiness to seek support and consultation; and the humility to accept one's personal or professional limits.

In this spirit of creative flexibility, we recognize that the group dilemmas the reader will face will not overlap precisely with ours, so we hope the recommendations in this volume provide a "good enough" fit, and encourage further consultation with others. To talk candidly with others about one's dilemmas is clearly a powerful process. Writing about the power of such talk, Diane McWhorter notes, "Any impression of an event I had formed on the basis of the gold-standard written sources would change about 30 degrees once I talked to the actual players—not because of their recall of any specific event but simply because of their complexity as human beings" (2004, p. 51). If the practice of group therapy teaches us anything, it teaches about the complexity of human beings—and the wisdom of treasuring such complexity even as it challenges us deeply.

References

Agazarian, Y. (1997). *Systems centered therapy for groups.* New York: Guilford Press.

Alonso, A., & Rutan, J. S. (1996). Separation and individuation in the group leader. *International Journal of Group Psychotherapy, 46,* 149–162.

Alonso, A., & Swiller, H. I. (Eds.). (1993). *Group therapy in clinical practice.* Washington, DC: American Psychiatric Press.

Bertalanffy, L. von (1968). *General system theory: Foundations, development, applications.* New York: Braziller.

Billow, R. M. (2001). The therapist's anxiety and resistance to group therapy. *International Journal of Group Psychotherapy, 51,* 225–242.

Bion, W. R. (1959). *Experiences in groups* (1974 Edition). New York: Ballantine Books.

Brightman, B. K. (1984). Narcissistic issues in the training of the psychotherapist. *International Journal of Psychoanalytic Psychotherapy, 10,* 293–317.

Cartwright, D., & Zander, A. (1998). *Group dynamics* (3rd ed.). New York: HarperCollins.

DeChant, B. (Ed.). (1996). *Women and group psychotherapy: Theory and practice.* New York: Guilford Press.

Dies, R. R. (1992). Models of group psychotherapy: Sifting through confusion. *International Journal of Group Psychotherapy, 42,* 1–17.

Dies, R. R. (1994). The therapist's role in group treatments. In H. S. Bernard & K. R. MacKenzie (Eds.), *Basics of group psychotherapy* (pp. 60–99). New York: Guilford Press.

Durkin, J. E. (Ed). (1981). *Living groups: Group psychotherapy and general system theory.* New York: Brunner/Mazel.

Ettin, M. (1992). *Foundations and applications of group psychotherapy.* Boston: Allyn & Bacon.

Forsyth, D. R. (1998). *Group dynamics* (3rd ed.). Belmont, CA: Wadsworth.

Fuhriman, A., & Burlingame, G. M. (Eds.). (1994). *Handbook of group psychotherapy: An empirical and clinical synthesis.* New York: Wiley.

Gans, J. S., & Alonso, A. (1998). Difficult patients: Their construction in group therapy. *International Journal of Group Psychotherapy, 48,* 311–326.

Horwitz, L. (2000). Narcissistic leadership in psychotherapy groups. *International Journal of Group Psychotherapy, 50,* 219–235.

Kaplan, H. I., & Sadock, B. J. (Eds.). (1993). *Comprehensive group psychotherapy* (3rd ed.). Baltimore: Williams & Wilkins.

Klein, R., Bernard, H., Singer, D. (Eds.). (1992). *Handbook of contemporary group psychotherapy: Contributions from object relations, self psychology, and social systems theories.* Madison, CT: International Universities Press.

Kutash, I. L., & Wolf, A. (1990). (Eds.). *Group psychotherapist's handbook: Contemporary theory and technique.* New York: Columbia University Press.

LeBon, G. (1920). *The crowd: A study of the popular mind.* New York: Fisher, Unwin. (Original work published 1895)

Leszcz, M., & Goodwin, P. J. (1998). The rationale and foundations of group psychotherapy for women with metastatic breast cancer. *International Journal of Group Psychotherapy, 48,* 245–273.

Lieberman, M., Yalom, I. D., & Miles, M. D. (1973). *Encounter groups: First facts.* New York: Basic Books.

MacKenzie, K. R. (Ed). (1992). *Classics in group psychotherapy.* New York: Guilford Press.

MacKenzie, K. R. (1996). Time-limited group psychotherapy: Has Cinderella found her prince? *Group, 20,* 95–111.

MacKenzie, K. R. (1997). *Time-managed group psychotherapy: Effective clinical applications.* Washington, DC: American Psychiatric Press.

Markus, H. E., & Abernathy, A. D. (2001). Joining with resistance: Addressing reluctance to engage in group therapy training. *International Journal of group Psychotherapy, 51,* 191–204.

Marziali, E., & Monroe-Blum, H. (1994). *Interpersonal group psychotherapy for borderline personality disorder.* New York: Basic Books.

McRoberts, C, Burlingame, G. M., & Hoag, M. J. (1998). Comparative efficacy of individual and group psychotherapy. *Group Dynamics, 2,* 101–117.

McWhorter, D. (2004). Talk. *American Scholar, 73,* 47–53.

Nitsun, M. (1996). *The Anti-group: Destructive forces in the group and their creative potential.* London: Routledge.

Piper, W. E. (1993). Group psychotherapy research. In H. I. Kaplan & B. J. Sadock (Eds.), *Comprehensive group psychotherapy* (3rd ed.) (pp. 673–682). Baltimore: Williams & Wilkins.

Roller, B. (1984). The group therapist: Stages of professional and personal development. *Small Group Behavior, 15,* 265–269.

Rosenberg, P. R. (1993). Qualities of the group psychotherapist. In H. Kaplan & B. Sadock (Eds.), *Comprehensive group psychotherapy* (3rd ed., pp. 648–656). Baltimore: Williams & Wilkins.

Roth, B.E., Stone, W.N., & Kibel, H.D. (Eds.). (1990). *The difficult patient in group: Group psychotherapy with borderline and narcissistic disorders.* Madison, CT: International University Press.

Rutan, J. S. & Stone, W. N. (2001). *Psychodynamic group psychotherapy* (3rd ed.). New York: Guilford Press.

Shay, J. J., & Wheelis, J. (2000). *Odysseys in psychotherapy.* New York: Ardent Media.

Smith, M., Glass, G., & Miller, T. (1980). *The benefits of psychotherapy.* Baltimore: Johns Hopkins University Press.

Stacey, R. D. (2003). *Complexity and group processes.* New York: Brunner-Routledge.

Toseland, R. W., & Siporin, M. (1988). When to recommend group treatment: A review of the clinical and research literature. *International Journal of Group Psychotherapy, 36,* 171–201.

White, J. R., & Freeman, A. S. (Eds.). (2000). *Cognitive-behavioral group therapy.* Washington, DC: American Psychological Association.

Yalom, I. D. (1995). *The theory and practice of group psychotherapy* (4th ed.). New York: Basic Books.

Author Index

Subject Index